Rich Girl
NATION

Rich Girl
NATION

*Taking Charge of
Our Financial Futures*

KATIE GATTI TASSIN

PORTFOLIO | PENGUIN

Portfolio / Penguin
An imprint of Penguin Random House LLC
1745 Broadway, New York, NY 10019
penguinrandomhouse.com

Most Portfolio books are available at a discount when purchased in quantity for sales
promotions or corporate use. Special editions, which include personalized covers, excerpts,
and corporate imprints, can be created when purchased in large quantities. For more
information, please call (212) 572-2232 or email specialmarkets@penguinrandomhouse.com.
Your local bookstore can also assist with discounted bulk purchases using the
Penguin Random House corporate Business-to-Business program. For assistance in
locating a participating retailer, email B2B@penguinrandomhouse.com.

Book design by Nicole LaRoche

LIBRARY OF CONGRESS CATALOGING-IN-PUBLICATION DATA
Names: Gatti Tassin, Katie, author.
Title: Rich girl nation : taking charge of our financial futures / Katie Gatti Tassin.
Description: [New York] : Portfolio / Penguin, [2025] | Includes bibliographical references
and index. | Summary: "From the founder of Money with Katie, a leveled-up finance
guide for ambitious women everywhere—and a rallying cry for a new
money movement" —Provided by publisher.
Identifiers: LCCN 2024056622 (print) | LCCN 2024056623 (ebook) |
ISBN 9780593718865 (hardcover) | ISBN 9780593718872 (ebook)
Subjects: LCSH: Women—Finance, Personal. | Finance, Personal.
Classification: LCC HG179 .G39 2025 (print) | LCC HG179 (ebook) |
DDC 332.0240082—dc23/eng/20250331
LC record available at https://lccn.loc.gov/2024056622
LC ebook record available at https://lccn.loc.gov/2024056623

Printed in the United States of America
1st Printing

Some names and identifying characteristics have been changed to
protect the privacy of the individuals involved.

The authorized representative in the EU for product safety and compliance is
Penguin Random House Ireland, Morrison Chambers, 32 Nassau Street,
Dublin D02 YH68, Ireland, https://eu-contact.penguin.ie.

To the anonymous guy who "works in finance"
that used to relentlessly comment on my nascent
website in 2018, urging me to quit writing
about money and "keep it to myself."

I hope you're well.

Contents

Rich Girl
NATION

The Invitation

A third tray of cubed cheese circulated past me. I reached over to add a hunk of white cheddar to an already crowded plate, intent on maximizing my free food consumption. Pinching a glass of red wine between my right forefinger and thumb and using the remaining three fingers to maintain a precarious grip on my cracked iPhone 6S, I glanced around the room vibrating wall to wall with women. Despite my awkward cocktail party "nowhere to set things down" dance, I felt oddly at ease in this crowd.

Normally I hated the milling and shouty small talk that accompanied networking-style functions, but something about this evening—the Dallas stop on the *Refinery29 Money Diaries* book tour—was different, even a little subversive. It was like the women around me were bringing all the energy and accoutrement you might expect to find at BravoCon to the boy's club world of finance. So far, this personal-finance-centric event seemed like everything I thought money wasn't: fun, spirited, and for *me*.

At twenty-two, I hadn't yet seriously considered my finances (beyond a vague desire to get rich enough to convincingly wear red-bottomed shoes to work), but my scrappy friend Kylie had insisted I join her that night. Up until that point, I was mostly met with sympathetic nods or blank stares anytime I broached the subject of money with friends—this was especially true for those who still used credit cards tied to their parents' checking accounts. But Kylie and I shared a mutual interest in making sure our credit reports weren't torched by our new matching Discover cards. She was the type of friend to whom you could bring just about anything and be met with unbridled enthusiasm: She was creative and unpredictable, someone who would tell you she tried a party drug at an underground disco in the same breath that she mentioned she was halfway through an online MBA program she was paying for herself with money she earned freelancing for ESPN.

At the time, I was making $52,000 and doing a decent job of shuffling a little extra into savings each month—otherwise, I felt financially rudderless. My excitement about becoming a high-powered career woman and stomping around boardrooms in tasteful patent leather heels evaporated almost immediately upon being lulled into the monotonous rhythm of an endless expanse of forty-hour workweeks. I was thrilled to be able to pay my bills, but the entire arrangement felt inescapably claustrophobic. By the time I walked through the doors of the *Money Diaries* event, I had a suspicion that there was something about savvy money management that could be transformational in paving my path out of dependence on a paycheck, but I didn't know much beyond that. Fortunately, Kylie managed to get me out of the house on a school night (!) in fall 2018, usurping my usual post-work routine of melting into my bed and scrolling Facebook (like I said . . . it was 2018).

When it was time to take our seats for the guests of honor, two women found their way onstage. The backdrop, decor, and accents in the venue looked as though they had materialized directly from the Instagram Explore page, dripping in the precise trendiness that only a millennial media company could conjure on short notice.

The younger woman's name was Lindsey Stanberry, the "Work & Money" director at *Refinery29* and author of *Money Diaries*, and the older woman's name was Manisha Thakor, the VP of financial well-being at Brighton Jones, a prominent wealth management firm that even I, in my ignorance, had heard of. It was clear that Lindsey was intended to be the bridge between the audience, a group of predominantly young women, and Manisha, who was an established financier with an intimidating pedigree. At every turn, Lindsey would offer a personal touch that made someone in the audience feel better—she was paying off student loans, had a child, and was *still* able to buy a home, she'd reassure, inadvertently highlighting how absurd it is that the presence of one thereby makes the other two achievements seem unrealistic. They shared intensely personal money origin stories— like the salacious details of Manisha's divorce proceedings, in which her ex-husband's mistress sent her a greatest hits compilation of their amorous email correspondence. (Her takeaway: Get a prenup.)

Having been in several preprofessional organizations in college, I was accustomed to forcing myself to pay attention to the subject matter at any given panel. My similarly ambitious classmates would seem genuinely riveted by speakers about crisis communication and earned media impressions; I was mostly feigning interest given the more earnest preoccupations of my early twenties (read: boys and parties). But that night, I was on the edge of my seat. I didn't have to pretend to listen—I was captivated by the two women onstage before me, knowledgeable and independent, rattling off the names of investment accounts and strategies with an ease and assuredness that mesmerized me. Manisha spoke with such fluidity and confidence that it made me wish, for the first time ever, that I had studied finance in school. The presence of Lindsey, our twenty-something translator, seemed to implicitly suggest that we, too, could become our own personal money managers.

At the end, they announced they'd be taking questions from the audience, and I was certain that a brief, awkward Q&A would be the stopping point for the evening. I was wrong. Hand after hand flew into the air. Here, in this room of hundreds of strangers, women asked questions that self-evidently revealed intimate financial details.

Amazed, I listened to questions with implications that reached far beyond the interest rate in a savings account. These were career-shaping, relationship-changing, and life-altering scenarios filtered through the lens of money—and here we were, a millennial-pink town hall, baring the souls of our asset allocations to the congregation and asking for guidance.

"I'm in a lot of credit card debt and I don't know how to break this cycle, but I hate my job and feel stuck."

"Should I be contributing to my 401(k) or trying to build an emergency fund so I can start my own business?"

"My boyfriend and I want to buy a home, but I have a lot of debt, and he doesn't know."

Whenever an audience member would ask a question on the simpler end of the spectrum that I knew the answer to, I had to physically restrain myself from interjecting. I didn't know other young women had these questions, let alone felt encumbered enough by them to attend a book tour on a Tuesday evening and ask strangers for help in front of a crowd. I learned more about personal finance in those two hours than I had in the previous twenty-two years of my life. It cost $15. (And there was free wine, which, at that age, would've lured me to a cookout where they were grilling women named Katie.)

Being surrounded by women talking about financial security felt like coming home to a place I had never been before. As the event ended, there were two things I couldn't ignore: a newfound conviction that if you want options in this life, you need to understand money—and that I felt a visceral, pure attraction to the subject.

"That was fun," Kylie chirped as we emerged from the air-conditioning into the warm Texas evening and crossed the street to our cars. She had launched into an out-loud pros-and-cons list of different options for a new investment account. As I listened to her, my friend in white go-go boots and elaborate feathered earrings discussing the intricacies of a Roth IRA, I was surprised that these two things could go together—then surprised at my surprise. Why did this scene feel so foreign to me? Why was this the first time I was having a conversation like this one?

As I drove home, the high of the night faded into a strange sadness: I didn't want to stop talking so openly about money, *especially* now that I could see other young women had the same burning questions and willingness to discuss them that I did. For 120 minutes, the paths of a few hundred women intersected in the venue space of an arts building. The lives of women who wanted—either desperately or just curiously—to know more about what they were supposed to do with the paychecks they were receiving every other week, about how to get ahead in a world where boards of directors bore uniformly white male faces and where questions about investing usually invited incredulous scoffs.

Many of the women there, I'm sure, were invited by friends who knew more than they did or simply felt more comfortable admitting interest in something not traditionally coded as "for girls." I felt determined for this to be the beginning—not the end—of my involvement in the world of women's personal finance.

A seed was planted that evening that I continued to nurture with a yearslong binge of financial information (the Money with Katie brand would be born eighteen months later). At the time, I had been running a personal blog for a few years as a fun side project, and I abruptly stopped posting musings about life and dating—and replaced them with energized revelations about personal finance that, upon reading now, sound almost manic in their enthusiasm. Just one month after I sat in the crowd before Lindsey and Manisha, I wrote a post titled "Why I Talk About Money" in which I marveled at my newfound knowledge:

> I felt like I was discovering all these secrets and philosophies that are utterly mind-blowing. At the risk of hyperbole, it was completely changing the way I thought about my income, the way I spent, and the path to wealth and freedom.

With a convert's zeal, I began studying compound interest charts. Every single one told me that being in my twenties was my superpower. All I wanted to do was share this eye-opening information with others: that you didn't have to have a six-figure salary or degree in accounting to build wealth, because damn it, a few wise investments and decades of time could do practically all the heavy lifting for you.

It wasn't until the early weeks of pandemic boredom in April 2020 that I decided to collect all my new knowledge and shut down my old blog in favor of a more formal project, which I called "Money with Katie" when I realized such a simple URL—moneywithkatie.com—was available. Instead of overthinking the purchase (something that had become commonplace in my freshly financially responsible worldview), I bought the domain for $20 and figured I'd spend a few minutes setting up the site navigation before taking a break to make some lunch and go for a walk.

Instead, I emerged from my room into the common area of my dark apartment in a fugue state eight hours later, having built out the entire site and written the first few blog posts. I didn't have a business plan or any grand monetization strategy, but I decided later that I'd commit to two blog posts per week for a year and see what happened.

By late summer, it was clear I couldn't keep subjecting my non-consenting personal Instagram followers to an onslaught of shares about HSA plans, so I made the @MoneyWithKatie Instagram account. Rich Girl Nation was born: a small but mighty force of smart, curious, and driven women (and some men!) who were down to indulge my rambling videos and gratuitously long blog posts in exchange for a budgeting hack. Over the next year, I accumulated around twenty-five thousand passionate readers and a community on social media. While I only ever intended to *write* about my methods for financial organization, these pointers sparked interest from others, who asked if I could just share the bare-bones templates I had already made for personal use. At first, I wiped my data from my janky spreadsheet and threw it on the site as a free downloadable. But one Saturday toward the end of 2020, I decided to spend a few hours tricking it out—and the first Wealth Planner was born. By the second half of 2021, Money with Katie's revenue from partnerships and digital product sales was outpacing my $66,000 salary approximately 5:1. In retrospect, the rush I felt in my body sitting in the crowd at the *Money Diaries* event in 2018 was an encrypted message from my future self: *Pay attention to this feeling. This is the path you want to walk down.*

In 2022, I took the venture full-time when I joined forces via an "acquihire" agreement with the business media brand Morning Brew, and together, we continued to grow the platform. Today, Money with Katie reaches millions of people every year. Because I was never classically trained in the financial world, my outlook was developed through other means: self-directed study, trial and error, and talking to thousands of women about their financial lives. This intimate style of learning taught me empathy and showed me that no two financial situations are the same. It also allowed me to observe patterns in thousands of money stories—I could scratch my every curious itch with data, sure, but I also got to see statistics firsthand, refracted through the personal narratives of individual women.

I am routinely blown away by the level of knowledge, grit, and open-mindedness in Rich Girl Nation—in late 2023, we did a survey of our audience to get a sense for how they earn, spend, and invest. We found that the median household income (among single- and dual-earner households) was a whopping $180,000. The median household net worth? $311,000. In the early days, I was mostly talking to other women who, like me, earned a mid-five-figure income and were interested in nailing down the basics. But several years later, it was clear they had grown with me—and were interested in taking their knowledge and progress to the next level. This group was at the forefront of my mind as I wrote the book you're about to read.

It's fitting, I suppose, that my baptism in the world of personal finance was by and for women, because I learned quickly that the game women are playing when it comes to pursuing financial freedom has a unique set of rules and regulations. Although the beginning of my journey was characterized by youthful optimism about our prospects, as I gained context, I realized the history of women and money is a rich text, no pun intended.

Because as we'll explore in the next seven chapters, there's no way around it: Women experience money differently than men. We face financial choices, obstacles, and pressures that are partially or entirely absent from the average man's experience. Not only do we exist in a cultural context that demeans women's ability to manage their money responsibly ("Women be shoppin'!"), assumes they're unable to grasp or uninterested in the technicalities behind financial principles ("bad at math"), and assigns them a sort of manipulative malevolence when it comes to their romantic interactions with men (the "gold digger" trope), but products marketed to women also cost more,[†] women are statistically less likely to earn the high incomes with which it's easiest to accrue wealth, and even women who are their household's primary earner are more likely to bear a disproportionate amount of the underpaid or unpaid labor that makes society function.

As someone who's reading a book about women and money, you're probably already well-versed in these discrepancies and

---

† In 2015, the New York City Department of Consumer Affairs conducted the first-ever study of pricing of nearly eight hundred gendered goods across five industries, from baby to senior products. On average across all five industries, products marketed to women cost 7 percent more than similar products targeted at men. Some of these examples were hilarious: Identical items in the boys' and girls' sections of a store would be priced completely differently.

double standards, but let's quickly review a couple key statistics: In the aggregate, households headed by women have just fifty-five cents in median wealth for every dollar owned by households headed by men. The Survey of Consumer Finances of mixed-sex marriages found that 56 percent of husbands were designated as "most knowledgeable about household finances," a statistic that's worse than it was in 1992 when only 53 percent of households reported this. Though this book will primarily use gender data to examine financial disparities, the evidence is clear that racial differences are just as significant, if not more so. While women's wealth lags men's across all races and marital statuses, married white women have between *two and three times* as much wealth as married Black and Hispanic men, both of whom have more wealth still than Black and Hispanic women. And while that statistic is specific to married people, it's indisputable that women of color face far higher economic hurdles in the United States than white women do—so when I highlight statistics that emphasize gaps between white women and white men, my intent is not to suggest that their inequality matters most, but to demonstrate how unequal things remain for even the *most* statistically advantaged women.

These high-level statistics are just the tip of the iceberg, and they don't answer the most important question: Why? And more critically, what can we do about it? In *Rich Girl Nation*, I'll explore what I perceive to be the six most pressing drivers of financial disparity in women's lives, as well as provide practical strategies for what to do with your money in the gendered system of labor, capital, and home life that we inhabit. My goal is to open the aperture widely enough that we can talk frankly about where statistics indicate women are more likely to draw the shit end of the stick and discuss methods for overcoming those outcomes. Let's look at the journey we're about to embark on together.

Where we're going in the next seven chapters

We'll begin our exploration by examining a few particularly pernicious consumer industries—beauty and personal care—that almost exclusively target women by manufacturing insecurities that one must pay to "fix." In doing so, we'll devise a road map for confidently navigating such a glittering minefield.

Next, we'll dive into the differences in how women and men earn, because deeply held cultural norms impact everything from a woman's outcomes in negotiations, to her perceived value in the workplace, to the family structures that are most likely to land a woman in the low- or middle-wage cycle.

Then, we'll focus on the key pieces of long-term financial planning that research shows are most likely to be abdicated to male partners, and therefore represent the biggest windows for impact early in a woman's life.

Next, we'll talk about what legally happens to your identity, assets, debt, and income when you get married, and how you can financially protect yourself before and after you say "I do," setting the stage for how family dynamics impact a woman's financial outcomes.

Because high-earning and highly educated women aren't insulated from these hazards: Women contributing at least as much income to their household as their male partner still tend to do more than twice as much of the housework, and earning potential drops after women become parents (in case it's not obvious, the same is not true for men). Understanding how to save and pay for help such that you're *not* automatically and singularly faced with the "well-rehearsed dichotomy"† of career versus family is the practical, necessary step we can take to avoid being pushed out of paid work and public life by default.

By the end of our journey, you'll probably have a richer understanding of how a lifetime of financial disparity creates different outcomes for men and women, and the way these differences become more pronounced over time. Women typically outlive men, are far more likely to find themselves in poverty following divorce, and retire with less than one third of men's median savings, so we'll address how to make sure your assets outlive you, and how smart, simple, and diversified investing can help you do it.

Finally, we'll learn how to implement a holistic and comprehensive financial plan today.

Women face off with a unique constellation of cultural norms, systemic shortcomings, and, in the US particularly, failures of policy. It's only after we understand the full picture that we can begin—individually and collectively—to paint a different one for ourselves and the women who come after us.

---

† The "well-rehearsed dichotomy" is a quote from an essay called "Maternal Instincts" about the so-called biological truth of women's propensity for housework and care work by Laura Kipnis. Here's the full quote, because it's worth including (emphasis mine): "Even with men doing more parenting than before, the majority of women are still left facing the well-rehearsed motherhood-versus-career dichotomy. **But it's *not* a dichotomy; it's a socially organized choice masquerading as a natural one.** There would be all sorts of ways to organize society and sexuality that don't create false choices if we simply got inventive about it—as inventive as we've been about equity in sexual pleasure—but there has to be the political will to do it."

Because as much as I wish it could, this book is not and cannot be a substitute for sweeping reform like universal pre-K or Social Security credits for caregivers. It won't fix the fact that one in three American workers earns less than $20 per hour, or the fact that women are overrepresented in that group. It won't heal our broken healthcare system that plunges hundreds of thousands of people into bankruptcy each year despite boasting some of the worst health outcomes and highest infant and maternal mortality rates of all high-income nations, with Black women dying during childbirth at a rate 2.6 times higher than white women. But what I hope this book *can* do is help the women who read it make more informed decisions; decisions that will inspire and change not only their lives, but the lives of the women around them, too. Everything I've learned over the last six years has led me to believe that addressing the most glaring manifestations of the financial power differential will help us create a more equitable cultural playing field on which deeper, systemic change is possible. We must address *all* the contributing factors: from individual decisions to cultural norms to systemic shortcomings. Individual solutions cannot cure our collective maladies, but they can equip individual people with the capacity and resources to make a larger impact in their arenas of influence.

Our financial decisions aren't made in a vacuum. Women in the US weren't even allowed to have their own bank accounts until 1974, so it's not like we've had centuries to perfect our collective asset allocation. Half the battle is looking around and behind us to become aware of these dynamics—only then can we begin to chart a viable path forward.

1

The Hot Girl
Hamster Wheel

*We don't consider the gender gap in time and money
spent on beauty, but time and money matter. They're
essential sources of power and influence and also major
sources of freedom.*

—DR. RENEE ENGELN, *BEAUTY SICK*

One of the more challenging tasks I set out to complete when my personal finance journey began was getting a *real* handle on my expenses. Surprisingly, I found that my fixed expenses (home, car, other needs)—areas I was warned were troublesome for most—actually weren't too bad. I had a roommate, my car was relatively affordable, and I lived in an apartment complex that was built in the '90s and looked like it. In many important ways, I lived comfortably beneath my means.

But there was one notable outlier: My Hot Girl™ category was staggering. Based on an early inventory, I calculated that I was spending:

- $200 every three months for my cut and color
- $100 per month on eyelash extensions

- $15 per month on eyebrow threading
- $100 per month on manicures and pedicures
- $500 per year on makeup

The first time I examined these expenses in their totality, I thought my calculator had added an extraneous zero. After confirming it was, in fact, a totally warranted zero, I knew I couldn't justify this superficial hemorrhaging any longer. So in 2019, I decided it was time to hop off the Hot Girl Hamster Wheel—at least temporarily.

The Hot Girl Hamster Wheel is a term I coined that describes the litany of rotating, recurring expenses necessary to make one "conventionally attractive." When you're on the hamster wheel, every dollar spent functions like a commitment to spend more in the future—your body will eventually reject the modifications, often leaving you aesthetically "worse" than you started (think chipping gel polish and brittle nails underneath or brassy, grown-out highlights that must be corrected). As a former Hot Girl™, I'm all too familiar with the financial trials and tribulations of attempting to maintain some semblance of an acceptable "feminine" appearance, and the most common iteration went a little something like this:

1. Feel bad about self for some generalized reason, then notice (in rapid, horrifying succession) that my roots were growing out, my ends were split, my gel nails were peeling, my legs were pale and hairy, and—oh yeah!—I was stressed.
2. Panic-schedule a full day of back-to-back primp appointments.
3. Attend said appointments in order: facial, eyebrow threading, cut and color, manicure/pedicure, spray tan and chill.

4. Feel increasingly uncomfortable calculating the accumulating 20 percent tips at each and every vendor (and swipe the AmEx with less and less enthusiasm).

5. Bask in glory of retaining Hot Girl status for another two to three weeks, and then quickly realize that not only do I feel no different, but it's already almost time to re-up.

I'm hyperbolizing, of course, but the general framework followed a predictable pattern. Perhaps the most unnerving part of this NASCAR-pit-stop-style tour of Dallas's beauty providers was the way in which these habits eventually became my baseline state: When I sensed I was deviating too far away from it, a crisis of confidence ensued, and the cycle would repeat anew.

When I annualized my spending and broke it down to monthly averages, I realized I was spending about $320 per month (**chokes** that's $3,840 per year) on *being pretty*. Depending on how much you earn, this number could be reasonable—but at the time, I was taking home about $1,500 every two weeks, which meant I worked for more than an entire month each year solely to maintain my Acceptable Feminine Appearance.

But while I was swiping, tapping, and inserting my chip card's merry way through the Tour de Texas Salons, there was something deeper at play. The women at my office had manicured nails. The women I spent time with on the weekends had full sets of lashes and highlights. In Dallas, most of the women I encountered on a daily basis were similarly pledging their time, energy, and money to keeping up appearances. Yet I didn't see my boyfriend at the time (now husband) traipsing to the salon every other month to get his color refreshed or schlepping to the pedicure chair biweekly to get his cuticles pushed back. Even before I learned about how beauty consumerism functions to keep women on the financial, metaphoric, and often literal treadmill, it always struck me as profoundly unfair that (what felt like) my default condition required so much more time, effort, and money than the men in my life spent on theirs.

When you itemize the expenses so plainly, it seems obvious that beauty consumerism's laser-like offensive on women's self-image will materially impact our financial outcomes. But when I was building my first budget, the topic was almost entirely absent from the instructional material I was mainlining. In her essay "In the Name of Beauty," Tressie McMillan Cottom summarizes this exchange of value perfectly: "If I *believe* that I can become beautiful, I become an economic subject. My desire becomes a market." If we want to make honest progress toward financial independence, that means taking a necessary hard look at how industries that exist to infiltrate our psyches (and checking accounts) are impacting our goals.

It's worth stating explicitly that these industries aren't the primary *reason* why many women don't make financial progress. A mani/pedi is expressly not to blame for wage stagnation or the shrinking middle class. But if you're a woman who suffers from money anxiety and has a self-care routine akin to 2018 Katie (who had a variety of acrylic products adhered to every surface of her body), I feel confident that your hard-earned income will serve you more powerfully from the safety of a Roth IRA than in a $50 vitamin C serum.

Calculating the true cost

For the sake of argument, let's return to my routine and pretend I had extended it over the course of my lifetime—or, at least, the next forty years. Tapping my trusty compounding returns calculator (a magical device that shows how your money can earn money over time), prepare to be horrified at the opportunity cost[†] of a lifetime of "conventional" beauty, at a sticker price of $320 per month. Had that money been invested each month for forty years in a cheap total US stock market index fund like VTSAX, returning a historically average return of around 8 percent per year, the opportunity cost is $1,001,728.88.

One million dollars.

For some nauseating context, an investment portfolio worth $1,000,000 is enough to reliably produce a monthly income of approximately $3,333 in perpetuity.[‡] The median American aged sixty-five through seventy-four hits retirement with around $200,000 in savings, and gets an average of $1,907 per month from Social Security. These are not costs at the margins; these are *retirement-supporting amounts.*

It turns out my spending was pretty indicative of the national average for women who report regularly spending on their appearance: The average American woman spends $3,756 per year on beauty (the figure for men who reported regularly spending on their appearance was $2,928 per year, which surprised me, as the men in my life are the quintessential "7-in-1 body wash" consumers).[§] If you assume the average American man is investing

---

† "Opportunity cost" is just jargon for "What do the opportunities that I'm giving up in order to do this cost me?" In other words, if this money weren't spent on these things, what could it have earned elsewhere instead?

‡ I'm calculating this by using the 4 percent rule, which says an investment portfolio invested "correctly" should be able to support a 4 percent withdrawal annually. Four percent of $1,000,000 is $40,000, or $3,333 per month. Hold on tight—we'll dig way deeper in Chapter 3.

§ There's some selection bias at play here. This report examined the average purchasing behavior of women and men who said they spend regularly on their appearance, so it doesn't do a great job of showing us what the average woman does, but the fact that the discrepancy exists within this group is telling.

only the cost difference of $800 per year for forty years, they'd hit retirement with $206,606 more. Even if we're comfortable with that value exchange in our own lives, I'm not sure many of us are aware that's the trade-off we're making. I know I wasn't.

Frustratingly, any mention of these budgetary inclusions was mysteriously absent from most of the personal finance books and blogs I frequented. How come many of my favorite writers, like Brad and John and Brandon and Nick and Jack, weren't covering how to cope with a balayage routine gone rogue?!

To fully understand what I was up against, I had to contend with the long, troubling history of the way aesthetic norms have been used to police women's behavior and access to resources in our post-industrial world.

Beauty, status, and billions

If all of this feels silly or superficial, consider the fact that beauty and personal care is a $100 billion industry in the US and a $624 billion industry worldwide as of 2024. The US is the top spender. It's big business, and those dollars are extracted from the personal wealth of (largely) women, in our effort to exchange our actual capital for the social capital one can derive from maintaining Hot Girl status. Beauty is the form of power that girls and women are socialized to value most. Unlike financial capital, which compounds and grows more powerful as you age, beauty is capital that—in our current paradigm's idea of "beauty," which usually just means "youth"—decays as you get older, requiring more and more money to extend its half-life. Investing your money in the capital of beauty guarantees a long-term proposition of deterioration.

While the exact breakdown of "culture" and "biology" that informs what's considered "attractive" isn't totally clear, history lends us some clues about what influences our changing norms. Western beauty standards are informed by Eurocentric ideals of beauty that treat whiteness as the default (and fetishize "exoticized" ideals of Black or brown beauty), which usually means a certain body type, a general appearance of hairlessness where hair "shouldn't be," and straight, thick, shiny hair where it "should be."

What's considered "beautiful" seems to track closely over time with whatever connotes upper-class status. "[In Victorian England,] women were literally powdering their faces with arsenic and lead to appear as white as possible," beauty and culture critic Jessica DeFino told me. "Paleness" was seen as beautiful because working-class people were outside all day in the fields, and they had tanned skin. This changed with the Industrial Revolution, when low-income workers shifted into factories and were no longer in the sun all the time. "The upper classes have leisure money, they're going on vacations," Jessica explained. "Coco Chanel was kind of the first one to popularize the tan. And the idea was that she was on a yacht, tanning, *because she was so rich.*" In other words, beauty is a system designed to reinforce hierarchies. Women are valued most highly in patriarchal societies when they assume the role of the selfless "giver," and giving your time, energy, and money to maintain an appearance that *conspicuously* signals your willingness to exert effort is rewarded, too. In *Hood Feminism*, Mikki Kendall describes how appearance-based judgments seep beyond the realm of the purely aesthetic for Black women, whose "appearances, speech, and sexuality" are measured against a subjective yardstick of respectability: "Any hint that a Black woman has failed to put effort into her appearance is met with ardent disapproval both inside her community and outside it."

Put another way, guidelines for the ideal physical appearance often map to what most effectively communicates an aesthetic of wealth or status—what's considered "beautiful" is usually just the thing that telegraphs proximity to capital. At the time of this writing, the "Clean Girl," "Quiet Luxury," and "Old Money" aesthetics are making the rounds on TikTok, all of which are animated by the same core principle. Suffice it to say, the connection between beauty and money runs a lot deeper than first meets the eye.

Beauty gets Goop'd

Conversations that openly challenge beauty standards have become more common in the last few years. Women were like, "Wait a second, how come *we* have to be gorgeous maidens with silken hair while 'dad bod' is the craze sweeping male standards of attractiveness?" As such, the beauty industry has been in the midst of a masterful pivot: repackaging many of the same beautifying wares as—wait for it!—good for you. Enter: the self-care industrial complex. *Just* when you thought we had this one in the bag.

If you assumed the concept of "self-care" was the product of a Poosh-funded advertising blitz given its cultural dominance in recent years, you may be surprised to learn its roots are far more complex and—crucially—not consumerist. Originally, self-care was rooted in the struggle for survival—it was a medical concept popularized during the civil rights and women's rights era of the

1960s and 1970s, and it was a term that broadly referred to health and community engagement—as in, *How can we help our underserved communities access the basic health and social services they need?* OG self-care was about activism and strengthening a community's efforts toward equality; Goopified self-care is the commercialized solution for the challenges endemic to our hyperspeed lives, and at the level of individual self-optimization—a philosophy that says you can outrun burnout if you wake up early with this $200 faux-sunrise alarm clock (accompanied by a subscription, obviously) and give heatless curls a spin.

Estimates of the size of the "self-care industry" vary wildly depending on which underlying sectors are included, but in its narrowest definition, it's probably worth around $11 billion in the US.[†] My own contributions to the self-care industry's growth mostly comprised gelatinous under-eye patches, face masks claiming questionable benefits, and too many body scrubs to count, purchases usually fueled by rampant Sunday scaries while meandering through the section of the grocery store that promised to ease my existential dread with something lavender-scented and lush.

On one hand, I'm glad that we're glamorizing (mostly) healthy lifestyle choices as opposed to *Euphoria* teen MDMA binges. Getting enough sleep, exercising, eating nutritious foods, and being hydrated are good things. But much of the industry deserves a dose of skepticism: If you scratch just a little bit beneath the surface, you notice that many of these products and processes have the (supposedly unintended) side effect of *also* upholding the

---

† The difficulty of quantifying it illustrates part of my point: Skincare is usually counted in "beauty industry" estimates, but even the most excessive and dubious products are increasingly being lumped in with "self-care." Like I said, a masterful rebrand.

conventional feminine beauty standard. *Hey, wait a minute—are these just Trojan horses with manicured hooves?*

After all, "That Girl" is in control of her life; she's wealthy, healthy, responsible, and gorgeous. When the pace of life is unforgiving, *anything* that promises a leg up looks like a life raft worth lunging toward. But the center of the Venn diagram between the beauty industry and the wellness industry is the section that says "profit from women's manufactured insecurities." And as with most normative cultural moments directed at women, it's still an implicit directive about who ~we ladies~ should be, and—importantly—how we should use our resources. In some ways, the only difference between commercialized self-care culture and something like the 1950s cult of domesticity (meant to use shiny appliances to lure women back into the kitchen after they got a taste of freedom working outside the home during WWII) is who all these routines and aesthetics claim to benefit. You don't have to have a perfect body or keep a perfect home for your husband anymore—now you get to do it for *yourself.* And you better like it!

While the beauty industry may invent new insecurities and then market products to address them (matte skin versus dewy skin, thin eyebrows versus feathery ones, etc.), the self-care industry is harder to dodge because it positions its products as the solution to legitimate human needs. You don't need paid sick time or *simply more sleep*—you just need these $25 gold under-eye patches for your dark circles. But therein lies the rub: The fancy facials and picturesque homeware and intricate rituals involving armaments of brand-name products catered to overburdened women are not likely to *actually* solve any of the implied problems they purport to address.

The troubling history of "pretty privilege"

You might intellectually agree with these ideas or believe that these industries offer consumerism-centric solutions to collective human problems . . . and still, that knowledge can pale in comparison to the magnetic allure of *feeling attractive*. By 2019, I had spent my entire adolescence and young adulthood accustomed to looking a certain way: a thin body wearing trendy clothes, fake eyelashes, blond hair, sculpted brows, pink nails. More important, I had grown reliant on how that appearance led other people to treat me: with attentive accommodation.

I've been writing and talking about this topic publicly for a few years, and I often hear from women who want to scale back on their beauty regimens but don't believe it's an option, pointing out that it feels dangerous to deviate. They often say something like this: *I know I'm spending too much time and money on this stuff, but couldn't it be seen as an investment in . . . I don't know, being more successful at work and finding a good partner? If it makes me feel good, what's the big deal?*

I asked Rich Girl Nation to share their stories about pretty privilege. One woman who wrote in, Kate, expressed the uneasiness of knowing that sometimes your looks are working in your favor: "Throughout my career, I've had a pretty easy time rising through the ranks. I happen to be thin, white, and fairly attractive. I never thought much of it until I noticed other extremely competent women being left behind because they have larger bodies or don't fit these standards. It's a bit humbling to realize that perhaps it's not my merit alone that's earned my spot, but also my looks." Another, Amy, wrote in to say she's experienced both sides of the coin in her life: "I went through a breakup and lost about 20 pounds and bleached my hair. Instantly, I saw an uptick in messages, not just from men on the internet, but also other women reaching out saying they miss me, asking how I am, saying how great I look and saying we should make plans. When I started dating my now-husband two years later, I grew my hair out and gained the weight back. I have seen firsthand that when you are conventionally skinny and blonde, people are just nicer to you."

Another woman, Ana Maria, described what it was like to be Colombian in a town that's 99 percent white: "I didn't experience any discrimination or negative interactions—instead, I felt like I was memorable, and people were interested in knowing me. Being Colombian became an asset, and I realized it was because I'm pretty and look rich. Another Bolivian student wasn't treated as 'exotic' like I was, and she wasn't nearly as 'known.' It's uncomfortable to voice that I feel I got the benefits of being an immigrant and having an accent (being memorable, getting special treatment at bars, restaurants, stores, etc.) without having to deal with the negative experiences."

As these stories illustrate, adhering to these very specific norms unlocks benefits in Western culture. As Jessica DeFino explained to me, "When a beauty standard is normalized, it is incorporated into what you could call 'pretty privilege'—what society expects of women in order to treat them with basic human dignity. Studies show that people who more closely adhere to the dominant standard of beauty are given more attention from teachers in schools and mentors [at work]. They're more likely to get the jobs they interview for. . . . They're more likely to have positive legal outcomes in the justice system. . . . They receive better social treatment, more options for romantic partners. What you look like does affect the type of life you lead."

If your natural state has always mostly adhered to conventional Eurocentric beauty standards and you've never given Brazilian blowouts a second look, you might be skeptical: Can we *really* quantify the benefits of being an "attractive" woman? The short answer is yes. One study from 2016 attempted to do just that, by grouping five thousand women in college into three camps: more attractive, average, and less attractive (this has to be in the top ten of "bleakest research methodology" I've come across). Women who were rated as "less attractive" had grades that were 1.5 percent lower than "average" women, and the most attractive women had grades that were 0.5 percent *higher* than "average." You might wonder whether this is merely a bias toward attractive *people*, but male students' grades showed far less correlation to perceived attractiveness. When the same analysis was done with online grades of students who never met their professors, almost all of the correlation with perceived attractiveness vanished.

Differences become even more pronounced when we group results by variables like body size or race. It wasn't until the 1990s that things like weight requirements for flight attendants (and more broadly, the way employers openly made hiring decisions based on appearance) finally became the center of successful lawsuits. But litigation alone is not enough to dissuade economic discrimination based on appearance: Women with a bachelor's degree and a BMI at or above 30 earn 12 percent less, on average, than their thinner colleagues (men in the same category experience a wage penalty, too, but it's lower, at 5 percent).

All that to say, when a woman's appearance doesn't conform to the idealized, gendered norm, she is punished for nonadherence. You'd be forgiven for assuming that your appearance matters, because you probably receive signals every time you leave your home that it does.

Renegotiating the terms of your agreement with the beauty and self-care industries

I know we've been going statistic-crazy, so let's take a breath and relocate the plot: The point is not that spending on things that scan as traditionally "feminine" is wrong, nor is it the "Women be shoppin'!" silver bullet that some like to claim explains why women lag men financially. That type of condescension feels like dunking on women for trying to live up to unrealistic expectations they have little control over. Damned if you do, damned if you don't.

But embodying these norms doesn't come cheap. Regardless of the purity of Estée Lauder's intentions, it's indisputable that creating insecurity (and then marketing to it) is an incredibly profitable business model. We talk at length about the psychological ramifications of such messages; we discuss the way the pressure to be beautiful often makes us *feel*. And the way we feel matters! Conventional beauty standards generate real, negative consequences. But we often gloss over the equally important financial implications (much the way I glossed over them at the individual level for years, assuming gel manicures and facials were just part of the Hot Girl Bill of Rights I was duty bound to uphold).

With the cold, hard numbers staring back at me in my first nascent Excel budget in 2019, I decided to conduct an experiment: I was going to extract myself from the Hot Girl Hamster Wheel one luxury at a time (because, realistically, that's what these things are: luxuries that the majority of women globally do not have the privilege of participating in) and see how each incremental reversion back to my ~natural self~ felt. And something funny happened.

I realized that while the financial benefits were palpable, what was immediately noticeable was the amount of *time* I gained back. My calendar had formerly supported a glossy Hot Girl Jenga. I was fitting in four-hour cut-and-color sessions on Saturday mornings and squeezing mani/pedis into lunch breaks every other week. I was paying to labor under beauty's terms. My routines had morphed and expanded slowly over time, so I hadn't noticed the water I was submerged in was actually boiling Chanel No. 5.

With each abstention, the fog of beauty's cold war lifted, and it was easier to assess what was worth it. I was comfortable parting with the eyelashes, nails, and facials—settling on a Latisse prescription for the short-term regrowth problem (hilariously, it was a medication originally developed for glaucoma patients that had an interesting side effect of giving all the grannies gorgeous lashes), deciding naked nails were fine, and developing a simple at-home skincare routine instead. But part of the challenge of renegotiating the terms of my agreement with the beauty industry was parsing what I was doing "for myself," and what I was doing out of a vague sense of obligation and ambient insecurity. I told myself for years that my routines were "for me," but realized upon further reflection that this explanation was a bit suspect: What were the chances that my unique self-expression *just so happened* to align almost perfectly with conventional beauty standards? (Houston, we've discovered a plot hole.)

The truth is, I *was* "doing it for me"—but not in the way I thought. I was doing it because the results, or the treatment it garnered for me, were personally advantageous. And as Jessica gently reminded me, "It's not bad to do things for other people. We are communal creatures. . . . What we have to examine is what we're communicating [with those aesthetic choices], and why." After all, not everything we do in life needs to be an explicitly feminist act—but it's worthwhile to resist recasting individual decisions as empowering simply because they make us *feel power-ful* in contexts where "power" means doubling down on the importance of being hot and thin.

I felt good about ditching most of my involvement with the Hot Girl Hamster Wheel, but there was still one thing I was having a hard time letting go of: my highlights. At the time, I decided to compromise. I'd continue to get highlights every three to four months, the sole survivor of ghosts of Hot Girls past. As the years wore on, I realized that even my internalized preference for blondness was inextricably tied up in a performance of class: Only 2 percent of the global population possesses naturally blond hair, but it's estimated that between 30 percent and 40 percent of women in the West bleach their way there.

Anyone who's ever attempted to keep up with a highlights routine understands that this is, in many ways, a wholly impractical aesthetic choice, as it's both time- and capital-intensive to keep the reality of your dark roots at bay. Artificial, salon-quality blond-ness signals what you *really* possess in the absence of naturally blond hair: time and money. It's a hair color that's inescapably associated with status. While admittedly a small sample size, consider that approximately half of the women serving as CEOs for S&P 500 companies have blond hair. Suffice it to say, even my uneasiness about giving up my Barbie-inspired ritual felt loaded— once I understood the subconscious reasons I preferred myself that way, it was hard to keep going and still feel good about it, so I'm experimenting with embracing my natural color.

If this recounting was resonant with you and you'd like to re-assess your own financial relationship with the beauty and well-ness industries, let's do a quick exercise.

Performing your own Hot Girl Detox

A Hot Girl Detox is about experimentation, curiosity, and self-inquiry: Which of these practices am I engaging in because it's a form of healthy self-expression, and which am I adhering to out of fear of deviating from the norm? More importantly, *what can't I justifiably afford right now?* Where am I using my money to uphold systems I don't support, instead of supporting *me?*

I asked readers and listeners to tell me how their lives changed after they began divesting from the beauty industrial complex: Sarah, who told me about how her upbringing placed a lot of emphasis on her appearance, has been saving around $500 per month since paring back: "You want to know what changed when I stopped? Almost nothing. My partner still loves me, I still got promoted at work, I changed jobs and still got hired. I've saved an extreme amount of time and money, and I learned how to love myself without all the extra stuff. It's been the best thing I've ever done for myself." Heather's savings weren't as extreme—only $100 per month—but her story of allowing her gray hair to exist naturally stopped me in my tracks: "When I look at my hair now, I think, 'I'm refusing to participate in a system that harms other women,' and I feel more powerful. I'm surprised my confidence has actually grown. I hope it impacts my son, and his understanding of what's important."

There's no hard-and-fast personal finance "rule" around beauty spending, but I'll draw one strong line in the setting powder: If you're spending more each month on beauty and personal care than you're saving, do not pass GO and do not collect your next round of overnight masks. Your financial future is officially being imperiled by the beauty industry's death grip, and it's time to renegotiate the terms of your agreement such that Future You's security isn't jeopardized.

To perform your own detox experiment, you can follow this framework:

1. List every expense you can think of that pertains to your upholding of appearances or broadly falls into the category of "self-care," and leave no Moroccanoil bottle unturned. You may find this category includes products and services for your hair, nails, brows, skin, or clothing.

2. Once you list all the services and products, do your best to estimate the frequency and *all-in* cost (that is, after tip). If the service is especially time-consuming, add an asterisk— your time is an important resource, too.

3. Annualize the costs. If something happens twice a year, count it twice. Once a month? Twelve times. Add up what all of it costs you each year.

4. Contextualize the costs with respect to how much you earn (you can use your pretax salary if you don't know your annual take-home pay, for simplicity). Divide your all-in costs by your salary and multiply by 100 to get a percentage— you'll probably get a number that's between 1 percent and 10 percent. (If it's higher than 10 percent, don't beat yourself up—but take the next two steps seriously.)

> *Pause:* At this point you may realize that you're either (a) exceptionally high-earning or (b) very low-maintenance, or perhaps both. If that's the case, you might decide steps 5 and 6 aren't necessary for you. It all depends on how much you want to experiment! Did someone say hashtag reinvention?

5. Rank your beauty expenses from most important to you to least important to you.

> You already know that, for me, hair color was a worthwhile expense that I was unready to part with at first (I blame being raised on a steady pop culture diet of Jessica Simpson, Christina Aguilera, and Britney Spears, something I'll take up with a therapist). I didn't need a compound interest calculator to tell me that. But when I weighed my other options—have polished nails and lashes that were 2 millimeters longer for the rest of my life or retire with an additional million dollars—I felt it was a lucrative compromise.

6. Starting from the bottom of the list and working your way up, begin removing products or services from your schedule (and financial obligations!) one by one. If you have appointments scheduled for the bottom-of-the-barrel services, cancel them. Test the waters and aim to remove another product or service every month. You may find you don't miss some at all, while others might end up being reprioritized above something else.

Remember, you have multiple levers to pull here: the binary yes/no *and* the frequency with which you're engaging. Maybe you decide you'll only do certain things for special events. Maybe you'll pare back other services to once a month, or every other month.

Apart from frequency, opting for lower-maintenance alternatives can be a middle ground if you're currently keeping up with the Kardashians. For example, some hairstyles require less frequent touch-ups than others. Other things are easier to replace at a more sustainable cost if you don't want to fully cut them out but know they're disadvantaging you financially.

Regardless, it's worth interrogating what you're getting in return for the money spent, and whether the opportunity cost is worthwhile. If you're like, *Piss off, money wench, the pedicure chair is the only place on earth where I feel God's peace and you'll have to pry the sea salt scrub out of my cold, dead hands,* by all means, please continue! Only you will know when you reach the right balance. Divesting from the beauty and personal care industries can be fraught because bucking many of these norms feels inherently vulnerable and dangerous. Still, the compounding returns calculators can certainly help contextualize what you're gaining from extricating yourself—because the final step of the Hot Girl Detox is putting that money to work for Future You.

After all, what's *really* driving our participation in these norms? It's probably a belief that these things will make our lives better—that they'll make us safe, secure, happy, and healthy. We exchange our money for these products and services because we believe they'll deliver those results. But you know what else makes you feel safe, secure, happy, and healthy? Financial stability within extractive systems. Why not cut out the middleman—spending on beauty—and invest in our futures directly?

In conclusion

It's possible this chapter feels entirely foreign to you—maybe you're like my mom, who's never been the type to care about appearances or black out at Sephora (my 2018 Discover statements can't relate). But what I know from years of admitting my own struggle to other women is that many of them have, at one point or another, felt the same way—and despite six years passing since I first set out to find answers, I still can't say it's a topic that gets much airtime in the financial world.

This lack of exposure is part of the problem. It's hard to collectively change something if very few people see the connection between beauty standards and economic oppression. When I saw through this matrix for the first time, I felt conflicted. After all, there's a bit of game theory at play: Sure, it's better for everyone if *everyone* disavows these ideals and stops participating—but if you're the *only* one who opts out, you've merely disadvantaged yourself. "The way that beauty culture works is that the more people who opt into a standard and decide to try to embody that standard, the more normalized it becomes," Jessica told me.

I have a few close friends who embrace aging, rarely wear makeup, and focus the vast majority of their energy on interests and goals outside of themselves. Spending time with them almost always reorients me accordingly, building up the areas of my psyche that have been eroded by an onslaught of cultural messages attempting to direct me to my nearest Juvéderm specialist to eliminate the unsightly laugh lines on my aging face. This highlights the way in which the beauty industry (and marketing more generally) might be a broad, far-reaching system with its tentacles puppeteering societal norms, but individuals have the power to influence one another with their choices to abstain. A system is only as strong as its participants. Disentangling yourself from the Hot Girl Hamster Wheel innately gives other women in your orbit permission to do the same, and reroutes our precious resources toward furthering our autonomy and power, rather than supporting systems that do the opposite.

The economics of being a Hot Girl come with a steep, seven-figure opportunity cost, and when they've been part of your life since puberty, these cuts can be some of the hardest to make—at first. We sense, whether implicitly or explicitly, that our non-adherence will be punished, so divesting feels risky. But once you commit to pausing the Hamster Wheel's relentless spin to re-assess your relationship to it, you may find yourself experiencing similar emotions as I did: that the reclaimed time and money helps offset any negative ramifications you might face.

It's also okay if you decide some of these expenses (or all of them) are still worth it to you. Part of leveling up financially is taking a closer look at where you're splurging and where you're abstaining so you can gain an intimate understanding of how your choices are *really* benefiting you (and what those benefits cost you and the people around you).

Whether our jaunt together on the Hot Girl Hamster Wheel felt uncomfortably resonant or like a round trip to Money Mars, where we're heading next should hit close to home regardless of your commitment to fleeting beauty trends: what we know to be true about the gender wage gap data, and the clues it leaves about how women can earn more money.

2

The Truth About
Earning More

I t didn't take me long in my first (or second, third, or fourth) role in the corporate world to notice something discordant about the organizations I worked in: While the fields I chose in my pursuit of professional fulfillment (communications, marketing, user experience, media) were predominantly female, things got increasingly pale and male as you traced your finger up the organizational chart.

While I was vaguely aware of the sinister force that is the gender wage gap, I wasn't worried that a man was being paid more to do the same job I was doing—because there really *weren't* any men at my level. The first large marketing department I worked in was 75 percent female, but the three highest-ranking (and highest-paid) people—the chief marketing officer and his two understudies—were men. I clocked this incongruity almost immediately in the first department-wide meetings I attended, and watched this disheartening pattern play out several more times as I switched jobs. When I heard the bewildering statistic that it wasn't until 2023 that women CEOs *finally* outnumbered CEOs named "John" in Fortune 500 companies, I wasn't surprised. I had never (and still have never!) worked for a company for which top brass is anything other than a straight white man. My career thus far has felt like that scene in the *Barbie* movie where Ken leaves the matriarchal society of Barbieland and finds himself wandering around a fairly average weekday corporate scene in Century City, quickly identifying—much like I did, but with far more glee, fist-pumping, and an equestrian motif—that "in the real world, men are in charge!"

This is still the context we exist within: Most high earners fit a vanishingly narrow profile. Within months of beginning my career, I went searching for something that would propel me past the frustrations I heard described at happy hours by the other more talented, experienced women in my office.

At first, I found salvation in the *"Lean In,* Boss Babe" playbook, a career prescription that I white-knuckled with great enthusiasm. This philosophy promised that with enough relentless rising and grinding, I could beat the boys at their own game—but eventually I grew cynical. It seemed to implicitly thrust gendered disparities like the wage gap back on women as an issue of inadequacy. As a result, I wrote off *anything* coded as "ladder climb-y" for a long time, rejecting this type of advice wholesale on the grounds that it was incomplete.

But the suggestion that earning more money will make your life easier is, ultimately, sound. After years of grappling with my complicated feelings, I realized it was the implied cause and effect of the philosophy ("Women are bad at negotiating, and that's why they earn less") that most spiked my blood pressure. It seemed powered by the notion that women *choose* to be underpaid, related to the "choice" defense of the wage gap, which says women earn less money because they self-select for lower-paid fields or just prefer to work fewer hours (we'll hop in our debunk-beds shortly to poke some holes in that logic). The point remains that two things can be true at once: Women do not earn less than men because they're "bad negotiators," *and* learning how to negotiate in a way that effectively navigates gender bias can help women earn more.

Income is the oxygen that enables all other personal finance advice to function. And while a lot of financial guidance laser-focuses on managing your expenses, it's important to stay grounded in the reality that ultimately there's a strong positive correlation between income and savings: People who earn more, save more, and those savings are what enable financial freedom.

But no conversation about how women can earn more money is complete without first exploring our cultural circumstances. Enter: the wage gap, and the historical, cultural, and economic factors that impact our careers and earning potential. Understanding *why* women who work full time tend to earn less than men reveals a few clues about where we need to focus our energy as we work toward earning more. After a tour of the state of the wage gap today, why it's so persistent, some of the most common myths surrounding it, and the perceptions that undermine women in the workforce, we'll spend most of our time in this chapter talking about how to strategically represent your financial interests in a variety of different situations as both an employee and an entrepreneur.

Understanding the gender wage gap

My Grandma Jean was a medical technologist in the 1960s and especially adept at zeroing in on the best vein for a blood draw.

After a few years in her field, she and some of the other women she worked with realized they were being underpaid, so they went to the doctor who managed them to request a raise (collective action queens!). He said no. "You're all married," he told them. "You have husbands to provide for you. You don't need the money." This attitude was explicit, unapologetic, and pervasive. Even though such a rejection would be legally discriminatory today, the same logic still subconsciously undergirds how "women's work" is compensated the world over: Think of any field that's traditionally staffed by women, and you're likely to hear that they "don't do it for the money" or are "doing it because they love it." Women, apparently, don't work for wages, but for personal fulfillment—and if they're just working for fulfillment, who cares what you pay them?

The earliest data about the difference between how all men and all women earn comes from the year 1960, when women who worked full time earned, on average, 60.7 percent as much as men who worked full time. In the sixty intervening years since, the gap—which actually widened at first, reaching its largest deficit in 1973 at 56.6 percent—has crawled closer to parity.

The state of the wage gap today

As of 2023, all women who work full time earn about 83.6 percent of what all men who work full time earn. Your mileage may vary based on your race, parental status, marital status, education, and age: For example, Hispanic women have the largest gender wage gap when compared to white men (65 percent), and mothers in their twenties have a smaller gender wage gap (80 percent) than mothers in their forties (73 percent) when compared to fathers, who are the highest-earning group. Somewhat surprisingly, the gender wage gap is actually smaller for high school graduates than for those with bachelor's degrees. But if you pooled *all* men's full-time wages and compared them to *all* women's full-time wages, the men are pulling in about 19.6 percent more money than women.

Google's predictive suggested searches on the topic are telling: The first is "gender pay gap explained," while the very next is "gender pay gap debunked." You don't have to venture very far down in the search results before things devolve from open-minded discussions about equal pay to anonymous commenters trotting out ahistorical talking points about hunter-gatherers, embracing the readily disprovable fantasy that, *good news, we can pack it up!*, bias from pay and family structures has been eradicated.

Because as with most large-scale, culturally embedded trends, things are more complex than meets the eye. The key data point at hand—that *all* women who work full time earn, on average, eighty-three cents for every dollar *all* men who work full time earn—is useful for indicating an issue, but in some ways, it raises more questions than it answers. As a result, the primary interpretation is that a man and a woman who do the exact same job will be paid differently, which isn't *technically* what the data represents (though this happens, too). This is the argument at which most "debunkers" focus their efforts.

Skeptics point to the "controlled" gender wage gap as a more accurate measure of equality, since it's an attempt at normalizing for things like years of experience, title, and industry to create more of an apples-to-apples comparison (though even this introduces points of contention, as part of the problem is that it's harder for some people to reach certain titles or levels of experience, so there's a selection bias present in only studying those who do). But even when controlling for as many variables as possible, you're left with inequity: While these numbers *do* look better in the aggregate, men and women in substantially similar jobs with similar work experience, education, and hours worked are still paid disparately in a variety of important fields.

Controlling for experience, practice area, and hours worked, female physicians and surgeons earn only 93 percent of what male physicians and surgeons do. The controlled gender wage gap for everyone from credit analysts to insurance sales agents, to first-line supervisors of production and operating workers, to "inspectors, testers, sorters, samplers and weighers," to claims adjusters and investigators is 91 percent.

Remember: These are outcomes for women and men doing the same job with the same level of expertise and experience, and working for the same amount of time. And while these are simply cold, indisputable data points, the *explanations* for this phenomenon are a sketchy playground after dark. The wage gap deniers might proffer a description of reality that attempts to justify male dominance at top levels of government and business as little more than the consequence of natural, run-of-the-mill personality differences between men and women—that they're biologically more fit to fill roles like chief executive officer, president, pope . . . you know, all of the most powerful positions in the world! What a convenient conclusion for *checks notes* men. It's in this playground that you'll encounter a lot of curious references to the aforementioned "hunter-gatherer" societies that seem to suggest upper body strength and physical speed are somehow paramount for success in the rugged terrain of a cubicle farm.[†]

---

† Even this conventional wisdom was called into question in 2023 when new archaeological research examined sixty-three societies in the Holocene era across cultures and discovered evidence that women were hunters in 79 percent of them. But I digress.

Instead of visiting this sketchy playground, let's debunk the most popular explanation for the wage gap—then look at the most likely reason it *really* persists today.

The "choice" defense of the wage gap

The most common rationalization for the wage gap is simple: Women just so happen to choose all the jobs that aren't valuable and don't pay as well. To understand this argument, let's take a trip down memory lane. The nation's first computers were programmed by six math whizzes: Frances, Jean, Kay, Marlyn, Ruth, and (another) Frances. That's right. The original tech bros weren't bros at all. But for decades, their work went unrecognized—until lawyer and digital-rights activist Kathy Kleiman stumbled upon archived images of a secret US Army project during World War II, the ENIAC computer. The ENIAC was "the world's first all-electronic, programmable general-purpose computer." But Kleiman noticed something funny about the pictures: Only the men's names were listed in the captions. Nobody knew who the women were. (At one point in her quest to identify them and understand their contribution to the secret project, she was told they were random models placed in front of the machines to make them look nicer.)

Since the programmers developing the nation's first computers in the 1940s and 1950s were women, the work was seen as unglamorous, rote, and, well, "women's work." As such, pay was low. But as more and more people began to see programming as complex, analytical, and challenging, career aptitude and personality tests steered more men into the field—and over time, the "brogrammer" was born. You know what happens next if you've seen *The Social Network*: The pay and prestige promptly rose, illustrating the way the *person doing the job* influences our perception of how valuable (or not valuable) it is.

This is known as "occupational segregation," and it's the explanation for what wage gap deniers often chalk up to women at large simply *choosing* lower-paying work (like "female doctor" and "female lawyer," as the joke goes). And while it's true that women are overrepresented in low-wage shift work (they represent nearly 60 percent of low-wage workers despite making up only 47 percent of the total workforce), we shouldn't assume this overrepresentation can explain the "eighty-three cents on the dollar" phenomenon. Claudia Goldin, a Nobel Prize–winning economist who is committed to more fully understanding the gender pay gap, found that women's overrepresentation in low-wage work is responsible for no more than one third of the gap. (In other words, if you control for job choice, the gap is eighty-nine cents on the dollar, not eighty-three.)

The idea that women in the aggregate *just so happen* to choose work that *just so happens* to pay less relies on a bit of willful historical ignorance. The data indicates the opposite is happening: Women don't choose lower-paying fields. Fields pay less *because* they're primarily staffed by women. When a field experiences an influx of women, it leads to lower pay. (One way to reliably reduce this effect for women at the aggregate? Unions. Women in unions make, on average, 22 percent more than women not represented by collective bargaining agreements, and the gender wage gap is smaller for unionized workers, at around 6.6 percent rather than 16.4 percent. Put another way, unionized women earn around ninety-three cents, not eighty-three cents, for every dollar their male counterparts earn. They're also more likely to have things like paid family leave.)

The curious impact of age on women's earnings over time

So then, what *can* explain the gap? It turns out my anecdotal experience in corporate America was quite telling. Claudia Goldin's research focuses not on direct gender discrimination as the primary driver, but on how the life experiences of women and men diverge as they age. She postulates that men who work full time might earn more than women because men tend to ascend to higher positions than women do as their careers progress. That is to say: More illuminating information is revealed about the wage gap not when you consider a snapshot of the data, but when you study how it impacts women *over time*. There's strong evidence that gender pay disparity is exacerbated as women get older, which can give us clues about what might be driving it.

A Harvard study of the wage gap among people with MBAs from the University of Chicago found that the wage gap was relatively small upon graduation ($115,000 starting salary for women and $130,000 for men, which doesn't sound all that small to me, but just you wait!) and widens considerably as time passes—nine years later, the women were earning $250,000 while their male classmates were pulling down $400,000. The study found that men in the dataset tended to have a longer "right tail"; that is, men in the 90th percentile of earnings thirteen years post-MBA earned $1.2 million, whereas women in the 90th percentile earned just shy of $400,000.

And we're talking about highly educated individuals with prestigious secondary degrees, which highlights the paradoxical reality that the wage gap is *larger* in highly paid, highly educated work, compared to low-wage work, where a "floor" (the minimum wage) tends to act as an equalizing force.

Overall, the gender wage gap is largest among fifty-five-to-sixty-four-year-old workers, at 77.2 percent. This is why I'm hesitant to celebrate an otherwise bright spot in recent developments: As of 2022, women under thirty now outearn men in 16 cities across the US (only 228 more to go!). While I feel encouraged by this, the fact that the trend is specific to *young* women—who, the researchers point out, likely have not yet started families—doesn't necessarily signal change for women as a whole. Why might growing older, getting married, and starting a family be particularly detrimental to women's earning potential but not men's? We'll spend most of Chapter 5 on that brain teaser.

Where "traditional" negotiation advice falls short

Now that we know how the gender wage gap changes as women age, there's one final borderline-depressing-but-totally-worth-examining explanation of why women earn less than men: You've probably heard that women simply negotiate less (a vector of the "women's choices and behavior are to blame" framework). But recent research gives us reason to believe that this conventional wisdom is probably bullshit. Research from 2014 found that when job postings stated that wages were negotiable, there was no observable difference between men and women's likelihood to negotiate—it was only in environments where the method by which "wage(s) [were] determined was ambiguous" that men were more likely than women to *try* to negotiate for a higher wage.

So naturally, you might conclude that the solution is clear: Even in "wage-ambiguous" environments, women should ask for more money. Problem solved! Except pump the brakes, Rosie the Riveter, because later research found that when women were *just as likely* to ask for a raise, they were *less likely to receive one*, on average. Artz, Goodall, and Oswald found that, "holding background factors constant, women ask for a raise just as often as men, but men are more likely to be successful. Women who asked obtained a raise 15% of the time, while men obtained a pay increase 20% of the time. While that may sound like a modest difference, over a lifetime it really adds up."[†] These results are often chalked up to women's supposed "lack of self-confidence"— that they simply aren't aggressive enough in their request. But unless you're a card-carrying misogynist, which explanation for this phenomenon sounds more reasonable?

1. Men on the aggregate level are just 33 percent better at their jobs (or negotiating) than women, and therefore 33 percent more likely to hear a yes when they ask for a bump in compensation.
2. The 33 percent difference in outcomes can be attributed to a subconscious but pernicious belief in number 1.

Even if you accept the flawed premise that women's behavior in the workplace is the problem, the advice to be more assertive at work doesn't work for women the way it works for men. Four different studies from Harvard and Carnegie Mellon[‡] found that people "penalized women more than men for attempting to negotiate for higher compensation." It didn't matter whether the

---

† The dataset used in this research came from 4,600 randomly selected employees across eight hundred workplaces in Australia, the only nation that the study authors found to have "really good information" on how much "asking" was occurring in wage negotiations.

‡ These high-level studies, while landmark, were done in the early 2000s. Many of the more recent experiments that attempted to study this phenomenon were conducted in specific fields, like academics or STEM, and affirmed the findings described here.

negotiation was in person or on video or on paper, or whether the study participants made observations from the role of hiring manager or objective, third-party viewer. Even *women* viewed the women who asked for more money less favorably, which underscores the uncomfortable fact that it's possible to feel bias against a group to which you belong.

Feminist philosopher Kate Manne writes about how women who desire "masculine-coded goods" are more likely to be punished for behaving in ways that subvert the gender binary. These goods include "positions of leadership, authority, influence, money, and other forms of power, as well as social status, prestige, rank, and the markers thereof." Since masculine-coded goods usually serve to reinforce some hierarchy of power, they're perceived as being zero-sum—and a woman who pursues something that's considered to rightly belong to men is seen as *taking* something that doesn't (and can't, per patriarchal logic) rightly belong to her. Because powerful women are "better tolerated when [their power] is wielded in service of patriarchal interests," the incentives are strong for women who eventually gain it to then *turn around and reinforce these very norms in order to keep it.*

I asked Kathryn Valentine, a negotiation expert who specializes in negotiations where research indicates that gender bias is likely to play a role, for her perspective. She's dedicated her career to understanding and addressing these dynamics. She confirmed the findings of the research I referenced earlier that "traditional" negotiation advice—aggressively and directly asking—doesn't quite work for women in the same way it works for men, for three reasons:

1. We generally expect different behavior from women and men (you should smile more!).

2. The general "I win, you lose," combative perception of negotiation in the media sets up women (for whom "agreeableness" is a more highly valued trait) in particular for failure (so . . . you should smile more?).

3. Perhaps most interestingly, *both* genders suffer pushback when negotiating things that feel "gender-incongruent." For example, a man negotiating for more flexibility or time at home is likely to experience the same negative effects that a woman negotiating higher pay might face.

This illustrates why the "Act like men to 'make it' in a man's world" advice is so self-defeating—women are penalized when they defy gender norms. Moreover, it presumes the so-called "man's way" is the *correct* way, that assimilation into traditional power structures is how we reach parity. So how can we navigate these dynamics?

Earning more money

At this point, you're probably like, "Well, shit, Katie, you're painting a pretty bleak picture here—what's next? You're going to tell us we should bag it entirely and resign ourselves to a life of cottagecore housewifery?" Lucky for you, my love of financial autonomy trumps my statistics-driven disillusionment, so let's push forward. Because while the "women's biology and preferences are to blame for the wage gap" theories that attempt to thrust responsibility back onto women range from absurd to insulting, knowing which tactics are most likely to generate an increase in income can help. (Not the least of which being: Join a union.)

I've experienced two distinct "phases" in my career: The first phase involved three stints in giant companies with massive compliance departments, and the second phase is what I'd call "fending for myself as a business owner." And while there are some principles that apply across the board, these careers-within-a-career taught me very different lessons about earning more money—so I'm going to break up my insights accordingly.

Much of the negotiation advice I've encountered deals a lot with semantic fancy footwork: specific phrases, argument structures, and Glassdoor stalking. And while those methods can be effective when implemented correctly, I've always found they're most effective when paired with a few high-leverage tactics. (And if you're not currently earning income from paid work because you're contributing to your household in another way, we'll talk more in Chapters 4 and 5 about ways you, too, can financially protect yourself.)

Negotiating for more money when you work for someone else

When you work for someone else, your compensation is determined by the market rate (what they think they need to pay to get you to stick around; this is external to you and your performance) and their perception of your "value" to the company (what you have some control over, and what we're trying to impact). Let's start by looking at your perceived value.

WHAT YOU CAN CONTROL: YOUR PERCEIVED VALUE IN THE COMPANY

There are three high-leverage components of boosting your perceived value to a business: socializing your wins, embracing the "extra yard" mentality, and managing up effectively. Taken together, nailing these three elements of corporate politics will amplify your excellent work and create rich ground for negotiation.

Socializing your wins

Workplaces are a little like glorified high school lunchrooms, which sheds light on why trends like "all-male boards" tend to reproduce themselves in self-perpetuating cycles of endorsement. The old dog sees himself in the young pup and takes him under his wing (we're mixing animal metaphors now, but the point stands). I've worked in fantastic environments and not-so-fantastic ones, but this fundamental truth has been pervasive in all of them: It's incredibly difficult to make progress without advocates (and if you've got a manager who has it out for you, get off that team or out of that company as soon as possible—because you'll be rowing upstream forever otherwise).

This type of politicking used to drive me crazy; if I was good at what I did, shouldn't that be enough? But humans are imperfect, so organizations composed of them will be, too. "Socializing your wins" (a term that's so jargony I gagged while typing it)—by which I mean finding discreet ways to highlight your victories at work to build an intentional, broad, public perception of *I get shit done*—is more powerful than quietly logging all your conquests in a spreadsheet to be revealed privately in a one-on-one. (That's why I believe the popular strain of advice that recommends tracking your wins at work so you can unfurl your scroll of badassery in a negotiation later is *good*, but incomplete.)

I once had a coworker—let's call her Bridget—who did this exceptionally well. Bridget was often the person communicating wins for her team or sharing learnings from side projects she had taken on. Everything was always disseminated in a tone that communicated she was just "sharing these interesting findings from a user experience session from last week, in case anyone else finds them useful," which felt less like a bragging montage and more like a person who *really* understood how to wield her work in a way that conveyed "I'm competent, on top of it, and here to make things happen." Bridget got promoted twice in the four years I worked for that company. (Though she's since left to become an attorney, which I think is hilarious—if you have an innate knack for presenting compelling information in a way that benefits you, you might as well hit up law school and cash in.)

This practice of sharing wins ladders up to a broader truth: What I've found to be the true needle mover, time and time again, is having an engaged network of advocates inside your organization. We're talking about other, more senior employees (ideally including your own manager) who are willing to go to bat for you.

Going the extra yard

So how do you assemble that coalition of natural advocates? This is less about the specific words you say or data you present in a private negotiation, and more about laying the groundwork over time. A core crew of people in your organization who look out for you can mean easier access to the projects and opportunities that put you in the high-visibility positions necessary to earn more. The fantastic thing I noticed in my time trafficking in slide decks and email threads? You don't need to go the extra mile to stand out—you just need to go the extra yard. Here are a few examples:

- If a deadline is Friday, hand over the deliverable on Thursday.
- If you have a standing one-on-one with someone whose opinion impacts your compensation, send an agenda ahead of time and manage up.

- If you're asked to pull a report on three factors influencing conversion, throw in a fourth.
- If you're bringing an issue to a manager, come prepared with a recommended solution you're ready to execute. (More on this in a moment.)

This doesn't mean you need to be on Slack on Saturday mornings firing off compliments to everyone on payroll—but the "extra yard" mentality goes a long way in establishing a disproportionately robust perception of your work ethic that makes building a network of cheerleaders (and sailing through negotiation conversations) much easier.

The five levels of managing up

I asked my friend Tara Reed—founder and CEO of the multimillion-dollar ed-tech business Apps Without Code, who spent her early years at Microsoft and Google—what she felt was crucial to know when it came to justifying promotions, and she laid out her favorite five-level framework. "When you go to your boss with a problem or challenge, how are you framing it? Communicating with C-suite level executives in a way that conveys you're making their lives easier puts you on a fast track." Here's how she breaks down the levels of "managing up":

Level 1: "Here's the problem."

Level 2: "Here's the problem. I've started to investigate, and I think this is what's causing it."

Level 3: "Here's the problem and its cause. These are a few possible solutions."

Level 4: "Here's the problem. These are a few possible solutions, and this is the solution I recommend."

Level 5: "Here's the problem and what's causing it. This is what I already did to address it. Just keeping you in the loop."

"If you work at a startup," she said, "Level 4 is the minimum contribution." This framework strikes me as especially helpful for someone who's trying to position themselves for a big step up in responsibility. "When someone's consistently performing at a Level 5," she told me, "the promotion happens effortlessly." *Jump cut to me withering away in shame as I reflect on all my Level 1 and 2 communications to past managers.*

Consistently implementing these three practices will create ultra-fertile soil for your negotiation, and you may have noticed that none of these internal influences involve hard numbers. The other element—the one that's external to you—is where hard numbers come in handy.

WHAT YOU CAN'T CONTROL AS EASILY OR QUICKLY: YOUR MARKET RATE

Your "market rate" is defined by the price you could command in the labor market (and helps demonstrate why things like collective bargaining are so powerful, because your power as an individual wage worker is inherently so much weaker than that of a giant corporation). In other words, what's the typical salary range that senior graphic designers with five years of experience working at medium-sized companies in the Bay Area are being paid? If your employer wants to compete in the labor market for the best employees, it's likely they're *trying* to pay somewhere in that range (though the range can be wide). Determining your market rate used to be a little trickier, as we had to rely on hushed conversations with coworkers and sites like Glassdoor. But as more states pass salary transparency laws, it becomes easier to gauge—in real time, for your company and companies like it—how your skill set is valued by the market.

Determining your market rate

As of January 1, 2025, businesses in California, Colorado, Connecticut, Hawaii, Illinois, Maryland, Massachusetts, Minnesota, Nevada, New York, Rhode Island, Washington, and the District of Columbia (as well as some cities in Ohio and New Jersey) are required to disclose some level of salary transparency data, though laws vary by state. In most cases, this means they're required to share the salary range in a job posting, which means you've got a treasure trove of data to pull from if you're trying to understand what the market has determined "fair compensation" to be for a role like yours. This data can help you triangulate a reasonable compensation figure to target when you go into a negotiation conversation. My favorite site for quickly comparing job listings is the "Jobs" section on LinkedIn, especially because it makes taking the next step of securing another offer—which *really* kicks things up a notch—a lot easier.

Securing another offer

While data around fair market rates for your role *might* be a compelling enough reason for your manager to increase your income accordingly, it's not foolproof. The best way to hold someone's feet to the fire and force the issue is to get another, higher offer from someone else. Having a better offer immediately tilts all the leverage in your favor. Unfortunately, this process can be annoying—applying and interviewing for other positions can feel like an unpaid part-time job—but I've found it's the surest way to secure the outcome you want, if the outcome you want is being paid more. (Even if your current company doesn't budge, you now have another option!) And since your company would incur costs if they had to replace you, (politely) threatening to leave gives you the upper hand—it takes time and money to find, hire, and train a new employee. When bringing a higher offer to your manager, it's critical to be intentional about your rhetoric: Instead of attaching the offer to a blank email with the subject line "Your move, assholes! Sent from my iPhone" and hoping for the best, ask for a meeting and share that you'd prefer to stay, as you see growth opportunities at your company—but you've received this offer for a similar role with similar experience and ask them what they think.

One of my favorite managers encouraged us to routinely apply and interview for roles at other companies to keep tabs on what we were able to earn elsewhere, as well as to keep the skills sharp. Interviewing and negotiating, like most things, takes a lot of practice, and doing it in low-stakes situations can be an opportunity to get reps. All that to say: It can be a pain in the ass to get a better offer somewhere else, but there are professional benefits beyond the immediate pay bump. And while this outcome is less likely, it's also possible you'll find that you're *already* being paid competitively (yeehaw!)—in which case you may decide you'd rather grow your skill set such that you're competing in a different pay band. Cue the JavaScript boot camp montage. I don't think there's a standard formula that companies use to determine compensation increases, but I have a feeling it's something like this:

WHAT THEY'RE WILLING TO PAY YOU

=

(the market rate allotted for the position)

+

(the additional cost they'd incur if they needed to replace you)^(*the special sauce you bring to the role*)

Some people skate through their entire careers inflating their compensation based solely on that "special sauce" exponent, so we often focus on that piece—but we shouldn't overlook the practical importance of the first two elements.

Having the negotiation conversation

If you've nailed socializing your wins, going the extra yard, *and* managing up masterfully, and you've targeted a competitive compensation worth fighting for, you're in a good position to set yourself up for a pay bump. How should you approach that conversation? Kathryn Valentine suggested a three-part framework:

1. **Think holistically.** If you're only asking for one thing, you're significantly limiting your upside. Think about all the places you can get more value: What would allow you to deliver more impact? What would lower your stress level? What would bring you more joy? What's sucking your energy right now that could get taken off your plate?

She offered a few examples: an additional work-at-home day per week, offloading a portion of the job that's especially draining, or a change in title that'll make it easier for you to get things done across teams (and therefore pave the path to a bigger jump later).

2. **Ask relationally.** Kathryn told me this one is her favorite. "If women can demonstrate that their request is both legitimate and beneficial for everyone, they virtually eliminate the risk of backlash," she said. To ask relationally, you mention past performance, you explain your vision for the future, and then—crucially—you stop talking. (She mentioned that because women are often socialized to put people at ease and prioritize the comfort of others, they're more likely to make an ask . . . and then begin negotiating against themselves.) An example of this done well: "As you've seen this quarter, I was able to increase our team's output by ten percent. Next quarter, I think I can hit fifteen percent growth, but to do that, I would like to talk to you about the working hours that'll make me most effective. What do you think?" (End of sentence.)

3. **Discuss collaboratively.** The collaborative approach is a proven best practice in negotiations and also has added benefits for women who are more likely to be penalized for being assertive. Rather than thinking about a negotiation as "you" versus "them," Kathryn said, it's "us" versus "the problem." "The problem" is anything that prevents you from delivering the highest impact at the lowest stress level. "People already expect women to be collaborative," Kathryn told me, "so using this approach that works for everyone gives women in particular a slight edge."

While we reviewed these strategies, I couldn't help but feel a gnawing agitation. Finally, I broke the glass fourth wall and asked Kathryn directly: "Do you ever feel annoyed that women have to perform these mental gymnastics to elicit the desired outcome?"

"Totally," she replied, "but these are good negotiation tactics regardless of gender. In twenty years, I have a feeling this is how my son will need to negotiate to excel in a more diverse workplace. This is how my husband, who's an introvert, negotiates. It's simply more comfortable." In other words, the world is moving in this direction—and women stand to benefit the most by being ahead of the curve in their implementation.

ADVANCED TECHNIQUES FOR HIGH-STAKES NEGOTIATIONS: MULTIPLE EQUIVALENT SIMULTANEOUS OFFERS

There's one other negotiation technique worth knowing, called "MESOs," or Multiple Equivalent Simultaneous Offers. The strategy works because you're structuring *options* for someone to choose from. Crucially, these options feel to your negotiation partner like choices for how to proceed . . . but you'd be happy with any of the outcomes.

My friend—we'll call her Mary—is a salesperson for a tech company, and her boss was recently fired. She knew her boss's compensation structure, and how it differed from her own. As luck would have it (as it often does in these types of forced re-orgs), her boss's boss wanted *her* to fill his role for the next six months while they assessed their options. They both knew she wasn't going to do it for free, but they weren't sure how to proceed. Mary decided to structure multiple equivalent simultaneous offers for him to choose from:

Offer 1: You increase my base compensation to match his for the next six months, but you keep my commission structure and bonuses the same.

This offer appeals to a desire to keep things straightforward and fair.

Offer 2: You keep my base compensation the same, but you give me one bonus now equivalent to three months' worth of the difference between his pay and mine, and the other half at the end of the six months, assuming I hit the performance targets we agree upon.

This offer begins to tie compensation changes to performance and might be beneficial for the company to pay out compensation differently than on biweekly paychecks, as different types of compensation often come from different cost centers.

Offer 3: You keep my base compensation the same, I keep my same, smaller bonus, but you increase my commission percentage.

This offer has the largest upside potential for her and the lowest downside potential for the company.

Mary also negotiated that at the end of the six-month period, if she hit the benchmarks they had agreed upon, she'd be offered the job permanently. She structured her stepping up to backfill the role temporarily as a sort of prolonged trial period, and she explained it as such: *You'll get to use this as a trial period to see how I do the job, and if I exceed expectations, this will be the outcome.*

Negotiating with a new employer, where you have no track record

But what if you're not already inside a company? What if you're negotiating with a hiring manager for a new job, where you don't already have advocates and a track record that you built through socializing your wins, going the extra yard, and managing up? There are a few flash points during the hiring process where you can most efficiently impact the offer, so let's unpack them one at a time.

"WHAT ARE YOUR SALARY EXPECTATIONS?"

While being asked this question during an interview can feel like a trapdoor, how you answer it depends on where you are in the process. Let's say you're only willing to leave your current company for $70,000 or more, but your true goal is $80,000. If the top end of their range is $60,000, you'd probably rather know that up front so you don't waste your time (and if there are other openings that are better suited for you in the company, they can shuffle you there instead). Refusing to give a number or deflecting can make it seem as though you're not sure what you're worth or what the role should pay, so if it's early in the process, I like to say something like this: "It's hard to specify a target right now without knowing more about what success looks like in this role, but I'd be comfortable landing somewhere in the (*here's where you give a very padded range!*) $75,000 to $85,000 range given my ten years of experience and the value I know I can bring to the team." It's unlikely you'll undershoot a realistic estimate if you've done your research on the role ahead of time, though there's always a chance they had you pegged at $95,000 and now they're looking at you with dollar signs in their eyes because they know you'll probably take $80,000. Still, it's a risk you can mitigate with proper due diligence.

Plus, if you're way over what they can offer, they'll tell you. I once went through a screening call where I told the recruiter I was expecting something in the range of $120,000 to $140,000 and they told me the cap for the position was $95,000, but that they'd keep me in mind for more senior roles in the future. If I had played coy, I would've wasted a lot of time in the hiring process only to learn the maximum salary was way below my target.

I know this runs counter to traditional advice, but in my experience, throwing out data-informed numbers that excited me has never backfired—and as you move further along in the process and learn more about what the position actually entails, you can adjust your estimates upward if you find it's substantially more responsibility than you had originally anticipated.

THE ART OF INFORMED "PADDING"

So you've almost got an offer in hand, and it's time to discuss compensation again. The single most important thing to remember when negotiating with a prospective employer who's just offered you a job is that—unless you are blatantly overqualified—it's very unlikely their first number is the top of the range they're authorized to offer. All that to say: They're giving themselves breathing room because they're *expecting* you to negotiate. I've found that the most comfortable way to have this conversation with a hiring manager is to rely on my (market-rate-informed, padded) current compensation.

When calculating your current compensation, consider:

- Your base pay
- Your old 401(k) or HSA match, if you have one

- Your old bonuses or profit sharing
- Any other benefits that have monetary value

If your base pay at your old employer was $60,000 but they gave you a $4,000 match, a $1,000 bonus, and a $500 stipend, your old compensation wasn't $60,000. It was $65,500. If your *new* offer from another company comes out of the gate at $68,000 and you know you want to land somewhere closer to $72,000, you can (honestly) say: "Thank you so much for the offer. I'm so excited about this opportunity, and I'm confident I'll be able to make an impact quickly. My current compensation is in the high $60,000 range, and in order to make this jump, I'm looking to increase my current compensation. Is $75,000 doable?" They might accept, or they might walk you down to the number you're hoping for, $72,000, which you can happily accept.

Relying on this exceedingly reasonable proof point—"I already earn that much"—has always felt like more solid ground than pointing to qualifications that might feel slippery and hard to quantify, or someone else's compensation (read: Glassdoor data), especially in the sociocultural context wherein women who ask for more money are more likely to be perceived as "aggressive." Importantly, you don't want to disclose your current salary (even a padded version of it) too early in the process—it's only *after* you've been offered the job, you're confident you know what it *should* pay, and that a padded version can get you reasonably close, that you'd gesture to your old compensation.

If you have other bargaining chips, like being decisively over-qualified or leaving your current company before a bonus hits, you could ask for even more. But, as in this example where we went from a salary of $60,000 to $72,000 with one (totally fair) request, you can use your old total compensation to significantly increase your base pay. An additional $4,000 more than their original offer is a blip for them, but a meaningful increase for you. Just make sure you're actually happy with the number you're proposing. If they agree to it, it's likely the negotiation ends there. It's hard to come back with, "Dope, so what about $78,000?"

The reality, though, is that you'll probably already get offered quite a bit more than what your current employer is paying you, so this trick only works if you can juice your current compensation enough to give yourself that realistically justified springboard— I've used this tactic three times and it's never failed me. If for some reason it doesn't work, you can try leveraging a bonus (or other reward) from your current position that you're forgoing in the job switch for a one-time signing bonus: "I'm excited to pursue this new opportunity, but in doing so, I'm forgoing a performance bonus I've already earned that would be paid out in [month] after I leave. It would be great if it could be matched in a one-time signing bonus. What do you think?"

Earning more . . . by working for yourself

The tactics I just reviewed represent the extent of the toolbox I was equipped with when I found myself on the other side of the table from Morning Brew's CEO, in way over my head negotiating an "acquihire" deal for my brand Money with Katie, its intellectual property, and forty hours per week of my time. I quickly learned that negotiating *deals* is a different ballgame entirely from salary negotiation. The last few years of my life have been a crash course in high-stakes negotiations, and I've been lucky to learn from people who have much more business experience than I do. (Every time I say "deals" I inadvertently adopt a Long Island–adjacent Trumpian accent, so please forgive me in advance for the repetition of that phrase—it's the broadest way I can reference all the different ways you might end up entering into business agreements with other people.)

In my own life, the key to earning a lot of money was entrepreneurship, and it's likely that other women will find this path to be more exciting and interesting to them, too, as it can sidestep some of this jockeying with the aforementioned pale and male org charts. But I'm going to resist the urge to position that path as the "best" way to earn a good living, because tax data tells us it's actually a rare way to "get rich." (Yes, despite what the ThinkBoiz on Twitter will tell you about the illustrious grind of "being your own boss," you're statistically more likely to earn a lot of money working for someone else than as a business owner.) A full 60 percent of top 0.1 percent earners are executives, managers, supervisors, or financial professionals.

To that point, I've aged approximately twenty years in the last sixty months learning how to successfully turn my side hustle into a real business. If you're interested in this path (or already on it), the following three hard-earned lessons are the things I wish I had known five years ago when I bought the domain for moneywithkatie.com. Because while we've focused a lot on negotiation already, being in business for yourself can similarly increase your income—but navigating these challenges requires an entirely different set of working knowledge.

LESSON 1: WHEN YOU'RE BUILDING A BUSINESS, FIGURE OUT WHAT YOU'RE OPTIMIZING FOR

You build (and scale) a business differently when you're trying to optimize for time, rather than growth. If your gut instinct was "I'm optimizing for money, obviously," great—my work here is done! (I kid, I kid—sort of.) When I was starting a business (read:

writing a blog in my free time for fun without *survey says* any discernible plan for monetization), the idea of earning money from writing felt like a pipe dream. All I knew was that I wanted to earn a lot doing something fun, to the tune of an ungodly goal income ($10,000 per month) and a blessedly unrigorous schedule. But I hadn't given much thought to what the end goal really was.

Once Money with Katie was off to the races in 2021, I went through an online MBA-for-creative-entrepreneurs-style cohort learning program in which we were forced to sit down and articulate *specifically* what we were trying to create, and I proudly told my group that my recurring revenue goal was $50,000 per month (this works out to a very respectable $600,000 gross revenue per year). The first question volleyed back caught me off guard: "Why?"

"Why?" I parroted back, my brain short-circuiting at the question's premise. *Well, why not?* I thought. *Isn't this what entrepreneurs do? They build a business, then try to make that business as big as possible?* By this point, Money with Katie was already consistently generating around $25,000 per month in gross revenue, so this doubled goal of $50,000 felt sensible, natural. After blowing past my previously unthinkable $10,000 per month, it took me approximately no time at all to up the ante.

But my small group pressed me on my suspiciously round number, and I realized it wasn't based on anything beyond stroking my own ego. After learning that my monthly expenses were quite low and my lifestyle required nowhere near $50,000 per month to support, another member of the cohort offered a suggestion: "What if, instead of trying to work harder to double your current revenue, you made your goal to earn the same amount, but by working for half the time?" This seemingly obvious reframing of the inverse relationship between time and money felt like a blurry lens finding focus: *Of course,* I thought. *Wouldn't it be better to work twenty hours per week earning $25,000 per month than forty-plus hours per week to earn $50,000?*

While that experience made me realize it was possible to optimize for lifestyle, it wasn't until I actually had a lifestyle business that I realized it was very hard to tamp down my ambition. I claimed I wanted to optimize for fun, freedom, and flexibility—and yet every decision I made was functionally prioritizing growth. Days full of meetings, saying yes to every opportunity that crossed my desk, and rarely working less than eight hours per day, seven days per week. It took me a year or two to recognize that, in my midtwenties and the early days of something I felt strongly about, the allure of seeing how far I could take my new enterprise was greater than having four-hour workdays. I didn't *want* that much free time yet—I was too excited to build.

All this to say, I wish I had taken a step back before I got too far down the rabbit hole and tried to figure out what, exactly, my end goal was: Was I trying to optimize for growth? Reach? The highest income possible? Sustainability? Or was I just trying to optimize for a certain lifestyle? At first glance, these questions can feel a little "soft"—but the reality is, once the train starts barreling down the tracks, it can be hard to change course.

For example, if you decide maximum growth and income is your goal, part of building will probably involve inviting opportunities (and the external deadlines they impose) into your orbit. In the media business, the moment you start working with advertisers, you introduce external deadlines to your process. You might "be your own boss," but you're ultimately accountable to a friendly media buyer who wants to see their placements on time, every time, and they want them compliance-ready, baby! On the other hand, if you wanted to optimize for lifestyle or depth, you might choose a media model in which you sell directly to customers (courses, digital products, or subscriptions): You largely define your deadlines. This means you can take breaks when you need them *and* have the flexibility to freely change course. A media solopreneur who ultimately wants to control their own schedule more readily should probably build a business that focuses on revenue streams they have more control over and that can be automated to become almost entirely passive after the work is front-loaded (like digital product sales or software, which can be fueled by content marketing that leads to automated email marketing that makes the sales "for" you).

LESSON 2: WHEN YOU'RE NEGOTIATING FOR OWNERSHIP, THE "INTANGIBLES" CAN BE THE BIGGEST QUESTION MARK— AND THE MOST VALUABLE ASSET

By the time I was in talks with Morning Brew to join forces, I was earning a total compensation of roughly $140,000 at my full-time job after several strategic jumps between companies and roughly $250,000 per year from Money with Katie on the side. Translation: I was bringing in far more money than I figured I'd ever earn, even in my wildest career ambitions. That put me in a position of great leverage to be selective going into a negotiation for the brand. I knew what I could pull down alone (though with quite a bit of context-switching, when what I really wanted to do was work on Money with Katie full time), so I had a solid basis for the numbers I was bringing to the table.

Still, an acquihire deal—in which a brand acquires your intellectual property *and* hires you—is a bit hard to navigate, because you're not just selling your labor—you're trying to put a value on a nebulous concept or body of work, too, and what it might be worth in the future. In my case: my nascent podcast, blog posts and website, social media accounts, audiences, and, of course, the brand itself. (Narrator: She was underprepared.) In that way, I wasn't just committing to *run* Money with Katie for Morning Brew—I was *selling* them Money with Katie, which was terrifying. (Morning Brew itself had been recently acquired by *Business Insider*, owned by the giant media conglomerate Axel Springer, and their four-million-subscriber email list, ad business, and intellectual property was valued at a reported $75 million.)

I didn't know how to value my intellectual property (or, frankly, what "intellectual property" even meant), but I knew how to value my time. With the Morning Brew brand powering Money with Katie, I knew we could grow it a lot further (and faster) together than I could alone part time, and that I'd learn a *ton* about media from operating within the bounds of a successful media organization—and at the time, that was the most important thing. While the deal has been fruitful, selling your business to someone else is always a risk, because it's often very difficult to claw it back should things go sideways. When it was time to renegotiate my contract after the first one ended, we added a new termination clause that specified how and when I could reclaim ownership of my intellectual property should we part ways.

If you find yourself in a situation wherein you've created something valuable and someone wants to buy it from you, remember: Everything is negotiable. To the extent you can retain *some* of your brainchild (whether that's a social media account, a customer email list, the rights to license back the name, or partial ownership of your business), it's probably worth conceding something else in the deal if you have reason to believe your business is truly worth something (and why wouldn't you?!). Here are a few things you might want to negotiate for:

- Termination clauses (if they end the relationship early, how much do they have to pay?)
- Exclusivity agreements versus intellectual property transfers (they get exclusive rights to your brand for the duration of your contract, but if the contract is not renewed, the material returns to your ownership)
- The right to access your own customer database if you go your separate ways
- Control over costs (in other words, the *L* on the P&L statement)
- Minimum guarantees (that is, you're guaranteed to take home $X), particularly if your compensation is largely based on factors outside of your control

I worked with a lawyer who specializes in mergers and acquisitions (okay, it was my brother-in-law) to build out my first contract, but even then, these were considerations I didn't see coming. Had I known that every single term is negotiable and there's no "one" right way to sell a business, I probably would've tried to be a little more creative about the intellectual property itself—versus focusing all my energy on compensation.

LESSON 3: ALWAYS BUILD IN
THE OPPORTUNITY FOR UPSIDE

Before I sold a business, I had never been employed in a way that wove the concept of "upside" into my employment agreement. *Upside* is a fancy finance word that I'm using to refer to any structure that allows you to benefit more directly from the potential rise in value of whatever you're building. For example, if you begin working for a startup and they grant you equity in the company, I'd consider that upside. The company IPOs? You make money, above and beyond your agreed-upon salary. The success (or failure) of the project impacts your earning potential. There are plenty of ways to build this in (whether it be a straight "revenue share" model wherein you receive a percentage of net revenue, or something more complex in which you retain an ownership stake), but I find it's a component of dealmaking that's worth considering when you're working in an entrepreneurial context because it can magnify the gains of your hard work.

Contrast this with a standard "fee per hour" model. Some people (think attorneys who charge $500 per hour like mine, now that I don't exploit my brother-in-law's time for free *sighs*) make an excellent living working forty hours per week—but ultimately, your time is the limiting resource that caps your income. An attorney who instead receives a cut of a class action lawsuit settlement isn't limited by the number of hours they work on the case (they could work for forty or four hundred; it doesn't matter) because they've got upside. The bigger the pie, the bigger their piece. Most freelancers work in a "fee per hour" or "project-based" model, and it's possible to create a great living this way—it's just much harder to scale that great living without hiring a team of people.

The last five years have shown me—repeatedly—that while my salaried life typically revolved around a few minimally negotiable terms (base pay, paid time off, minor concessions at the margins), there are endless ways to structure deals between two parties. Knowing a few key levers can help you reach agreements that feel fair *and* lucrative—i.e., provide a lot of upside. You want to retain as much of that pie as you can—you're the one baking it, after all. There are a few interesting ways I've seen this work:

- **Tiered models.** In a tiered compensation deal, your share of revenue rises as the project does better. For example, a salesperson might receive a small commission for the first $250,000 in sales driven—but for any sales beyond that, the commission rises by 5 percent. Tiered models are a win-win, because your incentives are aligned: Both parties benefit more if certain benchmarks are reached.

- **Percentage of revenue.** Service providers (in the online business world, think email marketers, agents, sales landing page designers or developers, point of sale systems, etc.) can structure client deals such that they do better when their product or service works better. Rather than charging you $200 per hour to write your website's landing pages and email marketing campaigns, I might charge you a small base fee for the project and 1 percent of sales driven through the email campaign for a predetermined period, like the first year or two. This is, admittedly, a harder structure to negotiate, but becomes easier once you have a solid reputation in a field for driving results—plus, it means ongoing streams of revenue that continue long after your work is over.

- **Minimums and price floors.** If you end up negotiating a revenue share or commission model as part of a deal you're working on and conceding a lot of "base pay" in the process, you can build minimums into the contract such that you're guaranteed to be paid out a reasonable amount for your time and effort—this is a win-win, since it ensures you don't get ripped off if something outside of your control blows up, but it also shouldn't theoretically cost any more for the other party in your negotiation. For example, you might agree to a deal for 10 percent of revenue that your negotiation partner expects will pay you $250,000 if all goes according to plan, which sounds good to you—but to protect your downside, you'd structure a minimum guarantee of $200,000. A price floor serves a similar purpose: For example, maybe you and I are partnering on a product for which you're providing most of the material and I'm focusing on distribution. We might agree that you're doing the lion's share of the work, but without me, it's not as likely to be successful—so we might agree to a 60/40 split, but *only after* you've already earned $10,000 from the project. The first $10,000 of revenue would go to you, while the 10,001st dollar would be split 60/40.

And if I can leave you with one last piece of advice, it'd be finding yourself the aforementioned stellar lawyer so you have legal representation "redlining" your contracts (line editing, in legalese) who's paid to have your best interest at heart and is looking around every corner for you. Regardless of which path you take, I've found that knowing how to represent myself in these types of conversations and understanding how to get creative gives me more confidence to ask for what I deserve in a way that feels beneficial to all parties.

In conclusion

In some ways, the relationship between wages and wealth is stupefyingly simple: You need solid wages to build wealth. Even if you ignore every other historical contributing factor to the current gender wealth gap (like women being legally barred from holding assets in their own name until the late twentieth century), the wage gap alone makes it unsurprising that women still have access to less capital than men do. If women earn less, they will own less—and find the road to economic autonomy more perilous. This is a problem, because economic autonomy is one of the most critical elements of women's liberation. It's why the women's rights movement of the 1970s spent so much of its time and energy focused on economic freedom via equal pay and employment opportunity, antidiscrimination work, and access to credit—and economic freedom begins with how we're compensated for the work that we do.

And while earning more money is not an inherently progressive pursuit, money often translates to time, power, and influence. One doesn't need to be rich to make an impact, of course, but it's hard to ignore the reality that someone working two hourly wage gigs and struggling to make ends meet likely isn't swimming in the free time necessary to, say, attend the local zoning meetings where they're voting to block the development of more affordable housing.

Could a woman become rich and powerful and pull the ladder up behind her? Of course she could. Men have been doing it for centuries! Having access to more money doesn't automatically mean you're going to wield that access for good, or that your freedom will make other women freer. But usually, some level of stability and autonomy are necessary when attempting to increase your impact in whatever sphere of influence you hold, and money confers that ability more directly and equally than just about anything else. I've observed a direct positive correlation in my own life between financial security and the ability to speak up, take risks, and make long-term decisions that prioritize things *other* than money.

Understanding the historical, cultural, and economic factors that impact our careers and earning potential helps us recognize more clearly where our efforts will go furthest. And if you succeed in making more, you might think that's where your money troubles end—au contraire. It *is* Chapter 2, after all! We're just getting started. Next, we'll talk about how to manage these increases in income headed your way. Because ideally, that money will go out and make *more* money for you so you don't have to trade your time and energy for money forever. To do that, we must get equipped with the knowledge to turn wages into capital, the thing that—in a system called "capitalism"—is most valuable.

3

Knowledge Is Power

reat, Katie, I've got Zach, who's in training, on the line for this call and I'll be stepping back to fill an advisory role," assured the deep voice booming out of my phone. I reflexively squeezed the button on the side to lower the volume.

Self-conscious that people in the surrounding cubicles would hear my conversation, I slipped into a nearby fishbowl phone alcove and slid the glass door closed behind me with a force that revealed my unfamiliarity with my new workplace's meeting rooms. Enclosed in the small, transparent nook, I settled into one of the cloth spinning chairs, stationed so I could look out at the passersby. Only a few months into my first full-time job, I was trying to figure out what to do with a steady paycheck. Most of my efforts felt more like LARPing adulthood than actual progress.

I cleared my throat after an awkward pause. "Sure, Jake, that sounds great," I said, trying a little too hard to sound comfortable.

"So, Katie," Zach began, with equally forced bravado, "what are your financial goals?"

"My financial goals?" I paused, considering a question that would've felt completely absurd only three months ago when I was still making minimum wage. "I guess I'm just trying to . . . figure out how much I can save every month?" I asked back.

Another long pause. *Does* anyone *on this call know what's going on?* I wondered.

I noticed two older men, both of whom occupied conspicuous leadership positions in my department, conferring in the dining area outside the fishbowl. I became suddenly embarrassed at the thought of them hearing my faltering side of a conversation with two financial advisers, as though I had been caught playing dress-up in my mom's clothes. *This is what adults do, right? They talk to financial advisers?* Again, a question.

"Well," I continued, my frustration with the entire ordeal transmuting into confidence, "I already know enough to know that I don't know what I'm doing. I just need to know how much I should save."

"Right!" Zach chirped. "Why don't you get back in touch when you know more about your financial . . . situation?"

And thus concluded my first bewildering call with a financial adviser in the summer of 2017.

The men on the phone were calling from a firm I now know to be more in the business of insurance sales than financial services. I didn't understand at the time why, in their position as financial professionals, they were unable to answer what was—to me—a simple money question: *How much should I save?* I had accepted their invitation to the conversation in an earnest effort to go through the motions of being an adult, skeptical that I hadn't been asked to pay for it ("How do you make your money?" I had asked, oblivious to both the industry and social convention).

Unsatisfied, I returned to my desk and pulled up a half-hearted attempt at a Mint budget I had created using Intuit's now-defunct, clunky-but-free online spend-tracking software. As I scrolled through my budgets, I wasn't sure I even knew what I was looking for. One hundred dollars a month for eyelash extensions? That's not that much, is it? Budgeting felt like writing your own rules and then leaving them up to yourself to enforce. What would happen if I made a shit budget? Even if I followed it perfectly, wouldn't the outcome still be shit? More than anything, I didn't really understand the point of tracking this information or determining how much to save. For the time being, I put my concerns on the back burner.

Being confused about money (and about how my friends afforded to attend an always-on rotation of music festivals in our early twenties) just felt like an adult rite of passage—but even if I wasn't talking to people about money explicitly, it was always present in the subtext of my interactions with my single and coupled friends alike. One thing was obvious: The men tended to default to the driver's seat in the couples, and the refrain I heard from most of my single friends was an admission of "not knowing enough."

The data indicates such a knowledge gap (whether real or perceived) is still a critical reason why many women struggle to reach financial freedom. As of 2021, even the most educated and high-income millennial women in mixed-sex relationships were not as involved as their husbands in long-term financial decision-making: Nearly half of the high-income millennial women surveyed said their husbands take responsibility for their long-term financial planning.[†] Only one in five couples reported making their financial planning decisions equally. The women who deferred to their spouses cited a few main reasons for doing so: They believe they lack the knowledge (82 percent), the interest (73 percent), or the time (78 percent), as they shoulder more of the other household responsibilities.

To understand this dynamic fully, we have to look at the other side of the equation, too: 70 percent of the men who reported "taking charge" said they just didn't trust their spouse to make good financial choices. The perception/reality gap is a two-way mirror: Only 11 percent of men reported that their wives were the primary decision-makers, while 30 percent of women claimed they were. In 2023, roughly half of women who were their household's primary earners reported that financial decision-making was just "less natural" for them than it was for their husbands. This language—"natural"—is interesting, because nothing about financial knowledge under capitalism is natural. All of it must (and can) be learned.

I realize including these statistics borders on preaching to the choir—*Yeah, Katie,* you might be thinking, *I'm sitting here reading your damn book about money.* But this finding—that four in five high-income women who defer financial decisions to their male partners do so because they feel they lack the *knowledge* to participate equally—is exciting, because we can impact this feeling directly and immediately, for ourselves and other women we care about.

---

† While the survey didn't specify the races of its 1,501 participants, they only worked with those ages twenty-five to thirty who had at least $250,000 in assets, those ages thirty-one to thirty-nine who had at least $500,000 in assets, and those forty and older with at least $1 million in assets. Because of what we know about the racial wealth gap, it's probably safe to assume this group is disproportionately white.

After all, it was only through acquiring more financial knowledge that I was able to recalibrate my relationship with my spending and begin investing aggressively. Knowledge is power, and in this chapter, we're diving headfirst into the world of saving and investing for financial independence. We'll ground ourselves in the relative magic of something called the 4 percent rule, which can show us how to live off our investments in perpetuity. We'll also explore the interplay between our income, spending, and assets, the three major puzzle pieces we need to identify a meaningful savings target today.

True financial freedom means freedom from *everything*, up to and including golden handcuffs that tether you to a job you no longer want, or—almost always more dangerous—financial dependence on another person. It's estimated that eight in ten women over age fifty will end up managing their finances alone.[†] Once you're making more money, the next step is *managing* more money—including how your savings habits and investing goals should take shape. It's paramount to understand the relationship between our income, assets, and spending habits *before* we start trying to make budgets and create an investment strategy. We first must understand how our spending behavior impacts our reliance on our jobs, our partners, and other situations where women have historically been trapped simply because they need the inflow of cash to keep the wheels turning. Knowledge can help pave a path away from that historic dependence. This is everything I wish Zach and Jake would've told me.

---

† Eleven million of the thirteen million widows in the US are women (more than 84 percent), which means a majority of women who never get divorced will still need to know how to manage their money on their own.

Saving your money

My initial approach (read: ignoring the question of my finances altogether) worked fine until one early morning several months after the conversation I had tried to forget with the insurance bros. I was walking into work, and it was already hot and sunny, the type of Texas summer day that smothers you with a thick blanket of humidity as you rush from one air-conditioned space to another. I wobbled through the parking lot in heels, the thin straps of my heavy laptop bag digging into one forearm while I used the other to squeeze my water bottle to my rib cage and hold my lunch box. As I performed my Bag Lady Dance across the parking lot, sweat collecting on my upper lip, it hit me: *Holy shit*, I thought, *I have to do this for the next forty years of my life.*

The unpunctuated expanse of time no longer felt limitless in its potential; it felt vast in its emptiness. I would have to traipse across this parking lot, holding these bags, wearing these shoes, for the next few decades if I kept running through my paychecks like they were an endlessly renewable resource. Despite enjoying my job, I felt trapped in modern adulthood in a way that genuinely freaked me out—not in my particular employment situation, but in working for a paycheck in general. *What was the point?*

In retrospect, I know this was something like a quarter-life crisis: I had finally arrived at the life stage I had spent my entire adolescence dutifully preparing for, only to learn it was just someone named Pam's fortieth birthday party with a couple of guys in button-down shirts standing around a punch bowl and talking about customer acquisition. I needed an exit strategy, and suddenly, it became conceptually clear why "saving money" mattered.

Of course, I always knew it was "important to save money" in the abstract sense, but it wasn't until I discovered more concrete financial planning information that I finally had an endgame toward which to orient myself. How was I supposed to get somewhere if I didn't know where I was going? Moreover, because I typically slid into the end of the month passing out portions of my checking account to various bills and expenses like the last slices at a drunken pizza party, investing a lot of money didn't seem possible. Exponential compounding defies our human intuition, and the "2 + 2 = 10" math of investing seemed out of reach given my lack of a formal financial education.

But one particular concept formed the basis for my wealth-building journey: the piece of the puzzle that, once clicked into place, transformed my relationship with desire and instant gratification so entirely that I could finally begin transforming my modest income into a nest egg for my future in earnest.

It's with great pleasure that I introduce the **4 percent safe withdrawal rate**, which we can use to determine how much money you need to save and invest to support your lifestyle in perpetuity *without* needing to work for income or rely on someone else. It answers the question that feels as though it supersedes all other financial concerns when you're striving for fiscal responsibility: What's the point of saving money? It can be difficult to delay gratification into the future when it's unclear *what*, specifically, you're gaining. What makes your sacrifice today worthwhile? Our goal is to self-insure your freedom using a nest egg you can rely on, rather than a job or person. This type of independence means you're able to make decisions about things like your work, romantic partners, and health without money being the primary consideration, so you can live a free, full life.

The 4 percent safe withdrawal rate clarified this path for me. The revelation of a "critical mass" beyond which the money would replenish itself faster than I was using it was the cornerstone on which all my good financial behavior was built. I finally had the information I needed to define "freedom" for myself—and better yet, a way to get there.

A brief history of the 4 percent safe withdrawal rate

For the uninitiated (oh boy, strap in), a man named Bill Bengen discovered the 4 percent safe withdrawal rate in 1994 while he was fooling around in some Excel data (as one does). Bill is a certified financial planner, and he was struggling with how to help his clients figure out what you'd think would be a very basic question: How much did they need to invest to retire? Because before Bill came along, there wasn't a widely agreed upon answer to this question. Some pundits relied on giant, round numbers ("$10 million!"), while others looked at the average annualized stock market return of around 7 percent per year after inflation and concluded that you should—theoretically—be able to safely use 7 percent of your assets per year without depleting them, because the average return would always replenish what you removed.

But Bill took this conundrum a few steps further: He analyzed real stock market returns over the previous seventy or so years, as well as real inflation data, and ran dozens of different scenarios with every overlapping thirty-year period to understand what the maximum safe withdrawal rate would have been—not in some hypothetical "average" version of reality, but in real life. His intention was to figure out how much his clients could safely withdraw and use from their savings each year without depleting their balance—no matter when someone retired or which stock market returns they were exposed to thanks to their retirement's proximity to crashes, bull markets, and inflationary periods. What percentage of their assets could *all* of these hypothetical retirees spend annually without running out of money during a thirty-year retirement? The number, he found, was approximately 4.25 percent—a number the media promptly (a) latched on to and (b) rounded down to 4 percent.

In practical terms, this means that in ninety-six out of one hundred historical scenarios, withdrawing and spending 4.25 percent of a retiree's assets every year "worked"—they didn't run out of money before thirty years were up. They didn't outlive their assets. But as Bill himself will remind you (as he did me, when I spoke with him), the *4 percent* withdrawal rate that became popularized in the media following his discovery had a *100 percent* historical success rate for the periods he studied. And the 4 percent rule was born, guiding investors like you and me to understand how we can determine a net worth target that really makes sense for us personally. Rather than indulging the impulse to hoard as much as possible, we can identify a quantitatively sound target of "enough."

Which investments "work" in this framework

Despite its elegant simplicity, any honest conversation about the 4 percent rule requires a brick of footnotes. Simply shoveling money into a savings account won't work with the 4 percent safe withdrawal rate. For this guideline to function as intended, the money has to be invested—and not invested in just anything. A portfolio comprising 90 percent TSLA stock and 10 percent Bitcoin doesn't qualify for the "4 percent rule" treatment.

Bill studied a range of portfolios with very specific holdings, namely somewhere between 50 percent and 75 percent US large cap index funds and the remaining 25 percent to 50 percent invested in US Treasury bonds (two asset classes we'll explore in more depth later in this chapter). When I interviewed Bill—who's now almost eighty years old—he appeared on-screen wearing a bright orange sweatsuit, perched in front of an enormous bookshelf full of binders with various years scrawled down their faded spines. These binders contained his historical data, I assume; he told me he does all his calculations manually, preferring that methodology to fancy financial planning software. "The original research just had two asset classes: intermediate-term US Treasury bonds and US large cap stocks. That was it. Not exactly a diversified portfolio, but you know, had to start from somewhere," he told me.

In 2020, he refreshed his analysis, but added a few more diversified holdings—and what do you know? The results improved: "I wanted to expand my research because I knew that a two-asset-class portfolio is not representative of what most people have or what most investment advisers use. So I added small cap stocks." (Small cap stocks have historically carried higher average returns than large cap stocks, despite being less popular.) He continued expanding his research to include a more diversified collection of asset classes: "Instead of three asset classes, I used seven. So I added micro cap [US stocks], mid cap [US stocks], international stocks, and Treasury bills. Those four asset classes raised the [safe withdrawal] rate from about 4.5 percent to 4.8 percent. I added even more asset classes, but I didn't get another big bump. That's why I'm indicating that we're probably approaching some kind of a limit, of 5 percent." Nevertheless, Bill persisted! A determined king. The original Freak in the Spread-sheets. The "seven asset class" portfolio that he used contained:

1. US large cap equities
2. US mid cap equities
3. US small cap equities
4. US micro cap equities
5. International (ex-US) equities
6. Treasury bonds
7. Treasury bills

We'll dive into what these terms mean and how to create a diversified portfolio later in this chapter, but I provide this backstory (and some of its finer points) because so much of our personal financial planning hinges—knowingly or unknowingly—on Bill's discovery. We know that if somewhere in the 4 percent ballpark is what we can safely withdraw from our assets to support our spending every year, we can reverse engineer an appropriate net worth goal accordingly.

How much money do you need to be "free"?

The best thing about the 4 percent rule is that it's inherently personalizable. For example, if you want to spend $50,000 per year, you just need to know how large an investment portfolio should be to safely spin off a 4 percent safe withdrawal of $50,000. What larger number does $50,000 represent 4 percent of? The easiest way to calculate this is to simply reverse the math and multiply your annual spending by the inverse of 4 percent, which is **25**: $1,250,000. This is your **financial independence number**. Once you accumulate $1.25 million in the asset classes that Bill described, you know you can probably withdraw $50,000 each year (adjusted upward for inflation annually) without ever[†] depleting your account.

It's easy to embrace this a little *too* earnestly and conclude that spending as little as humanly possible must be the solution if you want to be financially free quickly. But the permanence of this equation—that says your portfolio can maintain your existing lifestyle in perpetuity with between a 96 percent and 100 percent historical success rate—highlights why extreme sacrifices in the name of financial independence are probably self-defeating. If you can reach financial freedom faster by eating nothing but canned baked beans and Wonder Bread but you *don't* intend to eat canned baked beans and Wonder Bread for the rest of your life, well . . . the formula breaks.

That's why a proper discussion about your savings rate comes *after* discussing income: because it's only sustainable if your income is at a point where the savings rate you choose doesn't feel painful. We want to create a dynamic spending and investing plan that'll serve you for the long haul, and it's much easier for someone who earns $100,000 per year to save 25 percent of their income than for someone who earns $50,000 per year. They technically have the same timelines to financial freedom because these equations are all proportional, but the $100,000 earner is going to have a more enjoyable time simply because the remaining 75 percent they get to spend represents more money. If we're looking for balance between enjoying our lives now and saving

---

† Well, for at least thirty years. If you intend to be retired for longer (for example, a forty-year timeline), Michael Kitces's research ("20 Years of Safe Withdrawal Rate Research," 2012) recommends decreasing your safe withdrawal rate by 0.5 percent, to a safe withdrawal rate of 3.5 percent. This means multiplying your annual spending by the inverse of 3.5 percent, which is 28, instead of 25.

for the future so we're never "stuck" in a situation we no longer want to be in, the natural next question is: What's the "right" amount to save and invest? It all depends on how quickly you'd like to amass your "enough" financial independence number.

The "optimal" amount to save and invest

Finding this balance—particularly as you're earning more money—can be tricky. Go too far in either direction and you're sacrificing your current happiness for the sake of your future self, or vice versa. I wanted to know how to get the biggest bang for my buck, and where I would hit diminishing returns on my efforts. Because while there might be an ideal answer for each individual, I figured there was a good chance there was some number out there— some ideal percentage of our income to save—that would represent the top of the bell curve. I wanted to know what percentage would do the heaviest lifting for most people, most of the time.

To identify the ideal savings rate, we first need to translate "savings rate" to "years until financial independence." Fortunately, your save rate is the *only* thing we need to know to solve for *n*— the number of years between you and your freedom number. This is because your save rate, by default, defines your "spend" rate. And if I know your spend rate, I know what your freedom number is, assuming we're going to use the 4 percent safe withdrawal rate. And once we can nail down *those* percentages, it's relatively simple to figure out how many years it'll take to reach this freedom number that can support you, because we know how much you're saving every year. Since there's a point at which saving additional income does *not* meaningfully impact your future happiness, but it *does* begin to negatively impact your present happiness, we want to walk *right up* to that point—then stop short of it.

This equation applies to all incomes proportionally. Two people who are both saving (and investing) 50 percent of their income will be financially free in about fourteen years, even if one of them earns $100,000 and the other earns $1,000,000, because it's the percentage of income you're saving that reveals—in a roundabout way—how many years it'll take for your investments to accumulate to the point that they could support said spending. See for yourself, and remember, the $80,000 in the income column is a placeholder. You could put any income in that column, and the "years" column associated with various savings rates would be unchanged:†

POST-TAX INCOME	SAVE RATE	ANNUAL INVESTMENTS	ANNUAL SPENDING	FREEDOM NUMBER	YEARS TO GET THERE
$80,000	10%	$8,000	$72,000	$1,800,000	41
$80,000	15%	$12,000	$68,000	$1,700,000	34
$80,000	20%	$16,000	$64,000	$1,600,000	30
$80,000	25%	$20,000	$60,000	$1,500,000	26
$80,000	30%	$24,000	$56,000	$1,400,000	23
$80,000	35%	$28,000	$52,000	$1,300,000	21
$80,000	40%	$32,000	$48,000	$1,200,000	18
$80,000	45%	$36,000	$44,000	$1,100,000	16
$80,000	50%	$40,000	$40,000	$1,000,000	14
$80,000	55%	$44,000	$36,000	$900,000	13
$80,000	60%	$48,000	$32,000	$800,000	11

† This table assumes that the annual investments are generating an average annualized rate of return of 7 percent per year after inflation.

$80,000	65%	$52,000	$28,000	$700,000	9
$80,000	70%	$56,000	$24,000	$600,000	8
$80,000	75%	$60,000	$20,000	$500,000	6
$80,000	80%	$64,000	$16,000	$400,000	5
$80,000	85%	$68,000	$12,000	$300,000	4
$80,000	90%	$72,000	$8,000	$200,000	2

An easy way to interpret this table, going left to right in the top row, is:

1. Someone earning $80,000 and saving 10 percent . . .
2. Is saving (and investing) $8,000 per year, which means . . .
3. They're spending $72,000.
4. And since $72,000 × 25 = $1.8M,
5. And because we know they're investing $8,000 per year,
6. We know it will take **forty-one years** to accumulate $1.8M,
7. Which is the point at which their assets can support $72,000 per year in spending.

I feel like I'm in geometry class again writing proofs. Notice a few things:

- If you save **10 percent** of your income, you will reach your freedom number in approximately **forty-one years**. This is pretty simpatico with normal savings recommendations and traditional career lengths.
- Increasing your save rate from 10 percent to **15 percent** makes a substantial difference: You go from forty-one years to **thirty-four years**, shaving seven whole years off

the timeline with a small 5 percentage-point increase in savings.

- Going from 15 percent to **20 percent** shaves off another **four years**. Now you'll reach your freedom number after **thirty years**, not thirty-four.

You may have noticed that as the save rate increased, the relative impact of incremental increases diminished. When you were going from 10 percent to 15 percent, the impact of your increase was equivalent to seven years removed from the timeline. But by the time you're going from 65 percent to 70 percent, it only shortens your journey by one year. This exercise shows us that the lower your existing save rate, the more dramatically your increases will impact the speed of your progress.

Of course, depending on how much you earn, at some point in that ratcheting up of your annual savings, you're going to reach a point that's not actually realistic long-term. A 70 percent save rate on a $500,000 income means you still get to spend $150,000 per year. Fantastic! But a 70 percent save rate on $60,000 per year? I know very few people who don't voluntarily traverse the country in a tricked-out van that are capable of thriving on $18,000 per year. Before 2020, the average US savings rate was around 7 percent. As of the time of this writing, it's less than 4 percent. I'm aware even a 10 percent savings rate is aggressive, particularly for the lower half of the income distribution for whom saving at all is basically impossible given their exploitatively low wages.

Let's revisit our breakdown of save rates and timelines and try to identify the point at which diminishing marginal returns kick in most meaningfully (where, say, an additional 5 percent increase only gives us one or two years back). That way, even the most ultra-ambitious, high-earning readers among you will know when your additional effort is less likely to meaningfully move the needle.

Progress slows slightly at 40 percent

In trying to identify where we start to reach diminishing returns, we land on a **40 percent** savings rate. If we're investing 40 percent of our post-tax income, we'll be totally financially free after just eighteen years (that is: retirement ready), and any additional increases would only shave off two years at most. Now, 40 percent might be the number where you're hitting that maximum bang-for-your-buck point, but depending on how much you earn, it might make things way too tight. Is there a save rate that would walk that back a little bit to allow for more freedom (or saving toward other financial goals)? A solid compromise appears to be **35 percent**: At 35 percent, you'd be fully financially free after twenty-one or twenty-two years. A 35 percent save rate means someone who has worked hard to increase their income and begins investing for the first time at age forty-three could still retire "on time."

Of course, most people don't begin earning enough to save this much at age twenty-one, so this example is truly the "optimal" one—but remember, *when you start* is irrelevant to the number of total years it takes. Starting earlier just means you'll complete the timeline earlier in life. For example, if someone who begins earning $100,000 at twenty-one starts right away with a 35 percent or 40 percent save rate and someone else does the same thing at age forty-one, it'll take them both twenty years—the only difference is that the twenty-one-year-old will finish at age forty-one, and the forty-one-year-old will finish at age sixty-one.

For most people, most of the time, this will be a decidedly aspirational target—even if you're able to save 40 percent of your income, chances are that some of those savings will go toward other goals (like the down payment for a home, an offspring's college education, or a parent's retirement). Still, I include it because I know if you're reading a book like this one, that someday, in some life stage, you'll probably be in a position where you can pull it off, and I want you to be able to make informed decisions about your spending and saving choices (and how they're likely to translate to future outcomes).

It's important to see the diminishing returns of saving ever more income. After a certain point (i.e., in the range of around 40 percent), you're not *really* buying back a meaningful amount of Future You's time, but you probably *are* going to be cutting back a lot more aggressively in the present, and a healthy relationship with money requires prioritizing both.

Compounding is your best friend on this journey to independence

But wait, there's more! Because your savings will be invested, your money will start to do the hard work for you after the first few years. It's like a snowball rolling down a hill. At the top when you're just starting to add snow, your tiny fledgling snowball won't pick up much speed. But before you know it, the weight of its own snowball body will be driving most of the accumulation and speed, regardless of how much snow you're managing to pack on as you go. I haven't quite worked out the physics of how you'd manually add snow to a snowball as it rolls, but the metaphor stands.

For example, someone who earns $100,000 with a post-tax savings rate of about 35 percent will reach their "halfway to freedom" point (about $1.5 million) after eighteen years of investing. But once they have $1.5 million invested, even a 5 percent annual return on the money adds another $75,000 per year. All that to say: Each year, your money may be adding more money than you are. It may take eighteen years for this earner to build up the first ~$1.5 million of a roughly $3 million goal, but it only takes six additional years to reach the finish line.[†]

The only constant is change

Most people don't earn (or spend!) the same amount of money for their entire lives. You may find yourself hopping around on this save rate chart depending on how much you're making or your phase of life, which can speed up or slow down your progress. That's probably more reflective of how this works "in real life," since someone might not save at all in their twenties, then decide to really kick it into gear in their thirties or forties, then need to downshift again due to caretaking responsibilities. Taxes also make this scenario a bit trickier, because most people don't know their net annual income off the top of their head. If you want to be precise, use all post-tax figures, and remember that investing in tax-deferred accounts can help lower your tax liability so you're

---

† For my fellow nerds, this is assuming annual 3 percent increases in income, a 9 percent average annualized rate of return before inflation, which is consistent with historical averages, and spending increasing by 3 percent per year, with an 18 percent effective tax rate.

able to save and invest more of your money overall (something we'll cover in excruciating detail in Chapter 6). The money you're contributing to your retirement accounts at work counts toward this total savings rate, so if you're already contributing 10 percent of your paycheck to a 401(k), you've got a 10 percent head start.[†]

Part of what makes a recommendation for a static save rate (e.g., "Always save 35 percent of your income!") tricky is that most people *aren't* starting from zero dollars invested, which is what these timelines are intended to tell you: the time required to go from $0 to total financial freedom. It can be challenging to know exactly where your progress maps onto this timeline based on your existing investments without using more sophisticated math. The 35 percent goal save rate can be a great rule of thumb that strikes the balance between enjoying your life now and giving yourself the maximum flexibility later by stopping just short of diminishing returns, but there's one final formula that can help personalize things for *your* savings goals if you find your situation changing rapidly. Rather than just considering your income (which is what save rates are concerned with), we can take a wider view and consider the full scope of your financial picture by looking at your assets, too.

Income + assets: Personalizing your financial independence goal

As we've already seen, someone who spends 95 percent of their income will have a longer road to financial independence than

---

† If your employer matches your contribution, that's great—to factor a match into your personal savings rate, add the amount to both your savings (the numerator) and your income (the denominator).

someone who spends 65 percent of their income, but our current take-home pay is only one half of that equation. The other meaningful metric to be aware of when targeting a healthy savings rate is how much you *already* have saved and invested. You've probably heard the advice to "live beneath your means," but if you're an especially high earner, a more useful aphorism might be "live beneath your *assets*."

Consider this scenario: Let's pretend you're a charismatic twenty-three-year-old TikTok star who suddenly found yourself earning $400,000 per year thanks to the monetization of your sparkling personality (the fruits of late capitalism). You're making great money, no?! You've had your eye on the Mercedes-Benz G-Wagon for a while, a $140,000 car. Can you afford this vehicle, given your income? I suppose so—it's roughly one third of what you earn in a year, right? That's not too outrageous, relatively speaking. But wait—you only have $50,000 invested. *Now* does it make sense for you to buy a car that's worth nearly three times your entire life savings when there are so many less expensive options? Almost certainly not. You haven't been earning and saving a lot of money long enough to justify safely scaling up to such an extreme degree. By considering both of these metrics—your income *and* your invested assets—we can identify an even more meaningful, personalized target for your savings goals, especially if you're a high earner who isn't sure how much you can safely indulge.†

---

† Note that I'm using invested liquid assets, not total net worth, because many people own their primary residences, hold mortgages, or have student loan debt, which can either make your invested assets look (a) artificially inflated by an illiquid property value, or (b) artificially low with large, long-term, and potentially low-interest loans. Since the payments servicing these debts should already be accounted for by your financial independence goal equation in your total monthly spending, we're ignoring them here.

By considering the type of spending our current invested assets could safely support, we gain some perspective about how much progress we've already made. Using the 4 percent rule, we can ground our high income in the reality of our assets—never allowing the runaway freight train of luxury cars and Uber Eats to derail our progress completely. It lends weight to what's arguably the more meaningful, permanent variable in your financial life— your assets—as opposed to basing 100 percent of your spending decisions on your current, subject-to-change-without-advance-notice income.

One simple calculation I developed that strikes me as aggressive but still reasonable for a high earner striving for financial independence is aiming to spend no more than the average of 4 percent of your current invested assets and your current annual post-tax income (remember to add any paycheck contributions to investments back in when you calculate the latter).

For example, someone who has $250,000 invested and happens to have an income of $200,000 (let's pretend that's after tax, for simplicity's sake) would shoot for the following annual spending:

4 percent of their invested assets = $250,000 × 4% = **$10,000**

Post-tax annual income = **$200,000**

The average of these two numbers = ($10,000 + $200,000) ÷ 2 = **$105,000**

In this example, someone who earns $200,000 per year after taxes and already has $250,000 invested would find a reasonable "below their means" annual spend of $105,000 maximum. This allows them to enjoy their income without meaningfully disrupting their progress toward financial independence. Remember, if you're also tossing a giant chunk of money every month into something like a 401(k), HSA, 403(b), or another account sponsored by your noble corporate benefactor, don't forget to include that in your total income, too—it's still your income, you're just opting to save it before you see it.

The following table takes a few incomes between $50,000 and $250,000 and investment portfolios between $10,000 and $1,000,000 into account (our example is bolded) to give a sense for scale. If you're a high earner for whom the temptation to splurge is a little too real, take a moment to calculate this average for yourself and do some back-of-the-napkin math (read: divide the number by 12) to see if it's in line with what you spend each month.

A "Don't Outlive Your Assets" Calculation for Annual Spending Goals While Pursuing Financial Independence

INVESTED LIQUID ASSETS

POST-TAX INCOME	$10K	$25K	$50K	$75K	$100K	$250K	$500K	$1M
$50K	$25,200	$25,500	$26,000	$26,500	$27,000	$30,000	$35,000	$45,000
$75K	$37,700	$38,000	$38,500	$39,000	$39,500	$42,500	$47,500	$57,500
$100K	$50,200	$50,500	$51,000	$51,500	$52,000	$55,000	$60,000	$70,000
$125K	$62,700	$63,000	$63,500	$64,000	$64,500	$67,500	$72,500	$82,500
$150K	$75,200	$75,500	$76,000	$76,500	$77,000	$80,000	$85,000	$95,000
$200K	$100,200	$100,500	$101,000	$101,500	$102,000	**$105,000**	$110,000	$120,000
$250K	$125,200	$125,500	$126,000	$126,500	$127,000	$130,000	$135,000	$145,000

You might notice if you stare at this table long enough that the savings rates, in many cases, might skew above our 40 percent "diminishing returns" point, because this calculation was developed for high earners who are able to live on much lower percentages of their income. The average savings rate in the table is 45 percent, but they range from 10 percent to around 50 percent.

Here's the most important part: Running your financial life in this way will mean that after just a couple of years, you'll likely have more than $100,000 invested—an amount of money that immediately introduces optionality. **You don't have to be *literally* "financially independent" to operate independently of anyone else's influence and be more selective in your choices.**

This part-art, part-science formula

Originally, I developed this formula because I frequently heard from folks who were newly minted high earners but weren't sure what amount of "lifestyle creep" they could safely indulge without totally derailing their aspirations to become financially independent. At median incomes and lower, reality deals us a crushing blow—it's not realistic for most people with incomes of $50,000 or less to save anywhere close to 50 percent of their income. If the suggestion to shoot for a 35 percent savings rate was already ridiculous given your situation, don't let this table boss you around!

Regardless, for any of these fancy equations to work, our money can't be rotting under the mattress or languishing in a savings account—it must be growing, via investment.

Growing your money through investing

Now that we know how to make informed decisions about how much we're saving, we've alluded a lot to assets *growing* in our discussions of the 4 percent rule—and growing faster than we can use them. Growth requires investment, which can be another hard-to-clear hurdle in your financial journey.

Around the same time as my failed customer consultation with Zach and Jake, I had been spending a lot of time around a guy who was trying to code an app that would day-trade automatically based on opening price movement. Having approximately zero experience with investing, this struck me as extraordinarily sophisticated and impressive, and I watched, starry-eyed, as he quickly thumbed through flashes of red and green on his phone. This man really knew his way around Robinhood.

I, however, did not—and I didn't know the first thing about investing—so I texted my friend Haley, who quickly replied with a recommendation: "My brother said to buy VTI." I looked it up and saw that it had "stock market" in the name, which tracked. All was going according to plan! A markets whiz was born.

If it's good enough for Haley's brother I've never met, I thought, *it's good enough for me!* Through half-shut eyes, I took a deep breath and transferred $1,000 of my savings to the Robinhood app, completely unsure of what to expect next. After fumbling through a few too-easy-to-screw-up screens, I had placed a buy order for around $990 of VTI. I watched the price movement bob up and down on the screen over the following days, flashing intermittently between green and red as it climbed and dipped. Later that week at work, I noticed it was up around $4.

"Wait," I said, poking my head up from my desk to face the four graphic designers whose cubicles surrounded mine. "Once it's up $7, could I withdraw that money and get a burrito bowl?" Amused, they agreed that they were "pretty sure that's how investing works." I was hooked. Fortunately, Haley's brother hadn't led me astray with my first purchase, but things could've gone totally off the rails had I asked a less responsible friend (like the day-trader guy).

When our buddy Bill Bengen was discovering the 4 percent guideline, he used two asset classes. Over the years, he added several more to benefit from **diversification,** or the act of owning different assets that reduce your exposure to any one particular risk. At some point in your financial journey, you've probably heard something to the effect of "The stock market returns an average of about 10 percent per year over the last one hundred years." But when we reference "the stock market," we're usually talking about one of two things:

1. The S&P 500, a **cap-weighted** index that tracks the performance of the 503 largest companies in the United States, with larger companies (as defined by their **market capitalization,** which is one way to measure the company by the value of its total shares) representing larger overall shares of the index. When we say these indices are "cap-weighted," we're referring to the fact that the companies' market capitalizations determine how much "weight" they're given in the index. For example, as of the time of this writing, Apple represents 7.10 percent of the S&P 500. You're not getting 503 equal-sized bits and pieces of everything; if you buy an index fund that tracks this index, you'll own much larger chunks of the companies that are "worth" the most.

2. The total stock market index, which is *another* cap-weighted index that includes the entire US stock market (around 3,600 companies), but again lends preferential treatment to the companies with the largest market caps. For example,

the Vanguard index exchange-traded fund, or ETF, that tracks the Total Stock Market (ticker symbol VTI) has a 0.99 correlation to the index ETF that tracks the S&P 500 (ticker symbol VOO)—this means that even though the former includes the entire stock market and the latter is only the largest 500, they behave in almost the exact same way.

I think about these two indices—the US total stock market and the S&P 500—a little like the Plastics, the trio epitomizing early aughts high school popularity in Tina Fey's *Mean Girls*. If you're placing bets in the high school lunchroom about who's going to be popular next year, Regina George, Gretchen Wieners, and Karen Smith are a decent bet. But you probably don't own much Cady Heron, the scrappy startup from Africa who upsets the social order by usurping Regina's reign of terror one calorically dense Kälteen bar at a time. *Only* owning the Plastics means that when Regina gets hit by a bus, you don't have any Cady Heron in your portfolio to buoy the downswing in time for Spring Fling Queen nominations.

But we're getting ahead of ourselves—to make thematically accurate Lindsay Lohan movie analogies, we first must discuss how we classify various equities.

How we classify equities and equity funds

There are generally three high-level measures by which we judge equities, or stocks (for example, GOOG, shares of Google stock), and equity *funds*, like those that track the S&P 500 or US total stock market index:

1. The country or region(s) of the world (both previous examples are US-centric)
2. The style of investment (usually, the price of the stock is an indicator here; as in, are they **growth stocks** that are expected to get big, and are priced accordingly, or are they **value stocks** that are diamonds in the rough and potentially underpriced?)
3. The size of the company or companies they track (as in, market capitalization)

Usually, we see the latter two criteria—size and style—represented on a matrix, like this:

	VALUE	BLEND	GROWTH
LARGE		e.g., US total stock market	e.g., CRSP US Large Cap Growth
MID			
SMALL	e.g., small cap value		

Something can be large cap growth in the upper right-hand corner, but the equal and opposite is also possible: small cap value, in the lower left. (We'll unpack what that means in a moment.)

These classifications are important because they can help inform our investment philosophy. In other words, on which economies, sectors, or types of companies do you want to place your bet(s)? This is where individual investors take different approaches.

One popular way to invest: US total stock market or bust

My friend JL Collins popularized the "VTSAX and relax" approach in his book *The Simple Path to Wealth* in 2016, and his strategy is beautiful in its simplicity: By buying a US total stock market fund like Vanguard's VTSAX (or, he'll concede, its S&P 500 compatriot, VFIAX), you have all the diversification and risk you need to generate the average market returns you want (i.e., the aforementioned 10 percent per year before inflation).

At first glance, this might seem like plenty—after all, shouldn't owning only the "winners" generate the best returns? If the next twenty years are like the last twenty, I'd take that bet. But I've always been a fan of diversification beyond just US companies (or, more accurately, just large US companies), and I asked JL how he felt about his predictions that owning large US companies would always be sufficient to generate the best returns, without further diversification. (JL is almost in his seventies, so his investing time horizon is probably shorter than ours.) "I think the US is still probably going to be the best place to [invest] for the next decade or so," he told me. "But, for somebody like my daughter—somebody like you and your listeners—that's something I would keep an eye on. And at some point, I'd probably transfer to a [total world stock market] fund that includes the US."

His answer highlighted something important: There's no guarantee the largest companies in the United States will always give us the best results, particularly when we adjust for risk. In fact, it's not even fair to say that they've provided the best results in the past: Between 1900 and 2000, the US fell somewhere in the top 25th percentile globally. Equities in South Africa (6.8 percent),

Australia (7.5 percent), and Sweden (7.6 percent) all produced higher annualized real returns than the US (6.7 percent) over this period—the time period we often point to as illustrating US stock market dominance. Make no mistake: The US stock market did absolutely rip in the last century, but it's not the only country worth investing in.

I'd like to say I'm optimistic about the future of American capitalism becoming less cutthroat (viva la revolución) while somehow maintaining decent returns for investors, but I don't want to bet my entire future on it—so I like to invest in funds that focus on businesses in other regions of the world, too.

How returns are generated

Aside from the country or region of the world, many investors today place their bets on one type of investment style: growth. This is partially due to recency bias, because growth stocks (Apple, Amazon, Alphabet, Meta . . . the tech giants, you get the gist) have performed so well in recent years.

Part of what's important to remember when we're discussing the future of large cap growth investing is how your results are determined. Your returns aren't just about a company's continued survival or success—they're determined by how much a company continues to *grow*. Buying Amazon in 2010 (when its market cap was around $70 billion) is very different from buying Amazon in 2025 (when its market cap is, as of Q3 2024, $1.8 trillion), because the growth the company has experienced since 2010 was meteoric—it's approximately twenty-five times larger, with a compound annual growth rate of roughly 30 percent. In order for Amazon to grow that much *again* and create the same explosive returns for an investor who buys its stock today, it would need to become twenty-five times more valuable, growing from its current market capitalization of about $1.8 trillion to $45 trillion, which is more than the total GDPs of the US and China combined.

In other words, once a company is already gigantic, it's much harder for it to experience parabolic expansion. This is why many financial professionals tout the benefits of investing in indices that aren't large, too—those that grant you exposure to companies that total stock market index funds do not meaningfully represent, like micro cap, small cap, or mid cap funds.

Micro cap indices typically represent companies with market capitalizations of between $50 million and $300 million (not exactly your mom-and-pop bakery down the block), which is a fancy way of saying you're investing in businesses that are "worth" between $50 million and $300 million today. Small cap generally indicates a market cap anywhere between $300 million and $2 billion, and mid cap covers companies worth between $2 billion and $10 billion.

Another way to think about this: When you invest, whether the investment is successful depends not only on what the investment does, but how much you paid for it—did you buy Amazon at $5 per share or $100 per share? Your returns are contingent upon the answer. And when we're talking about big, growth-y, US-based companies, you're probably going to pay more to own them—because the market expects them to do well. But there's a **risk premium**, or expected additional return to be gained, associated with purchasing relatively cheap, little-known entities: The opposite of big, growth-y companies are small, "value" companies— companies with market capitalizations of less than $2 billion that are "undervalued."† (You could also buy "large cap value" or "small cap growth," but there's a historical sweet spot in this "small *and* undervalued" category.)

Professional investors whom I admire, like Paul Merriman of the Merriman Financial Education Foundation and Ben Felix of PWL Capital, have done excellent work extolling the virtues of small cap value index funds, which have traditionally outperformed the S&P 500 over the long term. Between 1972 and 2023, US small cap value stocks returned an annualized 13.6 percent per year, compared to the average annualized 10.5 percent per year for the total stock market overall.

The first time I learned about small cap value, I was blown away—a difference between 10 percent and 13 percent per year doesn't sound like much, but when we're talking about compounding returns, it means small cap value has absolutely kicked the pants off the S&P 500. If you were investing $100 per month for those fifty-one years and getting 10 percent per year, you'd have $1.5M. At 13 percent per year, it's $4.7M.

Small cap value funds can be more volatile and carry more risk because they track indices full of not-sure-things, but every big company was once small. When you buy companies that are small and underpriced, it stands to reason that some of them will experience explosive growth.

---

† There are a few different valuation metrics that can be used here, like the price-to-earnings ratio, which determines how expensive one share of a stock is relative to the company's earnings per share. This can get technical quickly, and there are a lot of varying viewpoints on how important (or unimportant) these metrics are.

So, how do you form your investing philosophy and construct your target investment portfolio?

Let's take things a step further with one of my favorite resources, the Callan Periodic Table of Investment Returns. Every year, Callan releases a report that shows the returns for eight key indices, ranked from best to worst performance. Those indices are:

1. Large cap equity
2. Small cap equity
3. Developed markets, excluding the US
4. Emerging markets
5. US fixed income
6. Corporate bonds
7. Global fixed income, excluding the US
8. Real estate

In the last twenty years measured (2004–2023), the S&P 500 (which would fit into the "large cap equity" category) was the top performer only 20 percent of the time. This is partially because the last twenty years were inclusive of what's known as "a lost decade," where large cap equity finished flat—if you had $1,000 invested in a total stock market fund in 2000, by 2009, you'd have a whopping $998.

The Callan Periodic Table of Investment Returns illustrates the same point that Bill Bengen made earlier in this chapter: Over long periods of time, diversification outside of "just the winners" can help boost your returns. Of course, it can also suppress your returns in times when the highfliers are flying high, but a solid portfolio that can withstand economic shocks usually owns a broad array of holdings, and investing in funds that track different indices is the easiest way to achieve that goal. Here's the tricky thing: You can't invest *directly* in an index. Instead, you invest in a fund that tracks an index's performance. Let's take a closer look.

DIFFERENT INDEX FUNDS AND INDEX ETFS YOU CAN BUY

Index funds and **index ETFs** are built to track a specific index's performance. Not all index funds or index ETFs tracking the same index are identical; fund managers make independent decisions about how much of the various holdings to include, but generally, it's probably not worth losing sleep over—most of the major players (Vanguard, Fidelity, Schwab, etc.) are in close parity when it comes to things like fees and their approach. Pick a brokerage firm or broker-dealer you like and let it rip. For the purposes of my examples, I'm using Vanguard.

Regardless of whether you choose to own one, two, or twelve different broad-based index funds or index ETFs, here are a few you can choose from:

1. Large cap equity, like the S&P 500 (at Vanguard, the associated ETF that tracks this index is called **VOO**)
2. Small cap equity (**VB**) or small cap value equity (**VBR**)
3. Developed markets ex-US (**VEA**)
4. Emerging markets (**VWO**)
5. US fixed income (**BND**)
6. Global ex-US fixed income (**BNDX**)
7. Real estate (**VNQ**)

Because portfolio construction can get a bit tedious, I like to use firms that allow you to buy preconstructed portfolios according to your risk tolerance. For example, a company called M1 Finance offers "portfolio pies" that are named for their level of aggression—from "Very Conservative" all the way to "Very Aggressive." Other companies, like Betterment, take this level of assistance a step further and consider things like your age, timeline, and goals to select a portfolio of low-cost, diversified index ETFs on your behalf for a small fee, usually around 0.25 percent of your balance per year.[†]

For example, here's what you'll find in the M1 Finance "Aggressive" portfolio, as of the time of this writing:

TICKER	INDEX	ALLOCATION PERCENTAGE
VEA	Vanguard FTSE Developed Markets ETF	29%
VOO	Vanguard S&P 500 ETF	26%
VB	Vanguard Small-Cap ETF	14%
VCIT	Vanguard Intermediate-Term Corporate Bond ETF	11%
VWO	Vanguard FTSE Emerging Markets ETF	6%
VO	Vanguard Mid-Cap ETF	6%
VNQ	Vanguard Real Estate ETF	5%
BNDX	Vanguard Total International Bond ETF	3%

Functionally, this means if I were to invest $100 into an M1 Finance "Aggressive" portfolio, I'd be investing:

† This is what's known as an AUM fee, or "assets under management." This is also how many financial advisers charge you for managing your money, but their fees can be upward of 1 percent per year. AUM fees compound like returns do, so it's best to proceed cautiously before engaging a professional whom you pay in this way.

- $29 in global developed markets
- $26 in the S&P 500
- $14 in small US companies
- $11 in US corporate bonds
- $6 in emerging markets
- $6 in US medium-sized companies
- $5 in US real estate
- $3 in global bonds

Within each ETF, there are hundreds (if not thousands) of underlying holdings. For example, in VEA (Vanguard FTSE Developed Markets ETF), the top holdings as of this writing are Novo Nordisk (healthcare), ASML Holding (a semiconductor company), Shell (oil industry), Novartis (healthcare), Roche (healthcare), Nestlé (food), Samsung (appliances), Toyota (automotive), and AstraZeneca (healthcare). Have you heard of all of these? Do you know enough about them to assess their fundamentals and what to buy? Almost certainly not (and if you do . . . maybe you're the one who should be writing the finance book). But thanks to index ETFs and financial technology, you don't *have* to know about them. You just have to buy shares of VEA.

If constructing your own diversified portfolio feels a little too complicated for your liking, there are perfectly reasonable alternatives:

1. Invest in a US Total Stock Market ETF (**VTI**) or Total World Stock Market ETF (**VT**) and call it a day.[†]

[†] Depending on your age and risk tolerance, a 100 percent VTI or VT portfolio might not be appropriate. Traditional finance advice recommends adding bond exposure (like the Treasury bonds Bill used in his safe withdrawal rate research) as you get closer to retirement since bonds are less volatile.

2. Use **target date funds or ETFs**. For example, iShares by BlackRock released the first target date fund ETFs in 2023 (formerly, they were only available as index funds), which means you can easily select a fund based on the year in the name. The iShares® LifePath® Target Date 2035 ETF, ticker ITDC, is allocated in a way that assumes you'll need the money in 2035. As of 2024, it's invested in 68 percent stocks and 32 percent bonds, but it'll slowly shift over time to become more conservative as your "target date" approaches. These ETFs have an annual expense ratio ranging from 0.08 to 0.11 percent, or between $8 and $11 for every $10,000 invested. Someone with large goals on various medium- and long-term timelines could theoretically open different accounts for each one, invest in the appropriate target date fund associated with each goal's date, and offload any manual rebalancing to the fund manager.

3. Use a platform like M1 Finance, Betterment, or Wealthfront to create a portfolio that weaves risk-appropriate, low-cost, diversified ETFs together for you.

How to invest in an ongoing way

One of the paradoxes of investing is that the times when it feels safest to do so (read: on the days when everything is "green" and things are moving up and to the right) is actually when you're paying more for the assets you want to own. For example, consider the effects of the global financial crisis on the housing market, which "bottomed" (when prices reached their lowest point nationally) in 2011. If you bought a house in 2011, you probably did so with an expired Best Buy gift card and a handful of milk chocolate coins—at least, it may have felt that way compared to the prices at the peak before the crash in 2007 and 2008. Buying a house in 2011 was scary. People thought real estate in the US would never recover, so pouring money into that asset class felt like the riskiest thing you could do. Dear reader, you've seen this film before—and if you're a renter in 2025, you probably didn't like the ending. In retrospect, buying real estate in 2011 was among the savviest things you could've done with your money.

The stock market works similarly, and here I'll quote Warren Buffett, an all-time legend[†] in the game of investing: "Be fearful when others are greedy. Be greedy when others are fearful." Market downswings have historically represented some of the greatest times to plow cash into assets, but it's at precisely those moments when it feels most dangerous to do so. How do we find a workable solution—a principled approach—that will allow us to invest consistently over time without allowing our emotions to interfere? The answer is **dollar-cost averaging**.

For the formerly uninitiated, dollar-cost averaging is effectively what you do by default when you contribute to something like a 401(k) plan: Every two weeks, you get paid, and your employer deposits new cash into your 401(k). It's happening on a regular interval—you're not trying to time your deposits based on what the market is doing, you're just adding the same amount of new cash as it becomes available to you.

This is in stark contrast with *buying the dip*, which refers to saving cash on the side and waiting for (what feel like) relative dips in the market when everything is glowing red and there's

---

† Buffett is that rare billionaire who's an outspoken critic of how ridiculously preferential the US tax system is to rich people like him, noting at various points that he pays a lower effective tax rate than his secretary and that he'd be happy for his business, Berkshire Hathaway, to pay a higher corporate tax rate. For this reason, when we eat the billionaires, we shall spare him (and—personal request—Taylor Swift).

blood in the streets to invest all your cash at once at (what feels like) a lower price. This method seems like it'd be ideal, except for the fact that (a) almost nobody can consistently and accurately predict the dips and (b) you lose a lot of compounding time waiting around on the sidelines for things to bottom, because the market spends more time "up" than "down."

One of my friends and the author of the book *Just Keep Buying*, Nick Maggiulli, conducted an excellent analysis where he found that "buy the dip" only outperforms dollar-cost averaging in periods of severe decline, like the crashes in June 1932 (the biggest ever) and March 2009. He back-tested "buy the dip" versus dollar-cost averaging over the last one hundred years and found something interesting: He compared the results of an investor who consistently invested every month (no matter what the market was doing) versus an investor who saved up each month and then only invested in the stock market once it dropped off an all-time high with perfect market timing.

More than 70 percent of the time, buying the dip underperformed the investor who just dollar-cost averaged—and remember, he gave the "buy the dip" investor perfect omniscience! (His analysis was titled "Even God Couldn't Beat Dollar-Cost Averaging.") Had you missed the bottoms by just two months, buying the dip underperformed dollar-cost averaging a whopping 97 percent of the time. It's an excellent case for a "set it and forget it" approach, instead of trying to hop in and out of the market—which is something most of us cognitively understand but have a much harder time implementing when Chicken Little is on CNBC loudly proclaiming that the sky is falling.

The biggest risk to your portfolio probably isn't some paradigm-shifting technology or changing world order (at least, it hasn't been yet)—it's your own human likelihood to hear about atrocities or crises on the news and assume it spells bad news for markets. Even an investor who invested everything in a total stock market fund like VTSAX at the "top" in the year 2000 before the dot-com crash, the Great Recession, and the COVID-19 pandemic would still have more than five times as much money today as they started with, despite their worst-possible timing.

The key takeaway here: As soon as you have investable cash, put it to work. Whether the stock market is "up" or "down" that day is, functionally, irrelevant. This means you're dollar-cost averaging into something like your 401(k) every time your paycheck hits by default, but it also means that if you come into a large sum of money, the data would suggest you're better off investing all of it immediately rather than putting in a little bit at a time.

Coping with uncertainty as you invest

Certainty is impossible to come by, so if you're interested in growing your wealth, calculated risks must be taken. Financial principles like the 4 percent rule and our historical best practices around investing lend an air of certainty and common sense to questions that often feel nebulous and unknowable, and when you speak to financial professionals, they're often quick to tell you that these estimates are just that: estimates. Part of the reason accurate financial planning is so challenging is because the variables we must use in our fancy-shmancy equations are effectively guesses at what the future holds. I *think* I'll have this many children, who will require $20,000 per year in additional expenses. I *think* I'll stay married to my current spouse and enjoy vacationing in Mexico forever. I *think* the US economy will continue to grow during my lifetime.

It would be a lot easier to plan optimally if we knew what the future held—after all, if you're saving as though you're going to live until you're ninety but you're diagnosed with a terminal illness (God forbid) in your forties (or the planet becomes uninhabitable before then), does your responsible plan to delay gratification into the future still look so wise? If you knew you were going to win the lottery at age thirty-five, would paying off credit card debt in your twenties still be a priority worth sacrificing Euro-trips for? But until Apple brings mass-produced crystal balls to market, we're stuck with statistics and our best guesses.

In the face of this uncertainty, I've often rested on my own (conservative) instincts about what I think I'm going to want in the future based on what I've wanted in the past, then invested accordingly. For example, my husband and I may spend north of $100,000 per year now as part of our excessive DINK lifestyle, so I might set a liquid assets target of around $3 million such that we could withdraw $120,000 safely. Another factor that impacts these calculations is how early in life you intend to pull the plug on paid labor (or how early you'd want the option to do so). If your nest egg needs to support you from age forty until death, you probably want to plan with a much more generous buffer than if you're hoping to rely on it from age seventy onward, when the research tells us our spending tends to decline. Precision will be impossible—what we're looking for is directional accuracy.

Maintaining your ethics amid the need to self-insure your financial safety

A discussion about investing in public markets is nestled within a reality that's a little more layered. Is it true that becoming a shareholder in profitable companies will directly enrich you? Yes. Is it also true that shareholder primacy and corporate personhood (i.e., the way we legally treat corporations as though they're people and grant them the accordant political rights) are the main sources of extraction of our time, energy, and money that create the need to invest in the first place? Also, yes.

Those who are not invested in the stock market—in other words, those who are not participating in the "capital class" that receives preferential treatment in our economy—stand to lose out, as is evidenced by the fact that the wealthiest 10 percent of Americans owns 93 percent of all wealth in the stock market (the bottom 50 percent owns less than 1 percent). Making matters more unequal, the wealthiest portion of the capital class primarily earns money from their investments, rather than their labor, which receive preferential tax treatment in the form of a top marginal tax rate of 20 percent, rather than 37 percent (how's that for a tax incentive?).

Anyone with enough income from their labor can buy their way into the capital class slowly over time through purchasing shares of stock traded on the public market—more than 60 percent of Americans own *some* stock—but the system itself, with its bloated profits and "shareholder first, customer second, humanity last" philosophy, is responsible for much of the pain and frustration we experience in everything from the world of for-profit healthcare, to flying on faulty airplanes, to food safety processes that cut corners to save money and make us sick. For this reason, some people choose to opt out of investing in the public stock market altogether on principle, deciding they don't want to profit from such a system.

My feelings about this choice are complicated, as the same game theory I mentioned in Chapter 1 arises, though with a difference: Is it better for everyone if everyone opts out? Sort of, though not until another less exploitative, long-term-focused system takes its place. Businesses need a way to access capital in exchange for public ownership, and people need a source of income that isn't directly tied to their ability to perform labor. Opting out *on its own* does little to improve the status quo, and a lot to make your life harder. As long as private ownership is the primary mechanism through which our economic system secures people's futures, it's still (paradoxically) the best way for regular people to benefit from the profits their labor is creating.

In conclusion

As you can probably tell, there's a lot to consider: deciding how much of your income you want (or are able) to save, how you want to invest it so you can create income and stability for yourself that isn't tied to your work, and how to deal with the existential questions of making these decisions in the face of uncertainty and inequality. Although there are no "right" answers, this knowledge allows you to understand the long-term implications of your choices for yourself, your community, and the world at large—so you can choose the best answer *for you*. Crucially, understanding these dynamics makes you the financial leader of your own life, rather than believing that someone else is better suited to make decisions about your financial future than you are. We've learned how retirement goals are calculated, how spending and saving impacts our timelines, and even how value investing can generate higher returns for investors—you now possess more financial knowledge than the majority of Americans. Wield your newfound power gently on the unsuspecting finance bros you encounter at dinner parties.

You may find that as you earn more, make progress toward

your net worth goal, and evolve in your career, your goals shift on purpose. It was only through an understanding of these financial principles that I was able to make intentional decisions with confidence. Financial fluency doesn't always lead to spending less—sometimes, it leads to spending more or spending differently. Had I not understood my own numbers, I might've irrationally clung to a lower cost of living out of fear or continued to prioritize wealth accumulation long past the point it was necessary or adaptive. This knowledge gave me more power and control over my outcomes and, more important, meant I didn't need to unilaterally rely on my relationship to another person, job, or situation to live a meaningful and self-directed life.

Now that we've discussed how to translate earning more money into progress toward financial freedom, it's time to explore what's likely to happen on your board game of Life before you tap-dance backward out of your boss's office: the big, expensive, and legally significant milestone that requires a lot of strategizing, and why it tends to affect women differently.

4

I Thee Wed
(and Spend Thy Bread)

As a little girl, I always told the adults who asked about my plans for the far-off adult future that I'd probably wait until I was *super* old to get married: "You know," I'd say, "like twenty-five." But when I got married at twenty-six (a whole year older than super old!), in some ways I still felt like a teenage girl playing "house" while her parents were out of town. Legally speaking, I had no idea what I was doing. I knew I wanted to marry my husband, Thomas, but I wasn't confident about much else.

Technically speaking, we got married twice: once in a courthouse in East Dallas next to a Denny's, and again in a much more indulgent party at the Garden of the Gods Resort in Colorado Springs. The former was less than $100; we paid for our marriage license, and a handful of close friends stood in the back of the courtroom and cheered as we said "I do" through masks. The latter was $50,000, took nearly a full year of planning, and was one of the more stressful experiences of my adult life. I didn't have a bachelorette party, bridal shower, or engagement photo shoot; we hosted sixty-five guests and didn't have photo booths, memory books, party favors, transportation, or a live band. We tried to keep things relatively simple but still luxurious—and at every turn of the planning process, I felt like I was failing a test. As the woman in my heterosexual couple, it felt like an unspoken given within our families and social circles that it was *my* responsibility to spearhead this professional special event, with delegated "help" from my husband.

In retrospect, there were many things I would've done differently. The night of, I realized I hadn't even gotten my dress bustled (why did nobody tell me I was supposed to do that?), so I swam around the dance floor for my first dances, trailing a pool of lace and silk behind me. We were way too laissez-faire with the DJ, who ended up playing hours of music that my older relatives were probably offended by (though it did produce a video of my eighty-year-old Grandma Jean fist-pumping to the early 2000s club anthem "Ms. New Booty" by Bubba Sparxxx, which might be worth $50,000 on its own).

Mostly, I regretted my approach. I was (and remain) so resentful of the process—the expense, the time commitment, the gendered labor of it all—that I cut corners wherever possible and didn't lean into the fun of the process. I realize now that I mostly just wanted nice pictures for posterity, and we could've gotten those without having an actual wedding. I obliged what felt like tradition for its own sake, even though the extravagant modern wedding "tradition" I felt compelled to uphold is barely forty years old. I found the ordeal to be mostly intense physical and emotional work masquerading as a good time, and while there were fun *parts* (like the food tasting!), it's not a process I reflect on fondly.

My haphazard courthouse wedding, on the other hand, remains an incredibly special memory: The total absence of pressure for the day to be faultless meant the laser focus of the experience was on marriage itself. I remember staring at Thomas with tunnel vision before the judge, heart thumping so loudly I was afraid everyone else could hear it, and crying, earnestly moved by the ceremonial but also legally binding words "till death do us part."

As attorney James Sexton said, marriage is the "most legally significant thing you will do, other than dying. . . . And you don't even get a pamphlet." It's a lifelong legally binding contract with nothing to read before you sign. If my wedding planning experience taught me anything, it's that it's freakishly easy to go into marriage unprepared—from figuring out prenups to planning the wedding itself to setting up your joint finances, you never hit a natural checkpoint where you're urged to think about how you'll protect yourself financially.

This is especially relevant for women, who are more likely than men to find themselves in poverty after a divorce (this is especially true of women with children). A married woman is also more likely than a married man to become an (unpaid) caretaker for her family members, thereby decreasing her marketability for paid labor in one of the cruelest twists of modern capitalism. We'll go further into detail about how *that* phenomenon impacts a woman's earning potential and lifetime access to resources in Chapter 5, but in the meantime, we should talk about what legally happens to your personhood when you walk down the aisle and sign that blessed contract with the state.

Even if you're already married, you can still play along. In this chapter, we'll review all the ways women can take care of themselves financially if they choose to get married, regardless of how that relationship status changes—after all, women couldn't even get a bank account without a man's permission in the US until the 1970s,[†] so these considerations are still relatively new, historically speaking. We'll discuss primary considerations *before* you say "I do," like which financial discussions to have with your beloved, and we'll unpack things with fancy legal names like separate property trusts. We'll also discuss more financial considerations for your wedding, if you have yet to plan one. And finally, we'll nail down a few things to keep in mind *after* you're married (like what to do if the prenup ship has sailed but you're still interested in contractually defining your "worst-case scenario" outcome) and options for organizing your finances together.

Before "I do"

What should you know before legally supergluing yourself to another person? We'll cover everything from planning conversations to prenuptial agreements, but first, let's take a quick look at how marriage has historically treated women to ground ourselves in some context. If you're already wincing in anticipation, you're one step ahead!

A very brief history of tying the knot

As with most major institutions in the world, there's a gendered financial history to marriage. Back in the day (think a few millen-

---

† Technically, women won the right to open a bank account in the 1960s . . . but many banks still required a signature from her husband, which meant two things: Married women's access to banking was controlled by their husbands, and unmarried women were often refused services outright. Women in countries like Canada, Sweden, Germany, France, Australia, and Japan had this right for decades by the time the US got around to outlawing credit discrimination based on sex. USA! USA!

nia ago), couples who tied the knot in places like ancient Greece and Rome were doing so in order to bind a woman to a man, such that the man could be sure her children were his and he wasn't #providing for some other dude's kids (he was, of course, still permitted to satisfy his sexual urges however and with whomever he pleased). As such, the betrothal ceremony metamorphosed the woman from her father's property to her husband's. Love that for us!

Fast-forward a few thousand years, and a man's superiority within the institution of marriage was codified legally in the early days of the United States in an idea known as "coverture," under which the woman's identity was thought to be legally absorbed by her husband's. (This is where we get the practice of giving up your name—it symbolizes dissociating from your former identity as your own person.) In this English common-law practice, the husband was seen as the "official public representative" of two people—an American woman who married a non-American man actually lost her citizenship.

It wasn't until white women got the right to vote—barely one hundred years ago, in 1920—that some women gained legal personhood, transforming marriage into the "union of two full citizens." Remember, at this point in history, the definition of "two full citizens" was incredibly narrow, meaning "a white woman marrying a white man"—interracial marriage wouldn't become legal throughout the US until nearly fifty years later in 1967,[†] and same-sex marriage nearly one hundred years later in 2015.[‡] But before the early twentieth century, *no* woman had a legal right to own anything in her marriage. She didn't have a right to her

---

[†] Per *Loving v. Virginia*, which said state laws banning interracial marriage were unconstitutional under the Fourteenth Amendment.

[‡] Also thanks to the Fourteenth Amendment, in *Obergefell v. Hodges*.

children. She didn't even have a right to her own body (horrify-ingly, it wasn't until 1999 that spousal rape became illegal every-where in the US). Suffice it to say, marriage has not been kind to women historically.

Thankfully, we live in the twenty-first century, so we have the right to vote *and* to full personhood under the law, sort of![†] For now! (Stay frosty.) This means the institution of marriage has modernized, too, and now most of us choose to get married for love, fulfillment, and partnership, not to align our royal families and strengthen a dynasty. Still, we often don't spend much time learning about how legal marriage changes our rights, and that means many modern women still experience the residue of this millennia-old asymmetric power imbalance.

If you're considering getting married, the first necessary step is having open financial conversations with your partner (I know, I know—this is table stakes—but it's my duty to include this).

What you should know about your significant other's finances before signing on the dotted line of your marriage certificate

Talking about money can be fraught territory, because we all grow up in families that treat it differently. If you and your part-ner hail from wildly different socioeconomic or emotional back-grounds, it's possible your respective levels of comfort with the topic will vary. But you've done the hard thing—found someone worth hitching your wagon to for life—so what do you need to know about *their* finances (and they, yours) before you superglue yourselves together?

---

† *Dobbs v. Jackson Women's Health Organization* (2022).

I'm no couples counselor, but I appreciate Ramit Sethi's philosophy on couples' finances: Start with building a joint vision around the type of life you'd like to live together. This is like a warm-up for the harder-hitting questions, so I'd recommend starting here:

- Where do we want to live?
- What type of home do we want to live in?
- How often do we want to travel, and where do we want to go?
- How often do we want to work, and what types of careers are we interested in having?
- What kind of food do we want to eat?
- Do we care about nice cars? Nice hotels? Nice restaurants?
- What's our ideal Saturday look like?
- If we're having kids, what type of education do we want them to have?
- What hobbies are important to us? What do we value?

I'll also take this opportunity to point out that even if you *aren't* getting married, these questions can yield important answers for you as an individual, too.

Depending on how long you've been together, you might have a good sense for a lot of the answers already—but it's fun to dream. My husband and I did a lot of budget travel when we were dating and engaged, but as our careers picked up steam and our responsibilities increased, our trips became fewer and farther between. I work from home, so we spend more money on our house than on trips. We like to eat delicious food, but we primarily cook rather than go out to restaurants. Our favorite activities are watching new shows together, reading, exercising, and playing music, so our hobbies are not all that expensive—but we *do* like to drive fun cars, and we want the option someday to hire a fleet of night nurses and nannies if we ever have kids.

Together, you're painting a poignant vision of your future that tees you up perfectly for the transition to the dollars and cents: *Great. So that's where we're going! Now, let's talk about how we get there from where we are right now.* Cue the throat-clearing and index-card-shuffling. Some of these questions will feel like common sense, but depending on your age, whether either of you have been married before, and how much life you've already lived, they might stir up some unpredictable answers:

- What outstanding debt do you hold? What loans are currently open in your name? (This can be a shame-ridden topic; it's important that anyone who holds debt in the relationship feels supported when discussing it. This debt is going to belong to both of you now, so you're on the same team and the debt is your joint opponent.)
- What's your credit score range? Do you have any prior bankruptcy filings? (I know, I should've warned you— things get hardcore quickly. Maybe ease into this one with a nice dinner date before interrogating your partner about their Chapter 7 filings.)
- What sources of income do you rely on? (Subtext: Are your parents or another rich family member secretly bankrolling your existence in a way that I should know about?) It's also good to make a mental note here of whose job is potentially more stable, for future planning purposes (e.g., the partner who works in the highly paid but volatile space of crypto platforming is probably more likely to lose their income than the partner who works a modest federal government job).

- What investments, retirement assets, and properties do you hold in your name, and will I have to tolerate Bitcoin manifestos every time it experiences a resurgence?
- Do you have any other financial obligations I should be aware of so we can plan for them? (Think things like support of another family member or friend, spousal support, or child support from a past relationship.)

Basically, let's get it all out on the table, yes? And, of course, you'll show them yours, too. There are probably even more financial conversations worth having at this point depending on your unique circumstances, but this is the minimum information you should gather before marching down to city hall and signing your name on a certificate that legally connects you to their "stuff."

It's worth repeating: It's critical that this discussion feels open, supported, and empathetic, which can take practice if you didn't grow up in a house where these discussions were modeled that way. You might be more financially savvy than your partner (or maybe it's the other way around), so talking about things like debt or a prior bankruptcy filing might feel akin to voluntarily stepping into unflattering fluorescent lighting and dropping trou. You're on a team now, so these challenges and goals belong to *both* of you—and if for some reason you find it's more advantageous to keep some things separate as a result (for example, filing separately on your taxes so one spouse's income doesn't impact another spouse's income-based student loan repayment), there are strategies you can employ once you know what you're dealing with—more on those later. But first, let's get to what we've all been waiting for: the prenup!

Getting your prenuptial ducks in a row

The time has come for us to dive headfirst into all the juicy legal talk I've been dangling like a three-carat engagement ring since we started this chapter. The **prenuptial agreement** is the legal contract that documents the nature of the property acquired before and during your marriage, and the division of property and income in the event of divorce, separation, or—the most metal way out—your eventual death. Usually, people write prenups to solidify their wishes for their separate property to remain separate, but if someone knows they're going to take a long career break to raise children, a prenup allows a couple to outline the legal and financial protections that the individual who works in the home would be entitled to ahead of time.

Despite the seemingly obvious and sterile nature of the suggestion to write your own marriage contract, the idea that modern couples—adults who are choosing to marry one another for love—should get prenuptial agreements still rubs some people the wrong way. A common rebuttal to the suggestion is "Isn't that like planning for your marriage to fail?" We don't often apply this same skepticism to the backup plans we make for other things. Is carrying homeowner's insurance planning for your house to burn down? Is wearing a seat belt planning for a crash? The reality is, everyone has a prenuptial agreement, because legally speaking, marriage is a contract between you (and your partner) and the state, and each state writes its own rules about what'll happen if your marriage ends. So, who do you want to write yours? You, your spouse, and your respective legal representation, or the fine folks down at the state capitol whom you've never met?

While there might be something romantic (in a tragic, Shakespearean, drinking-poison-to-prove-one's-love way) about locking yourselves together and swallowing the metaphoric key to the safety deposit box, I can scarcely think of something less romantic than staying married to someone because their name is on the deed and you don't have a paycheck job to fund a new start. Conversely, what's *more* romantic than fully choosing—and not feeling *financially obligated* to choose—to stay married to someone?

Once again, thank God we're all adult women in the twenty-first century! Equal rights under the law are cool and marrying someone simply because you want to is, too. What's more, making a decision—with the person you love, when you're feeling the most optimistic about your relationship—to say, "I love you so much that I want to legally ensure this is what you have in life, even if it's not with me someday, and I know you'll feel the same about me" can be more selfless than saying, "You signed on the dotted line—so if this doesn't work out, I'd like to torch our respective chances of moving on with financial integrity."

The intention of this process is to define how you'd want to handle a worst-case scenario and prepare accordingly. The makings of a prenup primarily deal with two major components:

1. **How separate property that you own *before* you're married is treated in the event of divorce.** Are you bringing assets into the marriage that you'd like to keep separate from your marital property, like houses, investments, or a business? The prenup can define what remains legally separate property after you get married.

2. **How property you accumulate *after* you're married is treated in the event of divorce.** In most jurisdictions, income from employment that either spouse earns after they get married is considered marital property, but a prenup

can more specifically define how that marital property will be split in the event of a divorce, as well as if one spouse is entitled to the other spouse's income after the split.

Got all that? Chapter over! Just kidding. Unless you're already a divorce attorney, this is a little more complicated than "two high-level considerations"—so let's dive into separate property trusts.

Separate property before you're married

Certified divorce financial analyst Kim Davis recommends setting up a **separate property trust** to kick off the prenuptial agreement process. Separate property trusts are like legal containers that you can place your personal assets in to clarify that you'd prefer legal ownership to remain yours and yours alone. They're used to avoid "commingling assets" after you get married. While it sounds like an advanced cuddling technique, commingling describes what happens when you get married and start mixing your financial lives together.

This type of revocable living trust is designed to hold property (property in the abstract sense, not necessarily in the "my beach house in Florida" sense) acquired outside of the marital estate whether before, during, or after marriage—for example, your high-yield savings account that you opened before you were married that's in your name only and funded with $100,000 that you earned, or a house purchased with your money and in your name only. It ring-fences the assets and says, "Hey, you see this stuff over here? I'd prefer to ensure that if we were to separate someday, half of this doesn't end up on the table."

When you're setting it up, keep in mind this can be tricky

business—it doesn't take much for assets to be considered officially commingled. For example, maybe you start using marital assets—e.g., your joint checking account—to pay the mortgage on the house you bought before you were married. Because marital property was used to pay for it, the house could be considered marital property now, too. (In one particularly unfortunate example, I heard from a woman whose spouse paid for *maintenance* on the home with his income and ended up with a legal claim to part of the value of the property.)

I asked Stacy Francis, a certified financial planner professional and founder of a 501(c)(3) nonprofit called Savvy Ladies,[†] if there were any administrative checks and balances we could all put in place to avoid accidentally commingling our separate property assets with marital property, with or without separate property trusts. "When you get married, open new individual accounts. Keep individual accounts from before marriage off to the side, and only add new, post-marriage income to the new individual accounts to keep it simple." This is because if you were to continue contributing income earned *after* the date of marriage to the individual account you opened and funded *before* marriage, that account now has "commingled" money inside it, which can create complications later. Since bank statements typically only go back several years, download your year-end statements for these premarital individual accounts so you can prove the funds were there before you were married (and that no new money was added to them after you got married).

---

† Savvy Ladies connects women with financial professionals for free if they're in a position where they can't afford help or they're in a financially abusive situation in which their spouse is blocking their access to resources. If you're interested, check out savvyladies.org.

There are a few common ways that funds accidentally get commingled:

- Depositing money into a joint account, regardless of where it came from (e.g., an inheritance that would legally be considered separate property can become marital property if it ends up in a joint account)
- A mortgage paid from funds in a joint account
- Investments or savings funded by both incomes
- Income of either partner *after* the date of marriage being deposited into individual accounts opened *before* the marriage

You might be perfectly fine with much of your income and assets becoming commingled—but generally speaking, some people who marry after they've already accumulated substantial assets (whether through saving and investing while they're young or because it's not their first marriage rodeo) prefer to place assets accumulated before marriage in a separate property trust to ensure that, should the marriage dissolve, they'll be able to walk away with those assets without having to legally fight for or split them.

Marital property after you're married

It's relatively straightforward to define and make decisions about premarital separate property, but it can be more challenging to know how you want to treat the assets and debt you accumulate during the marriage. Put another way, which assets will constitute your **marital property** that's jointly owned, and how will discrepancies in income or unpaid domestic labor affect a split if you get divorced someday? If someone quits their job to raise kids for twenty years and forgoes their ability to earn income, what do you want that partner to be entitled to if the marriage ends? Remember, after you get married, income earned by either spouse (and the assets that income buys) becomes marital property that belongs to both of you.

Your state's laws determine what'll happen in the event your marriage dissolves, unless you overwrite them with your own rules in a prenuptial or postnuptial agreement (and even then, enforceability here can be tricky if the court perceives the prenup's terms to be one-sided or unfair). Broadly speaking, there are two ways marital assets are split in divorce, depending on where you live: **community property** or **equitable distribution**. (It's the state you get divorced in, not the state that you get married in, that makes a difference in how your marital property would hypothetically be divided, unless otherwise specified in a prenup.)

In a community property state, both spouses are considered **equal owners** of the marital property regardless of who earned or invested it (which, again, does *not* include the assets owned before the marriage, or inheritances and gifts you received individually before or during the marriage, or assets that you hold in the separate property trust you set up earlier). This means that money you both earn or acquire during the marriage that's not already designated as "separate property" via a prenup is considered owned by both of you, regardless of whose name is on the paycheck, title, or account. It'll likely be split 50/50 if your marriage is dissolved.

For example, I was the sole earner of the income used to buy my car and the title is in my name alone. But since the money flowed through our joint account and was considered our marital property, if we were to split in a community property state, my husband would have a legitimate legal claim to half its value. If for some reason I *really* wanted to make sure the car wouldn't be up for the taking, I should've used funds that came from an individual account within a separate property trust to purchase it, and maintained documentation that proved the car was purchased using my separate property alone. Community property states include Alaska, Arizona, California, Idaho, Louisiana, Nevada, New Mexico, Washington, Wisconsin, and Texas. The rest are equitable distribution states.

Equitable distribution states are different in that they split a couple's marital property "equitably" or "fairly," which doesn't necessarily mean "straight down the middle." This can sometimes work against the nonearning spouse, whose contributions within the home might not be valued as highly as the earning spouse's (though things like custody and child support factor in here).

Splitting your marital property during a divorce can become contentious, but typically, both parties walk away with a reasonable portion of the couple's jointly held assets—even without a prenup. While the prenup can be used to refine your intentions around how you want your assets split, often the more important consideration is what will happen to a nonworking spouse if the marriage ends.

In 1980, Terry Martin Hekker wrote the bestselling book *Ever Since Adam and Eve*. It was an extension of a popular op-ed she wrote in *The New York Times* in 1977 called "The Satisfactions of Housewifery and Motherhood in 'an Age of Do-Your-Own-Thing,'" in which she made an earnest case for embracing the role of a "traditional" housewife and more or less dismissed the risks of financial dependence. Terry was the ur-tradwife, and she dedicated her life to creating a nurturing home for her family of seven. But as she tells it in a 2006 follow-up piece, on her fortieth wedding anniversary, her husband asked her for a divorce. While she had been raising wonderful children, he had been crushing it in his career and found himself a new, younger girlfriend. With no prenuptial agreement in place or job history to speak of, Terry was awarded alimony for just four years that amounted to less money than she typically received to pay their small, peripheral household expenses. Her story is sobering, but unfortunately, it's also incredibly common.

As her experience illustrates, a crucial part of writing a prenup is determining spousal support (also known as alimony) in the event of divorce if one partner plans to forgo their career (and ability to earn money) to focus on work inside the home. Writing terms around spousal support into a prenuptial agreement is an added layer of security that specifies what will happen if you, like Terry, spend many decades as a stay-at-home parent taking the lead in raising the children, managing the home, and enabling your spouse's career . . . and then they decide one day that they'd like to take their coworker to Sandals Jamaica. If you're relying on someone else's income for a long enough time that it would be hard to get your own again (particularly at a level that would allow you to sustain your standard of living), you need reasonable legal protection. Terms can be included in a prenup that outline a partner's right to receive a certain amount of spousal support for a predetermined amount of time in the event of divorce.

When Kim Davis told me this was A Thing™ in our conversation about prenups, I was relieved to hear that stay-at-home parents can negotiate some recourse *before* they leave paid work, and surprised by how creative the terms can be. To be most safely enforceable, terms about future spousal support should be written into a *pre*nuptial agreement, rather than a *post*nuptial agreement (don't worry, we'll get to those later in the chapter).

For Terry, as a bride from the 1950s, a prenup would have been a laughable notion. There was no expectation of equity protecting her if her marriage dissolved. And unfortunately, at the age of sixty-seven, after a lifetime of not working outside the home, the divorce court judge suggested she find work. (Terry recalls real-izing just how much she had lost when she was notified of her eligibility for Supplemental Nutrition Assistance Program [SNAP] benefits, and in 2009 she published a follow-up book called *Disre-gard First Book*.) A strong prenup and an awareness of these risks can help us avoid the same fate that Terry was forced to navigate when her marriage ended.

You might be totally fine with a 50/50 split of marital property in the event of divorce and feel comfortable forgoing terms about spousal support if you have no intention of quitting paid work, but if you want to modify the state's contract for your marriage, now's the time to do so. Once you and your partner have a sense for what you want the prenup to do, it's time to consult your own legal representation to execute it.

Best practices for prenups

Let's look at some of the things that will make this process flow as smoothly as possible. I asked Lisa Zeiderman, managing part-ner and certified divorce financial analyst at Miller Zeiderman LLP in New York, to share some of the common pitfalls she sees as a divorce attorney who deals with a lot of unenforceable prenups and postnups. She rattled off the best practices with the same pas-sion and confidence with which I've committed Taylor Swift's entire catalog to memory. Here are some of the greatest hits:

- Each spouse needs to be represented by their own attorney.
- There needs to be adequate negotiation regarding how things are split; a perception of one-sidedness can cause issues later (she mentioned the phrase "shocks the con-science": i.e., if you think a judge would read it someday

and go, "Nobody in their right mind would *ever* agree to this," you may run into issues of enforceability).

- Adequate time needs to be given for review and negotiation— if the process is rushed (or appears rushed), it can be over-turned later, which can happen when one side (or, more accurately, the family of one side) springs the prenup on the other shortly before the wedding in an attempt to shoehorn it in with little time for debate.

"The court has a lot of power to decide during a divorce pro-ceeding if something in a prenup or postnup shocks the con-science," she told me, and for a prenup to truly protect you, it must be legally enforceable. *Your* lawyer in *your* state should be aware of the finer points of these requirements, but her emphasis on this matter underlines the importance of each spouse working with their own real live attorney (versus going the DIY route) to improve your chances.

So now that we've barreled through all the juicy legal prenup-tial stuff, it's time to let down our hair and have a little fun. Let's talk about the wedding itself!

The wedding

While the institution of marriage itself has changed a lot, you know what else has changed dramatically over the last forty years? The wedding. Gone are the centuries of throwing on the nicest blue velvet dress you already own and smooching your affianced in your parents' living room before privately enjoying a sheet cake with your neighbors. No, the *Super Sweet 16*–ification of the modern wedding means you must select one of the obligatory themes ("Mumford & Sons, money, beach vacation, and gender" as my favorite meme suggests) and funnel as many of your resources (time, money, energy) as you can muster into throwing the most lavish party of your life, to celebrate legally binding yourself to another until one of you dies, amen.

Ideally, you're having conversations about what type of wedding you *both* want—because while none of this is required, anyone who's ever dabbled in the world of wedding planning (whether as the betrothed or as the guest of a wedding) knows it's a slippery slope, wherein each footfall comes at a 250 percent markup. You can set out to have a no-frills, totally chill, I'm-a-laid-back-bride ceremony, but the wedding industrial complex has a funny way of transmuting "I don't have a Pinterest-board vision for my big day—can I just have some white flowers and steak for dinner?" into a five-figure affair. The average cost of a wedding in 2024 broke down as follows:

First, you must select your wedding venue (average price between $6,500 and $12,000, without food included) and hire caterers (for between another $6,500 to $10,000, though you can take the convenient way out and choose a venue that *also* does the food; I combined the two and paid roughly $23,000 total for the room, furniture, food, and staffing). Next, you'll need to hire your favorite local jam band or fifteen-year-old DJ in training (speaking from experience on that last one; that tween spun bangers all night long) for between $2,000 and $7,000 on average. You'll want to hire a wedding planner (average cost $1,500 to $4,750, depending on how much of the work they're taking off your plate), and of course, you can't forget the people who will document your big day to provide photographic evidence for the rest of your life of just how stunning your blowout celebration was, at an average cost of between $3,500 and $6,500 for the photographer and roughly the same for the videographer. You can't have an unadorned space unless your wedding theme is "frat basement," so budget another $2,500 to $6,000 for flowers, and remember that your guests will need to be transported to your various venues, so budget between $700 and $1,200 for that. Your designer, non-Costco cake will run between $600 and $900, and music for the ceremony (because, yep, that's separate!) will rack up another $500 to $800. Finally, budget between $550 and $850 for bridal hair and makeup, because if you're going to be looking at these pictures for the rest of your life, you owe it to Future You to be as hot as humanly possible. And don't forget the centerpiece: The average bride spends around $2,000 on her wedding dress.

Keeping track? It's a total average cost of around $30,000, though it's become a bit of a joke among my friends that there's an observable marital arms race within some social circles, wherein each wedding you attend is somehow more outlandishly fancy than the last. That couple had professional flamenco dancers? Well, *this* couple had *two* surprise dance troupes! That couple had free toiletries and sandals in the bathrooms for guests? Well, *this* couple had free foot massages and pedicures on-site! (Seriously.)

This isn't to say there's anything wrong with prioritizing a big wedding if it's important to you or your culture—just that if it's *not* a priority to you, your family, or your culture, it's okay to recognize the modern wedding for what it's become: an exceedingly opulent party that is not correlated with the quality of the relationship it represents and celebrates. We all choose which nonsensically expensive rituals we want to partake in (mine just happens to be the shoe department at Neiman Marcus), and the wedding is no different. If it feels as absurd to you as paying more for shoes with a red sole, you don't have to.

Night of the wedding aside, the dizzying accompaniment of

purchases and activities *leading up* to the big day (engagement rings, engagement parties, engagement photo shoots, bachelor and bachelorette parties, bridal showers, etc.) impose a rigorous scheduling and financial burden not only on you, but on the people you love. I've never been more grateful that I have approximately two close friends than in this phase of life in which I receive a message every few weeks saying something to the effect of, "Help, I've been asked to be a bridesmaid in eight weddings this year, and between the bachelorette trips, travel, and required wardrobes, it's financially ruining me."

Ultimately, this is the larger problem with contemporary wedding culture: Its chiffon nuclear fallout doesn't just impact the budgets of the couple and their parents, but anyone in the blast zone (which is, usually, other people in their twenties and thirties with less-than-lavish bank accounts who can't comfortably swing a new $300 gown and $1,000 in cross-country travel every month). And while it's a joyful time, beneath the veneer of love and happiness, you'll often find a substantial amount of financial anxiety for all involved, unless your family and friends comprise the likes of Sofia Richie, with her trio of six-figure Chanel gowns and glam team imported from London. (Her wedding weekend allegedly clocked in at $4 million.†)

My wedding *felt* like it cost $4 million at the time, and given what I've already told you, you might not be shocked to learn that I'm quite pro-elopement, which can be breathtakingly romantic and a hell of a lot less stressful. Whether that's in a courthouse like my husband and me, on the side of a mountain like my dear friend Elizabeth who's been married to her husband for forty years, or alone in the living room of your new, empty home with one

---

† For the love of all that is holy, tax the rich already.

witness like my friend Paige, you don't have to go the big wedding route if it doesn't feel right to you. My advice for anyone who's going to have a "real" wedding is to truly commit and embrace the absurdity. In other words, if you're going to do it, *really go for it*—make it your own and have as much fun as possible. If you're feeling more resentful than excited about the process and expense before it even begins, you may find it hard to sincerely enjoy it.

At the end of the day, some families, cultures, and people are more interested in big weddings than others, and for them, it might genuinely be one of the most wonderful events of their lives that's worth the trouble ten times over (especially if you can pay for full-service wedding planning or have the money to approach it with the aforementioned blank check). For others, the escalating financial and logistical strain overshadows the few hours of fun and brings along with it big bills and stomachaches, so when you're facing down this choice, #KnowThyself and plan accordingly.

The silver lining is that conversations about how much you'd like to spend on a wedding ($5,000 for a backyard bash? $500,000 to rent out Versailles?) can be a good gateway to other more in-depth, transparent financial conversations, if you haven't had them yet. (Though, in a perfect world, the ideal time to have these types of discussions is *before* you're engaged.)

After "I do"

Congratulations, you've tied the knot. That was fast! What happens now? Let's talk about postnups (if you didn't sign a prenup), managing your finances together, and—clears throat—tax filing as a couple.

Because here's the deal: You're probably sitting there like, "Wow, I bet this chick's prenup is ironclad! I've never seen someone so excited about contract law!" But remember how I mentioned my naivete going into marriage? I don't have a prenup myself. I know, I know: How can a woman who feels so strongly about this not have a prenup? My husband is an attorney, and we had discussed how *it was the responsible thing to do* and *yes, we'll absolutely get one* and *oh, do you think they can add language about who has to go pick up the takeout when it's raining?* But . . . we never got around to it. Yep, that's the boring, embarrassing truth. Despite his law degree and my obsession with financial autonomy, neither one of us fully appreciated at age twenty-six just how utterly table stakes these agreements are in modern marriage. So, if you're like me and you also showed up late to this party, what can you do to remedy it now?

Postnups

If you're already married and prenup-less like me, playing fast and loose with your joint bank accounts, you can still draft a **postnuptial agreement** with an attorney. A postnuptial agreement is exactly what it sounds like: a prenup, but for people who are already married. If you're in agreement about the terms (most usually: money I earned and saved before marriage is separate property and so is yours; here's how we'll divide assets if we divorce, etc.), it should be a relatively inexpensive contract to execute.

While the laws around the enforceability of postnups vary more by state, Lisa Zeiderman assured me they can still be useful. I wondered what might prompt a married couple with, say, roughly equal assets and a willingness to split marital property in the event of a divorce to go through the process and expense of writing a postnuptial agreement. She told me it's most impactful if there's a major life change, like someone choosing to give up their career (and therefore stop earning money of their own). "Courts are not always kind about spousal support, and frankly, it runs out quickly. You may get assets, but I see people get divorced after twenty or thirty years out of the workforce and they have no income potential. It's a disaster."

The broader challenge with postnups is legal enforceability. For this reason, they can be more likely to be overturned, which is a risk to be aware of. Fortunately, you're still able to set up separate property trusts after you're already married for assets you acquired *before* marriage, but often you'll need to do a little forensic accounting (either together, or by *literally* hiring a forensic accountant) to ensure neither of you are inadvertently placing marital property in separate property trusts.

Another approach, especially if you're worried about enforceability of a postnup, is being extra-diligent about the organization of your household finances. This includes a few things:

- Knowing where you hold assets, jointly and independently, and what those assets are worth.
- Monitoring credit reports for irregular activity, which will call attention to nonpayments of debt or other delinquencies, or—God forbid—secret credit cards.
- Having a checking or savings account in your name that you can access at any time. While simply having an account in your name alone doesn't mean it's legally your sole property if the marriage ends, it's a good safety measure for ensuring you're never the victim of financial abuse or stuck in a situation you no longer want to be in for lack of access to funds.

These steps go an extraordinarily long way in protecting you after binding yourself to another individual. Fortunately, things like separate property trusts, prenups, and postnups are relatively one and done. But for the day-to-day management of your household finances after you're married, there are a few different strategies you might consider.

Separate vs. combined finances in marriage

Even though the brass tacks of how your checking accounts pay your bills isn't as sexy and controversial as the prenup, the plumbing of your financial life together is, in many ways, just as important to your long-term success. There are three major approaches to consider:

1. Total separation (also known as "the roommate model," wherein you split everything either 50/50 or proportionally but keep all money in separately titled accounts and combine nothing).[†]
2. Total combination (also known as "the traditional model," wherein you have no separate accounts and everything lives in joint accounts).[‡]
3. Half and half (also known as "yours, mine, and ours"— this is a favorite middle ground in modern marriage).

[†] It feels important to repeat here that even if you keep everything physically separate and titled in your own names, most income and assets gained after marriage are still marital property. In the absence of a strong prenup (and unique situation), actual separation is a bit of an illusion.

[‡] Note that retirement accounts are, by definition, individual, so those cannot be joint—therefore forming an exception to the total combination approach.

I would personally advocate for the third approach, for a few reasons:

- Keeping some accounts in your name alone, as discussed, doesn't impact who legally has a claim to them in the event of divorce without other precautions, but it *does* ensure you always have access to funds if something unexpected happens.
- Usually, married people have joint goals—like paying for a kid's education or funding a six-month trip or buying a home. Saving and investing for these goals in joint accounts is, in some ways, just simpler and more fun than trying to manage it separately if there's no other reason to keep funds separate.
- If you live with your spouse, the practical day-to-day expenses of running a household, taking care of dependents, and feeding yourselves is probably easier to manage out of joint accounts so you're not Venmo-ing one another $5.60 for your half of the toilet paper.

In other words, I think it strikes the right balance between practical and morale-boosting. If you're having open financial conversations with your spouse and you're protected with the proper pre- and post-marriage legal steps, strategically combining swaths of your financial lives often means attacking debt and growing your assets more quickly. Don't get me wrong—climbing Net Worth Mountain is fun to do alone, but climbing it with a partner makes the whole ordeal go faster if you're on the same page (key words: *same page*).

Bill Nelson, a certified financial planner professional and

certified financial therapist, shared some wise words: "Using separate accounts strategically in the context of a clearly defined plan to achieve your life goals as a family is great. . . . What I don't like, though, and where I see people get tripped up with this, is if [they're] using separate accounts as a way to not have those conversations." In other words, if you're operating with totally different money mindsets and unwilling to get on the same page, that often portends trouble more than the physical separation of funds itself does.

Essentially, separate financial lives can create a veneer of safety and insulation from one another's choices that isn't real—especially if you have radically different approaches to saving and investing. For example, you're investing like your life depends on it, but bae is diverting 60 percent of their paychecks to DraftKings. You might be pissed thirty years down the road when funding your joint retirement is a burden entirely borne by you and your sacrifices. "You don't want one person to be living like a pauper to save money and the other person to be living lavishly," Savvy Ladies founder Stacy Francis told me.

All that to say—it's the intent that matters, and some couples decide it's more efficient to keep the majority of their finances separate for organizational reasons. Just be careful about using separate accounts within marriage as a Band-Aid for avoiding uncomfortable conversations, because as Bill shared, that can be a red flag.

To break this down, "yours, mine, and ours" implemented well might look like this:

STEP 1: MANAGING YOUR DAY-TO-DAY CASH FLOW WITH INDIVIDUAL ACCOUNTS

You and your spouse each have individual checking and savings accounts with your respective emergency funds (or other fun money) for purchases you want to be able to make freely. (You may have individual accounts from before your marriage in separate property trusts, and new individual accounts *outside* of them for post-marriage income.)

STEP 2: MANAGING YOUR DAY-TO-DAY CASH FLOW WITH JOINT ACCOUNTS

You and your spouse have a joint checking (and maybe joint savings) account where you contribute your paychecks or hold a joint emergency fund, but there are different ways to fund accounts at this step. For example, my husband and I deposit our paychecks into our joint checking account, but some people choose to deposit their paychecks into the individual accounts mentioned in step 1, and then make transfers into joint checking for agreed-upon amounts. The latter approach might make more sense for a couple who's decided to keep their fun money separate.

Regardless of how it's funded, the joint checking account is used for regular bill pay—things like housing, food, childcare, entertainment, and travel. Since my husband and I both deposit our paychecks into our joint account, we have a predetermined amount of money set aside each month for guilt-free spending that we're both entitled to—we consider all the money in the joint account as belonging to both of us, so we aren't regularly adding money to (or making purchases using) our individual accounts. This is a matter of personal preference, and this works best for us.

If you decide to direct your incomes to your individual accounts and then transfer money for your joint expenses to the jointly held account, you might decide that a "proportional" approach is effective if earnings are disparate. This involves calculating what percentage of total household income each earner is responsible for—say, 60 percent you, 40 percent them—and applying those proportions to your expense burden. In this example, you'd be responsible for covering 60 percent of the joint expenses, and they'd cover 40 percent.

STEP 3: HOOKING UP CREDIT CARD AUTOPAYS ACCORDINGLY

Depending on what you decide in steps 1 and 2, any credit cards you both possess will be designated as intended for either "joint expenses" or "individual expenses" and get automatically paid by the corresponding checking account. (Whether or not your credit cards are jointly held is another story, and we'll unpack that in more detail in the debt section.)

For example, my husband's credit cards are tied to his name, Social Security number, and by extension, credit report, and mine are tied to mine. But since all our expenses—regardless of what it is, or who buys it—are paid by our jointly held income, all our credit card bills are set to autopay from our joint checking account.

STEP 4: PAYING OFF OTHER DEBT

Depending on how you've decided to attack debt, you may be making payments from individual accounts (funded by individual incomes) or joint accounts funded by both incomes.

STEP 5: INVESTING FOR YOUR FUTURE

You and your spouse each have your own retirement accounts (think 401(k)s, IRAs, etc.) that are funded with paycheck contributions or take-home pay, but you may also have brokerage accounts that are being used to invest for other goals, whether independently or together.

For example, my husband and I each had individual brokerage accounts before we got married. We didn't combine them retroactively, nor do we contribute to them anymore, so they remain separate property. Once we got married, we opened a joint brokerage account for our future desires (we named it KGT/TMT World Domination Fund) and any money that's left over at the end of each month in joint checking gets routed to the joint brokerage account.

We had to sit down when we opened the account to talk about how we were going to invest the money and arrive at something we both felt comfortable with, so we compromised and did it my way! (Kidding.)

How marriage impacts debt

Debt—and more specifically, who's legally on the hook for it—is tricky within marriage and depends on where you live, but it's important to know that once your credit cards are commingled, it's very difficult to untangle them. American Express doesn't care that you're separated and your husband's responsible for paying the Platinum Card bill—as far as they're concerned, you're liable for it if he doesn't. In my mind, this isn't a reason not to open joint credit cards, but it's good to be aware so you can close accounts if necessary.

In community property states—those glorious lands of 50/50 splits—you may be found liable for your spouse's debt *even if your name isn't on it*. Here, common sense is important:

- It's in your best interest (both of you!) to be fully aware of what's happening across all credit accounts every month, so carve out time to talk through it periodically.

- You'll want to review balances either manually or using a spending aggregator app that can collect everything in one place and ensure nothing is ballooning (you wouldn't need to manually check transactions if that feels a little privacy invasion-y, but you can keep tabs on overall card balances between you to confirm nothing is snowballing).

Even if you decide to maintain separate finances and your spouse assures you that they're managing their own just fine, it's important to understand your legal liability in community property states. If you divorce, their debt could be half yours. To me, this is a perfectly reasonable justification for checking in with one another at least once every few months to validate that nobody's balances are spiraling out of control. Because even if you maintain separate financial lives, as long as you're legally married in a community property state, you assume legal liability for your spouse's financial decisions.

I asked Stacy Francis if she'd ever seen this play out in real life, and she confirmed it's common (and messy) but that there's recourse in worst-case scenarios: "[If you find yourself in this situation], talk to your lawyer about **marital dissipation**, which is how we refer to using marital assets for nonmarital purposes. If you can prove this happened, you can typically get a 'credit' [during an asset split]. So let's say your spouse gambled away $100,000 you didn't know about of your marital assets. You can often have your lawyer negotiate to get you a $100,000 credit, so you're not footing the bill for this person's bad behavior. Before you sign any settlement agreements, make sure that debt is paid off from the assets that *they're* going to receive, because then you know that if they don't comply, you're still off the hook."

Married filing jointly vs. married filing separately

We've looked at the legal infrastructure you'll put in place before getting married, the day-to-day management of your money, and how your debt obligations are changed by walking down the aisle. But what about taxes? The "jointly vs. separately" question finds its way into my inbox regularly, which is interesting, because the US is one of the only countries in the world that strongly incentivizes you to get married via tax breaks (that is, the "married filing jointly" tax status). The use cases for filing separately are unique, but in some cases, they might serve to protect you legally or lower your expenses elsewhere.

For most, your tax return will probably be a lot rosier if you file jointly. If you're unsure, I recommend working with a CPA who can help you make this decision with confidence (and bring your spouse along, since they'll need to get on board, too). A few common reasons why you might choose to file separately:

- One spouse has income-based student loan repayment that will be impacted dramatically by a much higher household income (though this consideration should be weighed against the potential for a higher tax bill from filing separately). For example, you might have student loans and earn a lot less than your spouse. If you were to file jointly, your *entire* household income would impact how your monthly payments are calculated, which could inflate them substantially. Filing separately means your monthly payments will be based on your income, and your income alone.

- One spouse has high medical expenses and/or a much lower income that makes them eligible for certain tax credits that they'd be ineligible for if they filed together.
- One spouse is retiring early and plans to draw down on tax-deferred investment income while the other continues to work, and the retiring spouse doesn't want their partner's earned income to impact the tax rates they pay on their investment income. (Again, you'll just want to confirm the overall tax bill won't be higher by filing separately.)
- You suspect your spouse is engaged in some Gordon Gekko–level fraud or tax evasion and you feel dicey about signing a joint tax return, as that's legally equivalent to saying "I hereby verify that I can personally vouch for what's in this legal document and will suffer the repercussions therein if it's full of cocaine and lies."

As a fun aside, your marital status on December 31 is what determines your filing status for the entire year, so if you get married on Christmas, you can still claim married filing jointly status for the entire year. Fortunately, for most people, filing jointly will lower your tax bill and increase your household income—so maybe the New Year's Eve wedding is a good idea after all?

In conclusion

For nearly the entire ~4,500-year history of the institution of marriage, women didn't have the option to play an equal role in managing their own resources. Marriage necessarily meant surrendering your autonomy, and this continued until relatively recently in the twentieth century. The sediment of these power dynamics persists, and we must actively choose to resist them. As with most things, simple risk awareness and proper planning can go a long way.

No matter which approach you and your partner adopt for building your financial life together, I hope you enter marriage (should you choose to) less naively than I did. Financial autonomy, organization, and respect within marriage aren't just good for your *financial* outcomes, I learned from Bill; they also bode well statistically for your marital outcomes (bonus!). Much like we carry health insurance in case we face catastrophic medical expenses, we can take basic, commonsense steps to protect ourselves legally within our marriages, too.

Still, there's one thing we briefly alluded to in this chapter that deserves its own chapter, because it's a choice that economically impacts women in a drastically different way than it impacts men, statistically speaking: the decision to become a parent.

5

Every Mom Is a Working Mom

I don't yet have children, which obviously makes me an expert on child-rearing. But as a young woman curious about the prospect of becoming a parent, I pay attention to the cultural messages I receive about what it means to "be a good mother." I'm consistently struck by the impossibility of the proposition.

Eve Rodsky opens her book *Fair Play* with a telling anecdote called "The Case of the 30 Calls and 46 Texts," in which she describes gathering with female friends and family in mixed-sex marriages, only to find that—like clockwork—the frantic communication from their respective husbands flooded their phones after about an hour. *When's the babysitter arriving? When are you coming home? Where's Josh's soccer bag? What's the address for the kids' birthday party? Do the kids need to eat lunch?*

When I first cracked open my copy of *Fair Play*, I was sitting in the aisle seat of a United flight coming home from Mexico. In the middle and window seat sat a young mother and her squirmy baby. Opposite us, her husband was sitting with their older child, who was quietly entertaining herself with a blue foam-rimmed iPad.

"My mother-in-law gave me that book," the woman told me when she saw me reading it. "Do you have kids?" she asked, jangling various toys and stuffed animals in front of her baby, trying to keep her occupied.

"Oh, no," I responded, suddenly embarrassed to be caught reading a book that's ostensibly about caretaking equity in public. "My sister-in-law sent me this." (Are our husbands' female family members conspiring against them?)

"Yeah," she sighed, adjusting her grip on the baby, who was attempting to scale the seat in front of her. "I don't know. I haven't really had time to read it. My husband is pretty good at trying to help me out." I glanced over at her husband, who was scrolling on his phone, unaware of our conversation. She continued: "We both work for [impressive software company], but I recently downshifted so I could have more time to take care of them," she said, gesturing at her two kids. "It just made sense."

Though I wanted to, I didn't ask why it made more sense for her to downshift, or why she was the one sitting with the child who required constant surveillance on this four-hour flight. It was none of my business, but the circumstances felt a little too on the nose given my reading material. There was nothing out of the ordinary about this scene: the primary female caretaker and the helping husband. (Describing an equal partner as "helping" with a shared responsibility is telling.) As we talked more, she opened up about the family they had just vacationed with.

"She's a stay-at-home mom. And she's waking up early in our rental each morning, roasting carrots and shit . . . meanwhile, I'm tossing Puffs at my kids between emails. I just feel like I don't have the time to be that kind of mother, even with doing less at work."

"Puffs?" her husband repeated from across the aisle, catching the word and offering the canister to her.

"No, sorry, we're good," she responded.

"Want me to take over?" he asked, gesturing at the baby. Again, she demurred, and he went back to his phone.

We talked for most of the flight. It was clear my seatmate loved her kids, and I also got the impression that she really enjoyed her work. But this person was also very clearly overburdened trying to manage both. Given the state of work and care in America, it's possible (probable, even) that her husband felt the same way, but over the course of our conversation, she made her feelings clear: She was the one making career sacrifices to accommodate their family life. Because the United States lacks the family-oriented federal amenities like paid parental leave, universal childcare, and subsidized eldercare that are provided via publicly owned programs in our peer nations, women typically bear the brunt of these costs behind closed doors. Sociologist Jessica Calarco explained it most concisely: "Other countries have social safety nets. The US has women."

This chapter is intended to discuss how to plan for paying for childcare in the US, so you're *not* automatically faced with the "career vs. family" dichotomy that seems to disproportionately impact women. Of course, that means this chapter will be most practically useful for women who don't yet have kids, but the infrastructure of identifying and planning for a medium-term savings goal will be applicable regardless of whether the desired outcome is a child or a midsize SUV. As much as I wish they could, the strategies outlined in this chapter won't cause social safety nets or meaningful legislation to materialize—but I hope an awareness of statistical inequity in caretaking and other domestic labor might help guide your expectations for yourself, and what "fairness" really means. We've already explored the state of the gender pay gap, but as you likely know if you run a household, the time, energy, and executive functioning demanded by life's mental load are not "free."

The "feminine" role of caretaker

The man largely credited with inventing marketplace capitalism, Adam Smith, lived at home with his mother. While he wrote *The Wealth of Nations* in 1776, she cooked and cleaned for him. This juicy morsel of history makes for such perfect satire, I can hardly stand it. How *magnificent* that the person responsible for defining what's necessary for capitalism to function had unpaid help at home making his life possible. Notably, the necessity and value of domestic labor was absent from his reflections on men acting in their own self-interest. These were the real "invisible hands" in Smith's accounting of the market, and their conspicuous exclusion is hardly surprising: The subjugation of women is a treasured pastime of white, patriarchal capitalism. It was a foregone conclusion that a woman's biologically predetermined role was to be the de facto caretaker of society, and that this work would not be paid.

It takes time to unwind this dogma. As I write this book in 2024, women are still more likely than men in heterosexual couples to do the work that never ends—the work that must be re-completed every single day, as Silvia Federici writes, a feminist who founded the Wages for Housework movement in the 1970s. A 2021 profile of Federici summarized the message of her life's work: Unpaid domestic work is a form of gendered economic oppression, and in some ways, the core exploitation upon which all of modern capitalism is built. In her 1975 book *Wages Against Housework*, Federici wrote, "We have cooked, smiled, fucked throughout the years not because it was easier for us than for anybody else, but because we did not have any other choice. . . . We want to call work what is work so that eventually we might rediscover what is love." She rejected the idea that a "labor of love" existed, or that any person in society was preordained to be more naturally subservient.

For all our progress, women continue to consistently shoulder more than their fair share of the load. A study from Pew Research Center aggregated years of data from the Bureau of Labor Statistics' Time Use Survey and found that the (very small) contingent of stay-at-home fathers barely performs more household labor than their breadwinning wives who work full time. They spend only four hours more per week than their working partners on housework, and about two hours more per week on childcare. Yet their leisure time is nearly double that of their partners: forty-three hours per week for the stay-at-home father versus twenty-three hours for the working mother.

By contrast, when moms stay at home and dads work for money (the more common arrangement), the moms spend *more than three times* as many hours as their working partners on housework and caretaking, and only have four hours more leisure time than their working partners, rather than twenty. This means that—regardless of whether a mother stays at home or is the sole breadwinner—she's bearing an unfair portion of unpaid household and caretaking duties.

When both parents work for pay (whether part time or full time), the effects are even more exaggerated: While the average employed man spends fifty-seven more minutes per day doing paid work than the average employed woman, the average employed woman performs about one hour and ten minutes more unpaid household and caretaking labor per day.

If you want to know how a woman is spending her time or see

an explanation for *why* she might be spending less time and energy doing paid labor, well . . . there you go. The answer is: She's doing unpaid labor.

My guess is you're having one of two reactions right now:

1. "I didn't need some fancy data table from a government agency to tell me this, because I live it every day."
2. "What's so wrong with taking care of a family? Isn't it a good thing to be a primary caretaker?"

Here's the challenge with conversations like this one: In an attempt to clarify inequity in caretaking, it often inadvertently sounds as though caretaking is a *bad* thing. The opposite is true. What's problematic—and worth calling out explicitly—is that, if life is a big group project, women at the aggregate level are statistically and consistently shouldering more than their fair share of the load and ending up with fewer resources as a result. As one way to measure the financial consequences of these differences, consider that women today retire with approximately 22 percent less Social Security income than their male counterparts, and about 57 percent as much retirement income overall.

Other countries have social safety nets; the US has women

So what does it matter if women are more likely to forgo paid work so they can do more of the unpaid caretaking labor in their households? Someone has to do it for free, right? Not outside the US. The US's approach to care work, with its obsessive emphasis on the nuclear family, treats child-rearing (and eldercare) like a private, personal matter to be sorted by each individual parent or child, as opposed to a public good that benefits all of society. Despite care work being a universal need, as ubiquitous and necessary for life as infrastructure like roads, the US invests practically nothing in caretaking—leaving parents and children to fend for themselves in the private sphere or for-profit market.

Comparatively, every other high-income nation in the world provides some form of help to its populace through publicly funded social programs—such as universal childcare, a year of paid parental leave, subsidized higher education, or all three, and then some. The fact that the US is the sole notable outlier should be a clue that something is working abroad. The Swedes may pay higher tax rates than we do, but nearly three in five American parents spend 20 percent or more of their household income on childcare. A tax increase to expand the public school system to include daycare would have to be enormous to be a worse deal than what we've got now. (Not for nothing, Sweden's gender pay gap is less than half the size of the US's.)

Navigating our current paradigm requires a huge expense and serious sacrifice, and the majority of US households find life without two incomes to be too precarious. Seventy percent of families are dual income—and therefore need assistance to care for other family members while they're at work—compared to 49 percent in 1972. It's not just that more families have two earners now: Of these dual-income households, women earn as much or more than men in 55 percent of them.[†] Despite this progress, Nobel

---

† Women are the sole provider in 6 percent of mixed-sex US marriages, while men are the sole provider in 23 percent.

Prize–winning economist Claudia Goldin found in her research that one adult often leans into their career and keeps the "greedy" job, as she calls it, that may be more demanding and higher paying. The other adult typically downshifts, and while they may stay employed in some capacity, they tend to be the one who's on call to leave work to pick up a sick kid from school, take care of the laundry duty, coordinate the goodie bags for the class party, and—ultimately—defer the type of paid work that would lead to the accumulation of resources.

And let me ask you: As you read that last paragraph, free of gendered pronouns, and imagined this arrangement, which parent fulfilled each role? If you imagined the man on work trips and the woman taking the more flexible schedule, you'd be statistically correct—between our discussions about women tending to earn less than men and the data we've reviewed about how the average working woman spends her time, this outcome is unsurprising. In a perfectly egalitarian world, there'd be no gendered assumption of who performed what tasks in a two-income household, nor would we see any of these disparities in the data. And as we'll examine next, the status quo creates serious financial consequences for women later in life.

Being financially prepared for these circumstances can provide more optionality when you face them

The practical reason many women in the US today find themselves in a position where they must downshift or leave work altogether to raise children is because of the absurdly high expense of childcare. Taking your unpaid domestic labor and transforming it into someone else's *paid* labor costs money, and many couples look at their respective salaries and choose to forfeit or deprioritize the lower paycheck so that one parent can save the family the cost of care. Make no mistake: Some people *prefer* this arrangement; some choose it regardless of the availability of another choice. Others feel it's their only rational choice. It's the latter group we're concerned with.

Understanding how to save and pay for childcare such that you're not automatically and singularly faced with this career-versus-family trade-off is a practical, necessary step we can take to prevent women from being sidelined in the workforce as a gendered default. Saving for kids before you have them might mean you're also able to use more of your household income to pay for other help, like cleaning, meal preparation, a laundry service, and any number of the other responsibilities of running a household that often fall on women to bear "for free."

Right now, these are almost always low-wage jobs, which means they're almost always worked by women: An unbelievable 94 percent of childcare workers and 97 percent of prekindergarten and kindergarten teachers are women. Black and Latina women are disproportionately represented in this group, comprising shares of the early childcare sector that are nearly twice as high as their shares in the overall workforce. When it comes to the people who clean our homes and workspaces, like housekeepers and janitors, men are overrepresented in the jobs that clean our commercial spaces—66 percent of janitors are men. Women, on the other hand, make up 86.5 percent of people working as "maids and housekeepers," work done in the domestic sphere. This work is undeniably valuable—but it's not currently *valued*, and it won't be until we begin paying fair wages for the labor that allows the rest of society to function.

Let's take a closer look at the real costs women face when forced to downshift or give up their paid jobs.

The hidden price that women pay

Everyone's priorities will be different, of course, but the simple explanation for what women give up is this: Going years (or even decades) without any "real" earnings translates to zeroes in the Social Security work records, which means forfeiting access to Social Security payments of your own, as well as an inability to save for your own retirement.

Farnoosh Torabi, a personal finance expert and mother of two, navigated this dilemma when deciding how she was going to approach having kids. She noticed a lot of the parents around her often defaulted to shifting more of the burden onto the spouse with the lower salary, which usually meant the woman would leave her job to take care of their kids. "One person says, 'Well, you know, I guess I'm not going to work because childcare costs so much.' And that math isn't *wrong*, in the sense that childcare sometimes does exceed (or is at least equal to) some people's post-tax salaries. But I think that calculus isn't fair. You have to look at the bigger math."

By "bigger math," Farnoosh is referring to the way that continuing to work for pay is an investment in your own lifetime earnings: It might be a net wash in the short term, but being out of the game for many years often makes it difficult to reenter later. Financially speaking, staying in the workforce while your children are young is an investment in higher lifetime earnings (and any aspirations you may have outside your role as a caretaker). Conversely, Farnoosh felt that investing in her career while her kids were little meant having more flexibility, time, and money later when they were older and would likely benefit from her presence even more.

In many ways, awareness of this financial vulnerability should not be gendered: Men who stay home and don't work for pay need to be just as aware of this risk. But in our current paradigm, in which the vast majority of stay-at-home parents are mothers, the financial ramifications of marriages that go south are mostly borne by women. Approximately one in five divorced women ends up in poverty, a rate 56 percent higher than that of divorced men. And lest we fear that we're creating correlation where it doesn't exist, 61 percent of women report that they left paid work for "family responsibilities," compared to 37 percent of men. It's this overrepresentation of women getting the short end of the financial stick, particularly when this outcome is painted as a gendered inevitability, that's concerning. (And I don't think we'll see better legislative support for parents until more men are represented in this group, or more women are represented in Congress.)

Because women tend to spend more of their time doing unpaid domestic care work in their households and mixed-sex couples are more likely to defer to a man's career, Claudia Goldin theorizes that *this* is the primary reason the wage gap widens as women age and their familial responsibilities increase. It's the reason why more men end up in leadership positions; why men are far more likely to be high earners than women (a staggering 95 percent of top 1 percent earners are male): Because becoming a husband and father doesn't automatically mean your career gets put on the back burner in the same way that becoming a wife and mother does.

In summary: When cultural attitudes dictate that women are society's "natural" primary caregivers, not only is their *paid* labor valued less, but the attitude directly enables a complete dearth of public support for families—why do you need childcare or paid family leave if a woman's natural role is "full-time mother"? As such, the universal logistical and financial burden of childcare falls on individual parents, with the lower-earning partner, often the mother, more likely to downshift their career to accommodate their family's needs, thereby all but guaranteeing a lifetime of financial disparity. Before you know it, many women who would otherwise have chosen to maintain their careers—and could have, had quality childcare not been so expensive and onerous to find—are out of the workforce for a decade, not contributing to their Social Security benefits, stalled in their career, and finding it difficult to jump back in. It does not have to be this way. This is why the conversation about the "choice" to stay home is so hollow: How can one make fully autonomous choices in a system that structurally incentivizes one path over another? This is not a discussion about our choices. It's an examination of which real options are available to us in the first place. Our true goal is not a superficial "choice," but liberation from the systems that limit which paths we feel we can choose.

Of course, as I said at the outset of our journey together, this book can't change the American obsession with rugged individualism or the alliance between regressive gender essentialist values and fend-for-yourself policy. Since this is a personal finance text, I'll share my best advice for an interim Band-Aid until we achieve broader social change. At the individual level, how can we financially plan for kids now if we want to stay in the workforce? First, we need to understand the costs of childcare.

Rodsky's *Fair Play* covers many tactics one can use within the family to more equitably distribute the work of running a household. Perhaps unsurprisingly, it centers around making the "invisible work" visible (using a playing card system for every task, big or small) and abundantly open communication about expectations: everything from what's a "reasonable standard of care" for certain tasks to recognizing when resentment is beginning to seep in. Rodsky's approach boils down to making the discrepancy feel obvious, unavoidable. If two adults working full time find that, of one hundred household tasks, one partner is shouldering eighty-five of them, any reasonable person can see that something has clearly gone off track. Equitable families aren't just good for women's financial outcomes, but for the health of marriages and family dynamics. As Rodsky makes clear, resentment is the silent killer of love, and nothing breeds resentment quite like consistently working unpaid overtime while an oblivious teammate has their feet up.

The cost of raising kids

My friend and feminist writer Caroline Burke noted the stark difference in the cultural and consumer messaging she sees on social media (as of the time of this writing, she's not a mother) compared with her sister, who already has kids (and is pregnant with another child). Caroline immediately noticed the absolute deluge of promotions with which her sister was inundated: ads for things that would diminish the stretch marks on her supposedly unsightly stomach, organizational tools that would render her home acceptable, water bottles that would transform her into the most hydrated version of herself, the NASA-approved stroller that'll fix acne and cure depression. She describes how baffled and disturbed she felt by the onslaught—sponsored and organic!— assuring her sister at every turn that she was not and did not presently have enough, but that through *this* one-click purchase, she could be one step closer to empowerment and satisfaction. Caroline clocked the irony of this urging immediately and told me about the urgency of her realization on an episode of *The Money with Katie Show*: "The number-one thing that empowers women is access to capital, and the signals we are getting at all times to just flush any money that we have down the drain is baffling to me. . . . I feel like [I have] a pretty healthy relationship to products, but it's only because I now feel so certain that I want to spend my life doing things that matter to me, and in order to do that . . . I have to be hypervigilant. I refuse to get a divorce over children, over childcare [inequity], and I refuse to be a full-time stay-at-home [parent], which means that I have to be vigilant about making sure that we have money for childcare."

Being realistic about what we're up against, as Caroline demonstrates, is the first step in giving ourselves options. I'll never forget the way I sat, slack-jawed, listening to a parent who works in Boston detail the $4,000-per-month daycare costs they incurred for their two children for years. At the time, I was just *barely* past the phase in my life where $4,000 eclipsed my monthly take-home pay, so I could understand why someone in that position might consider it a wash and throw in the towel.

There are dozens of competing philosophies about the "best" way to raise a kid, but what most of them have in common is a hefty price tag: an oft-cited statistic claims that it costs $300,000 to raise a child from infancy to adulthood in the United States, which—bewilderingly—doesn't include the cost of higher education.

To get as clear-eyed as possible, let's unpack that six-figure sum. The MIT Living Wage Calculator's 2024 data allows us to compare the living costs of a household without children to that of one *with* children and analyze the additional costs incurred for housing and childcare in 384 metro areas. In the fifty largest US metros, it's least expensive to raise a child in New Orleans–Metairie, Louisiana, where the annual cost of one child was $17,887 in 2024—a far cry from number one, Boston-Cambridge-Newton, Massachusetts, which recorded an annual cost per kid of $37,758.

In general, the primary costs associated with having kids break down as follows:

Childcare

If you're a dual-income household, covering care from ages zero to five will likely be one of the largest expenses that goes from zero to sixty overnight. If you're lucky enough to have paid parental leave from your employer, you may get a break for the first few months of your kid's life, but soon enough, a nanny, au pair, or daycare will need to fill in the gaps. In the fifty largest metro areas, the average annual cost of childcare was $13,187 per year.

The cost breakdown varies dramatically by region, but depending on how many kids you have and the method of care you choose (part time or full time, in or out of the home, etc.), budgeting somewhere between $10,000 and $15,000 per child per year until school age is likely a safe starting point that'll dramatically reduce the cost burden when the time comes.

Incremental costs of housing

The data also estimates an increase in the cost of housing, as many people upsize their living arrangements when they start a family, which they may not have done otherwise. Depending on where you live, the estimated increase in housing costs ranges from $1,656 (in Birmingham-Hoover, Alabama) to $7,056 (in San Diego–Chula Vista–Carlsbad, California) per year.

Education

While the cost of caring for children has risen modestly in real terms over the last few decades, the cost of a college education at a public four-year university has tripled in inflation-adjusted dollars since 1980. Just when you think you've successfully navigated the trials and tribulations of birthing, housing, and caring for your kids, you face the biggest challenge of all: funding a college education, if that's of interest. College is, in some ways, like home ownership, in the sense that recent spikes in price have changed the cost-benefit calculus and transformed it into a decision that requires considerably more strategy to get right. The average cost of a four-year public university undergraduate education as of the 2020–2021 school year is $21,337 per year, though it can reach many multiples of that depending on the institution.

Still, parents benefit from one tailwind while planning for something like higher education: time. If you know you want the option to send a kid to college someday, you can begin investing for it (whether in a taxable brokerage account or 529 plan) early in your child's life and let time and compounding do the bulk of the work over the following ~18 years. Assuming prices continue rising at an average annual rate of 8 percent per year,† you'll incur around $300,000 in kid-related costs before college, and then pay another $300,000 or so for college itself (assuming you're paying for it).

Six hundred thousand dollars to raise and educate a brand-new human? Seems totally reasonable! But really, how does one even begin to plan for such a massive (and lengthy) outlay of funds?

How we'll approach medium-term saving

For the purposes of this exercise, we're focusing on how you'd set a financial goal that maps average childcare expenses to your current timeline. And of course, there's a wide range of volatility depending on how often your kid is going to $10,000-per-year sleepaway camp or if they attend a private school (or if you simply live in Massachusetts or California, apparently).

If we're using averages, we'd probably expect to see a moderate spike in the early years, then a period of relatively low necessary expenses (heavy emphasis on "relative"), followed by an enormous spike for higher education. As we've highlighted, the enormity of said spike is entirely dependent on education costs

---

† I have sincere doubts that things can carry on this way for another two decades. I think the education bubble will burst long before prices have a chance to climb that high, because there would simply be so few people who could afford to go to college that demand would plummet. The ROI would only make sense for a very small selection of high-paid careers.

continuing to rise as they have been, as well as the assumption that you're the one paying for it.

It's also probably worth noting that because—inexplicably— the school day and normal workday hours don't coincide, there are likely incremental care costs from the time school ends until the end of the workday for several years as well, though because that isn't reflected explicitly in the data, I'm not including it. (For what it's worth, Claudia Goldin's work suggests that shifting the school schedule to match standard working hours is one change that would put a big dent in the gender pay gap.)

Our "saving for offspring" game plan

In that sense, the type of saving we do for something like a child probably requires two major components:

1. **An enhanced cash cushion in a high-yield savings account** (or in CDs set to mature every twelve to eighteen months) that can produce around $10,000 per year for five years to help support the average daycare costs of $13,187 per year. (If you're actively planning for such an expense in your lovely hometown of, say, San Jose, California, I would recommend following this same playbook with your *actual* numbers.†)

2. **Investments in a taxable brokerage account or 529 account** (I could make an argument in favor of either, depending on your state income tax bracket) of roughly

---

† You can access comprehensive cost-of-living data about your city at livingwage .mit.edu.

$7,200 per year ($600 per month) on average to end up with around $300,000 after eighteen years, assuming an average 9 percent annualized return before inflation, beginning whenever your kid is born.

It's at this point that you might be like, "Wait a second, these numbers seem totally untenable," to which I'd say, "Yes, precisely." It's utterly mystifying that the average American family makes this work, and I can only imagine that the vast majority are either using debt or not saving at all to make ends meet. But even if these numbers are far outside the realm of what you're able to manage right now, even if you only contribute a small percentage of what you see here, you're still softening the financial blow of childcare and other expenses for Future You. And if you don't have any plans next weekend, let's form a Rich Girl Nation coalition and lobby Congress to stop this ridiculousness. In the meantime, we're reminded of why focusing on increasing income is such a valuable use of our energy . . . and of one other *non*financial consideration that feels worth acknowledging.

Many of the parents I talk to tell me the only reason they're able to make it work (financially and logistically) is because they live close to other family members (often their own parents) who volunteer to help in a part-time capacity. It takes a village, so it stands to reason that *having* a village seriously eases the financial, psychological, and physical burden of raising children alone as one or two working adults. Parents may live with other family members, or more commonly, in the same town. After noticing this theme appear time and time again in my conversations, it strikes me as a more realistic model for family structure in this sticky in-between time when daycare costs are becoming more and more untenable for most average people but families can't thrive on one income alone.

Part of this outcome is predictable: The atomized nuclear family model is actually quite new in modern history (see also: "It takes a village"). While the highest incidence of "extended family households" peaked around 20 percent in the US in the 1850s and 1860s, multigenerational living (wherein children, parents, grandparents, and sometimes aunts and uncles live in close proximity or under the same roof) is still very common in other cultures. While not every family situation will lend itself to this arrangement, over the years I've heard from more and more young people devising creative living solutions to ease the burden and help one another. For example, one Seattle couple in Rich Girl Nation told me they share a home with another family with young children. They take turns cooking and cleaning and split the energetic and financial costs of the household labor and care work among the four adults. As it becomes more expensive to raise children and our government fails to meaningfully address it, leaning into community might be the next best option.

With that said, we've now reached the exciting part of this chapter where we'll chart our path forward.

Creating the cash cushion necessary for Future You's childcare support

Step 1: Identifying your approximate timeline

The first thing we need to do is identify a rough timeline for when you might need childcare.

Unless your personality closely mirrors that of Jane Ryan in *New York Minute* with her color-coded closet and daybook of plans in fifteen-minute increments, you probably have a general sense of when you'd like to have a kid, but not a date circled on your calendar that says CONCEIVE NEW LIFE. For the purposes of planning, getting within a year or two of accuracy is fine. For example, "three to five years from now."

Step 2: Identifying your intermediate-term goal amount

We know that, for each kid, we're looking at an *average* of around $13,187 in childcare expenses each year, for roughly the first five years. This is the primary expense associated with bringing new life into the world, and the expense that comes first (aside from the astronomical cost of giving birth in a hospital with or without insurance, #ILoveItHere).

Our goal is to save enough to have about $10,000 available to us each year roughly three to five years from now. We also know we're probably going to be operating within a high-yield savings account with a guaranteed rate of return of around 4.2 percent (as of the time of this writing) or certificates of deposit that'll "mature" every twelve to eighteen months, as needed.

If we know childcare prices tend to rise over time, the first thing we'll do to find our target is look at the current costs adjusted for five years of 3 percent annual inflation: What costs $10,000 today will likely clock in around $11,592 five years from now.

Assuming we start and end at the latest possible points on our desired timeline, that puts our total "childcare goal" amount around $60,000, to be deployed slowly over time versus used all at once. This gives our plan a bit of an edge.

If you're planning to have a baby with someone you're already in a relationship with, you could split these savings goals. Surely this'll generate a better outcome than that cursed viral Reddit post from the woman whose husband—with whom she maintained separate finances—wanted her to independently cover the costs of having their baby, since she opted for the "fancy medicine" (Your Honor, it was an epidural). Jail.

Whether saving independently or together, the mathematical good news is twofold:

1. We're saving in a high-yield savings account earning approximately 4.2 percent, which means it'll grow as we save.
2. Since we're going to be using chunks of this account as we go, the remaining funds will sit in the account and continue to grow—which means we don't need to save the full equivalent of "the cost of daycare × 5."

If you're shooting for five years from now, saving $897 per month between now and then will have you covered (or, if you're saving with a working partner, $448 each). The chart below assumes your average desired daycare savings buffer is $10,000 per year and adjusts upward by 3 percent annually. If you find yourself racing the clock, don't let the chart freak you out—keep in mind this is a savings plan for accumulating almost the entirety of five years' worth of daycare money before your kid is even born, so saving just a fraction of the recommended amounts (the fourth and fifth columns) will help.

YEARS UNTIL BIRTH	AMOUNT NEEDED IN FIRST YEAR	TOTAL NEEDED OVER 5 YEARS	MONTHLY SAVINGS NEEDED	MONTHLY SAVINGS PER PARENT	TOTAL CONTRIBUTIONS	TOTAL INTEREST EARNED BY THE TIME YOU BEGIN WITHDRAWING
1	$10,000	$53,091	$4,340	$2,170	$52,077	$1,014.27
2	$10,300	$54,684	$2,188	$1,094	$52,515	$2,169.00
3	$10,609	$56,325	$1,471	$735	$52,949	$3,375.57
4	$10,927	$58,014	$1,112	$556	$53,379	$4,635.59
5	$11,255	$59,755	$897	$448	$53,804	$5,950.69
6	$11,593	$61,547	$753	$377	$54,225	$7,322.53
7	$11,941	$63,394	$650	$325	$54,641	$8,752.85
8	$12,299	$65,296	$573	$287	$55,052	$10,243.39
9	$12,668	$67,255	$514	$257	$55,459	$11,795.97
10	$13,048	$69,272	$465	$233	$55,860	$13,412.44

And again, for no reason at all, I'll take this opportunity to note that the United States is the only high-income nation that expects parents to figure this out on their own. It looks ridiculous and unreasonable because it is.

Step 3: Seeing the bigger picture

Something we glossed over in this breakdown is that we *stopped* contributing to this savings account once the baby was born, thereby freeing up those savings for something else while we draw down on our balance to pay for childcare. Whether that money is used for more discretionary spending, additional food or supplies for an infant, or something like future college savings is up to you (if you recall, to end up with $300,000 in eighteen years, you'd need to invest $600 per month). In an ideal world, I like to think the money would be spent making life for the new parent(s) easier. You also might decide to continue to save it for supplemental childcare once your kids are in school.

This exercise highlights why starting to save small amounts early (even if this isn't really on your radar yet) can allow time to chip away at a problem, whether the problem is supplementing childcare costs or accumulating a down payment. For example, in the "five years away" scenario, you'll end up disbursing $59,755 from the account over the five years you use it, $5,950 of which is interest—a little like having a third earner contributing for a whole year.

Two important takeaways

1. When you break down financial goals as a series of steps you can follow to generate the outcomes you want, the parameters around spending become a lot clearer. A Rich Gal taking home $5,000 per month might feel like the $2,000-per-month one-bedroom apartment is manageable, until she considers the home she'd like to buy, the baby she wants to have, and the retirement aspirations that are a couple of decades away. Then, she can weigh present sacrifice versus future reward. Maybe living alone is worth delaying these other things. Maybe it's not! But if you understand the trade-offs, you gain more information with which to choose.

2. In the world's most obvious statement, two earners make things half as difficult.

In conclusion

I want to let you in on a little secret: When I was conceiving the informational structure of this book (interesting word choice given this chapter's subject matter, I know), one of the challenges was how to address the subject of motherhood's impact on one's finances. It felt like such a big topic that it deserved its own chapter, yet simultaneously so interconnected with nearly every other discussion (particularly the one about the wage gap in Chapter 2) that I found myself struggling not to lay all my cards on the table three chapters ago. So while I alluded to it earlier, I want to state it plainly here: It is almost impossible to separate a woman's ability to earn and invest effectively from her role as a caretaker, which is fundamentally different from the career <> family calculus that men typically face.

It's this reproductive disparity that keeps our progress stalled, and based on the quantitative and qualitative evidence, I believe it's the driving force responsible for the vast majority of the gender wealth gap we observe. What seems important to me, then, is that this sacrifice is borne by *all* people in a society—that the hard work and expense of care is *not* primarily felt by women, who are statistically more likely to sideline their other aspirations to privately manage the load of raising the next generation or caring for the previous one to avoid burdening anyone else. As such, you shouldn't be the only person sacrificing to save this money. As Eve Rodsky wrote, we must make the invisible work visible.

When the other half of society faces the "family vs. career" dichotomy as directly and intensely as women already do, it's more likely that legislators will feel the pressure that women in the US have long somehow managed to balance. The types of cultural and political change that could really impact life for parents in the US, who are the most cost-burdened in the world, will look as obvious as they already feel to working mothers everywhere. Whether it's shifting the school day to match the workday, including preschool in the public school system, adjusting to a four-day workweek, turning daycare into a public good, or mandating paid family leave policies, there are plenty of areas where we could start.

Regardless of whether you're saving and investing for children, there's one major long-term goal that *everyone* needs to prioritize: your eventual retirement.

6

Don't Outlive
Your Assets

My Grandma Jean is a human firecracker (see also: her Bubba Sparxxx dance interlude in Chapter 4).[†] When she turned eighteen in 1958, all her high school girl-friends were already having babies and getting married—it was the standard life path for a white teenage girl in Wisconsin at the time. But she was determined to go to college.

She achieved her goal and got her diploma, marrying my Papa John during her final semester. Shortly after graduating, she became pregnant with Mary, her only child (my mom), and had to put her nascent career on ice. When my mom was eleven months old, Grandma Jean went back to work part time ("Three days a week!" she told me when I called her to fact-check) until my mom was old enough to be at home by herself, at which point she transitioned to full-time work. My grandparents both earned the

---

† moneywithkatie.com/yes-i-actually-want-you-to-see-it

income that supported their small family. Grandma Jean became the de facto administrative lead in the home who paid the bills and balanced the checkbook, and Papa John managed their investments, insurance policies, and other long-term financial planning. They were happily married for sixty years.

But in April 2020 (a famously calm and precedented time), I received a call from my mom and dad that Papa John had been diagnosed with acute myeloid leukemia. They suspected he'd had it for a while, because things had taken a turn for the worse. The next day, I got on an empty flight to Nashville, Tennessee, and within a few hours of my arrival, he passed away.

Grandma Jean was about as distraught as you'd expect a woman who suddenly lost her life partner to be. The night he passed, I slept in their bedroom to keep her company, unaware that she was silently lying next to me panicking until she told me the next morning. She realized she had been left with a major, unanticipated problem: She had no idea what financial position they were in. "I don't know what we have," she told me, wide-eyed and terrified.

The next few days were a blur. My dad and I burrowed ourselves in their office, distracting ourselves from grief with forensic accounting. We sorted through hundreds of papers, folders, and notebooks, trying to piece together their financial history. It took a full week to pull together a semi-coherent picture of their assets, but we managed. When my grandparents had first married, they'd been so poor that they shot squirrels in their backyard and fried them on a hot plate for dinner. Papa John's earnings peaked at $60,000, and Grandma Jean's hourly wage never got higher than $10.50. But by the time my Papa John passed away, they had managed to accumulate a respectable nest egg across various IRAs, life insurance death benefits, and a pension. Fortunately, my Grandma Jean was taken care of. Many women who lose partners to death or divorce are not so lucky.

Three in four divorced or widowed women report finding a "negative financial surprise" in the aftermath of this life-changing event, and as we noted in Chapter 5, women retire with about 57 percent as much retirement income as men do. Women older than sixty-five have higher rates of poverty than their male counterparts across all races.[†] My Grandma Jean found herself in the heartbreaking position of outliving her spouse, an unfortunate but not uncommon scenario for women in the US, who tend to outlive male partners with lifespans that are 6.5 percent longer on average. Taken together, this means women are statistically more likely to suffer the consequences of poor long-term financial planning.

And lest you assume that outsourcing all financial planning to a spouse is merely an issue for generations who were born before women could have lines of credit without a man's approval, a woman in her early twenties approached me after a speaking engagement in 2022 and told me I had inspired her to ask her partner for the password to their bank accounts. Even if you're never in a relationship that goes south, having no control or awareness of your financial standing is, frankly, dangerous.

As my friend Caroline Burke said in the previous chapter, in the world we live in today, the thing that empowers women most is access to capital. Prioritizing your long-term financial independence is, in that sense, radical. In doing so, you make yourself unable to be exploited or backed into a corner—and whether you've made one year of progress or twenty, simply enacting a

---

† Despite this, white women's poverty incidence rate is still lower (9.1 percent) than that of Black (16 percent), Asian (11.2 percent), and Hispanic (17.3 percent) men.

long-term wealth-building strategy creates more flexibility and options.

So, if women tend to outlive men but retire with less (and, sometimes, find out they don't have enough at a time in their lives when it's much harder to generate more income), what can we do *right now* to ensure our future selves are covered? The good news is, it's surprisingly simple to execute a sophisticated, strategic long-term plan that can all but guarantee you'll be taken care of regardless of what life brings. The strategy we're going to review in this chapter packs a punch that's proportional to how early you retire, but make no mistake, it will benefit you no matter how long or short your timeline until retirement is.

Meet Early Retiree Katie

In Rich Girl Nation, we believe retirement isn't necessarily an age. It's a mindset! A way of life! And most importantly for our purposes, a number in the bank. We discussed how to calculate your financial independence number at a high level in Chapter 3, which means you likely already have a general sense of where you're headed. And once you know where you're going, you can start looking for shortcuts nestled in the tax code. The strategy we're about to review can—all else held equal—shorten your timeline by about 15 percent.

Investing in tax-advantaged accounts (which we'll be covering in-depth in this chapter) is like giving yourself a raise, because it makes each dollar that you've saved go just a little bit further. When you're talking about a long-term game like investing for financial freedom, every little edge you can give yourself compounds. The advice to "contribute to your 401(k)!" is table stakes

in the personal finance world, but it's important to grasp why—
after all, if you're going to save, shouldn't you do so in a way that
creates even more savings?

For the purposes of detailing such a plan today, we're going to
follow the journey of Early Retiree Katie (no relation; a name
picked totally at random). Katie has a lot of potential, and we're
going to maximize it:

- She's thirty years old, earns $150,000 per year, and lives in
  Texas.
- She hasn't started saving and investing for retirement yet,
  because she wasn't aware this was something she should
  be prioritizing, so her long-term savings are $0.
- She's married and her spouse also earns $150,000 per year,
  putting them in the 24 percent marginal tax bracket. To
  keep this example streamlined, we're going to ignore her
  husband's income and savings behavior (we're only including his income to acknowledge how it impacts her tax
  rate). But keep in mind they could absolutely play this
  game on two-player mode if her husband mirrored her decisions, which, depending on how they chose to execute
  the strategy, could:
  - halve the contributions she needs to make but take
    the same amount of time,
  - keep her contributions the same and add his to
    make it go twice as quickly, or
  - do the same thing for the same amount of time but
    end up with double the money.
- Her "retirement" goals are less about sipping micheladas
  on the beach and more about insuring herself so that she
  can spend the second half of her life pursuing meaningful

work that doesn't necessarily pay her anything, as well as other hobbies and interests. Her goal is to tap out of work by age fifty (twenty years from now).

The plan

The crux of my plan relies on taking full advantage of your largest pretax account, calculating your tax savings from doing so, and *investing* those tax savings in other Roth or taxable accounts. The obviousness of this strategy hit me early one Saturday morning. I had stayed up late the night before reading FI/RE (financial independence, retire early) blogs, and I remember waking up suddenly, as though a few synapses had connected in my sleep, and going, "Wait a second—can't we use our tax break to invest *even more?*" The puzzle pieces came together, and I've since pressure-tested the approach with friends who have CFP certifications (and the accompanying math and software chops). It seems to check out in *most* scenarios, though we'll talk briefly about when it might not.

My strategy exploits the way traditional and Roth contributions and withdrawals are taxed to create the largest amount of investable income possible now, and the lowest lifetime tax bill, using the various tax-advantaged accounts available to you. For most people, the biggest bucket they're working with is an employer-sponsored 401(k) plan or equivalent account. My thesis is straightforward: By contributing to a traditional 401(k) now, you generate tax savings this year. If you know what your tax savings are, you can turn around and invest them in a Roth IRA or taxable brokerage account, creating net more investable income. Most times, you'll fare better doing this than if you'd just contributed the maximum to a Roth 401(k) and called it a day.

Looking at Early Retiree Katie and her spouse's household income of $300,000, a $23,500 contribution to her 401(k) (the maximum in 2025) lowers their tax burden in a way that a Roth contribution would not. Here's how a full Roth 401(k) contribution would break down, leaving them with $203,057 in take-home pay:

TAX TYPE	MARGINAL TAX RATE	EFFECTIVE TAX RATE	2025 TAXES
Federal	24%	16.83%	$50,493
FICA	2.35%	7.65%	$22,950
Total Income Taxes		24.48%	$73,443
Income After Taxes			$226,557
Traditional 401(k) Contributions			$0
Roth 401(k) Contributions			$23,500
Take-Home Pay			**$203,057**

If instead she contributes the same amount to a traditional 401(k), they have $208,697 in take-home pay—$5,640 more.

TAX TYPE	MARGINAL TAX RATE	EFFECTIVE TAX RATE	2025 TAXES
Federal	24%	14.95%	$44,853
FICA	2.35%	7.65%	$22,950
Total Income Taxes		22.60%	$67,803
Income After Taxes			$232,197
Traditional 401(k) Contributions			$23,500
Roth 401(k) Contributions			$0
Take-Home Pay			**$208,697**

Looking at her "half" of the equation alone, we can do some rough calculations:

- Her gross income is $150,000.
- She puts $23,500 of it into her 401(k).
- Taxes take another chunk of roughly $34,000.
- She's going to invest her tax savings, $5,640, somewhere else.
- This leaves her with around $90,000 or so to spend or invest.

If you'd like to play around with your own income, filing status, and contributions, check out smartasset.com/taxes/income-taxes, where you can input your zip code to see how your state and local taxes will be lowered, too. (Since Early Retiree Katie and her husband live in Texas, she doesn't pay state taxes, but if she lived in California, they'd save an additional $2,353 in state taxes.)

This additional $5,640 in income *could* be spent, but to take advantage of our strategy, we're going to invest it instead. But before we do, let's take a step back and learn a little more about how your income is taxed.

Marginal vs. effective tax rates

I've given you the TL;DR already about how my plan functions, but it's important to understand *why* it works this way in order to fully grasp how you're going to use the money later. You've probably heard traditional and Roth accounts framed in one of two ways during your financial life:

1. Do you want to pay your taxes now or later? Or,
2. Do you think you'll earn more later than you do now?

The first distinction is correct, but it buries the lede. The second is a little more misleading, as most people don't understand how they're taxed in retirement. It's less important to focus on "now or later" or "pretax or post-tax," and more valuable to focus on how much *control* you have over how you're taxed now and later.

Your contributions to Roth accounts are taxed this year, top down, at your **marginal** tax rate. Your marginal tax rate is the *highest* tax rate you pay on your earned income, because we have a progressive tax system in the US. The beauty of Roth contributions, though, is that you can withdraw them *and all the growth they generate* tax-free later, which many point to as all the proof you need that Roth is unquestionably superior across the board. On the other hand, your contributions to traditional accounts aren't taxed until you use the money later, creating a tax savings today at that same marginal tax rate. When you use the money later, your withdrawals from a traditional account will be taxed *bottom up* (colloquially, you can think about this like being taxed at your **effective** tax rate, which rises as you declare more income), like you're paying yourself a salary that you control based on how much you need to spend.

In 2025, here's how Early Retiree Katie's household income of $300,000 would be taxed:

AMOUNT OF MONEY	RATE	TAX OWED
The first $30,000 of income (the **standard deduction** for married couples in 2025) . . .	. . . is taxed at 0%	$0
Next $23,850	10%	$2,385
Next $73,099	12%	$8,771
Next $109,749	22%	$24,144
Next $187,899 (the last $63,302 of their income falls in this bracket)	24%, their **marginal** rate	$15,192
Total Income: $300,000	*Effective Tax Rate: 17%*	*Total Tax Owed: $50,492*

A contribution to a Roth account would come out of their top marginal 24 percent bracket today, which means it takes a 24 percent haircut. Early Retiree Katie probably doesn't have much control over their tax rate today, as their income determines it (and ERK wants to earn more, not less).

But as you can see in the table, their effective tax rate refers to the overall percentage of their income that went to taxes, and it's inclusive of every bracket their income touches: 0 percent, 10 percent, 12 percent, and so on. Their $300,000 household income has a marginal tax rate of 24 percent, but an effective tax rate of 17 percent.

This is important, because their income in retirement—that is, when they start paying themselves a "salary" from their investment accounts—will be taxed overall at whatever effective tax rate that amount of money produces. If Early Retiree Katie and her spouse make $300,000 today (or, if Katie were single and made $150,000 alone), her *entire* contribution to a Roth account would land in that 24 percent income tax bracket. But when she's retired and *withdraws* an inflation-adjusted $300,000 while married (or $150,000 single) from her 401(k), she'd pay a 17 percent tax rate on the withdrawal. (And this is, of course, assuming they need to pay themselves the same amount in retirement that they earned while working, which is unlikely given their income while working had to pay for their lifestyle, payroll taxes, *and* their savings. Most financial planning experts suggest you'll only need between 70 percent and 80 percent of your preretirement income.)

Times when this strategy might not be ideal

As of 2023, 88 percent of employers offer a Roth 401(k), and if you find yourself in the 12 percent marginal tax bracket (which is especially common if you're early in your career), you'll probably want to focus on Roth contributions rather than traditional, even in your biggest accounts, because as your income and lifestyle expand over time, you may find it difficult to beat a 12 percent tax rate later in life. But once you graduate into a tax bracket above 22 percent (or you live in a high income tax state), the benefits of using your current-year tax savings become too powerful to ignore.

Some financial advisers don't love the traditional 401(k) because of something called **required minimum distributions**, which refers to the way the federal government looks at your age and account balance (beginning at age seventy-three) and goes, "Hmm, you've got a *lot* of tax-deferred money in there—time to start withdrawing!" . . . and forces you to begin taking *required* minimum amounts from the account every year, which makes it harder to control your tax rate in retirement. This is a legitimate concern, but one that can be mitigated through the strategic fancy footwork we're discussing in the second half of this chapter.

Now that we've seen an overview of the plan and have a better understanding of how our two tax statuses function in our working years and retirement, let's meet the major players in this tax-hacking game. Here's a snapshot of what Early Retiree Katie will be using, but depending on what you have access to, your financial independence stack might look different:

- A traditional 401(k) at her job to which she's contributing the maximum allowable amount of $23,500, generating tax savings of around $5,640 that she's going to invest in . . .
- A Roth IRA, for additional retirement income and tax flexibility later, plus . . .
- A taxable brokerage account, for the contributions she wants to make beyond the annual contribution limit in the Roth IRA (her income is high, so she's going for gold).

The following are the major options you might have access to as you implement your own plan.

The vehicles we'll be driving on this journey

Depending on how you earn and who you work for, your tax-advantaged vehicles might be different from Early Retiree Katie's. Let's do a quick overview of the different accounts you might be using on the road to retirement.

Employer-sponsored retirement plans

You're probably familiar with employer-sponsored retirement plans by now, so we won't spend too much time reviewing the basics—but if you're a W-2 employee like Katie, this is probably the largest tax-advantaged bucket you have available to you. In the year 2025, your employee contribution limit is **$23,500**, which makes for a big tax break opportunity. These plans usually function the same way regardless of where you work, but they might have different names depending on your employer, including the:

- 401(k), at for-profit companies, private companies, and corporate employers
- 403(b), at public schools, hospitals, and nonprofits
- 457(b), at certain state and local governments and other tax-exempt entities
- TSP, or Thrift Savings Plan, available to employees of federal government institutions like the military

How to make sure your employer's plan provider isn't fleecing you

An important side note: Employer-sponsored plans have a few downsides, chief among them a lack of control over your investment options and the fees you pay. Fortunately, most of the time, your fees will be more than offset by the substantial tax benefits (and any company match you may receive), but you can look at your quarterly statements to learn what your 401(k) plan provider is charging for the privilege of managing your assets. To do this, you typically log into your online account and locate the section called something like "Statements and Documents." From there, choose the most recent statement, and you'll probably see something that either says "expenses" or "plan administration fees." If you're not in the mood to play Paperwork Nancy Drew, you can ask your benefits department or person for more information on the plan fees. Generally, anything near (or more than) 1 percent is firmly dicey territory, as the fee's effect on your account balance will compound over time, and after the account becomes large enough, the fees will negate the tax savings. For example, if your tax savings on your contributions are $4,000, a 1 percent annual fee on a 401(k) with $400,000 would be about $4,000. (Most people don't have to worry about this, because most people don't have $400,000 in their 401(k) plans, but say it with me . . . "Hashtag manifest.")

The other downside is a lack of investment options, though most 401(k) plans allow you to invest in the major indices we discussed earlier. My own 401(k) is invested 90 percent in a target date fund (the Vanguard 2065), and the other 10 percent is in a riskier small cap value fund, a portfolio known as the "Two Funds for Life" strategy courtesy of the Merriman Financial Education Foundation.

If you're *your employer*

You might think you're SOL if you don't have an employer, as we've already noted how valuable these employer-sponsored plans can be. But because the cost of living has been steadily climbing for the last zillion years and wages haven't, most people I know have a side hustle (or have abandoned corporate America entirely to become self-employed). I used to think extra income was the best benefit of self-employment, but then I met the solo 401(k) and SEP IRA—two self-employment retirement plans with massive contribution limits.

Whether you're fully self-employed or you're just a side hustler with a little extra change in your pockets, these accounts can lead to *massive* tax savings and shouldn't be ignored.

THE SOLO 401(K)

The solo 401(k) is exactly what it sounds like: a 401(k) plan that you can administer yourself if you're self-employed. To be eligible for a solo 401(k) and be your own plan administrator, you must:

- Have an EIN (this is like your business's Social Security number); you receive one of these when you form an LLC, or limited liability company.
- Have no employees (except for your spouse; for some reason, that's allowed, and your employee-spouse can also contribute to their own solo 401(k) plan).

If you meet those requirements, you can contribute up to $70,000 per year to a solo 401(k): $23,500 of which is considered your employee "elective" deferral (just like at a day job). Since you're your employee *and* your own employer (did someone say girlboss?!), you can give yourself a fat employer match: It works out to about 20 percent of your net business income. For example, if Early Retiree Katie was self-employed and her *business* made $150,000 of net profits in 2025, she could contribute up to $23,500 as her own employee and approximately $27,705 as an "employer match" to herself. That's a whopping $51,205 in pretax contributions! Since her entire contribution would've been in the 24 percent marginal tax bracket, she would've saved approximately $12,289 in taxes. (The calculation to determine precisely how much you can contribute is a little more complex, so I recommend working with an accountant to determine the exact contribution number—this example is solely intended to provide a sense of scale.)

There's only one thing for my side hustlers to be aware of: Your "$23,500 employee elective deferral" is, in the eyes of the IRS, per *person*, not per job, which means if you're already contributing the maximum to your 401(k) at work, you can't *also* make a $23,500 employee contribution to your solo 401(k)—you're limited to "employer contributions," based on the ~20 percent of net business income calculation.[†]

This is because the "employer" portion of your contributions are per source of *income*, not *person*, so you're free to fill up the entire bucket if your business is that lucrative (I know—the complexities abound).

THE SEP IRA

The SEP IRA works similarly, except it's "employer only," which means there's no elective employee deferral. There's *only* the opportunity to contribute 20 percent of your net business income.

[†] To estimate your allowed contributions to a solo 401(k) or SEP IRA, check out the calculator at aarp.org/work/retirement-planning/self-employed-401k-calculator.html.

For this reason, I typically think the solo 401(k) is a better choice, but SEP IRAs can be easier to open and manage because they don't require an EIN and are available at most robo-advisers. Sometimes— if you weren't planning on contributing that much anyway—people prefer them for simplicity. It blows my mind how few self-employed people take advantage of these accounts, and my hunch is that it's simply due to a lack of awareness. But now you know!

Other opportunities for pretax investing

If you're not self-employed but you *are* employed by an organization that doesn't offer you an employer-sponsored retirement plan, you might think you're totally out of luck in the "generating tax savings with pretax investing" game. Fortunately, there are two other common options you might want to consider.

TRADITIONAL IRAS

If you don't have access to a 401(k) or equivalent account at your W-2 job but you're hell-bent on making some pretax contributions to lower your tax bill, you may consider a traditional IRA instead—there's no income limit to contribute if you're not covered by a plan at work, but unfortunately, the $7,000 IRA contribution limit applies across traditional *and* Roth accounts, which means you can only contribute $7,000 total between them each year. Let your tax rate guide this decision: 22 percent or above, I'd probably use the traditional IRA and invest my tax savings in a taxable brokerage account.

THE HSA

You may also have access to an HSA if you have a high-deductible health plan, which will allow you to contribute between $4,300 and $8,550 per year as of 2025, depending on whether your plan covers you alone or your family. In my opinion, the HSA doesn't get nearly enough hoopla. It offers a range of substantial benefits:

- It's the only pretax account where contributions *also* aren't subject to payroll tax (the 7.65 percent that's taken out of your paycheck).
- Your HSA isn't subjected to those pesky required minimum distributions in retirement like your other pretax accounts are, which makes it an incredible place to grow your money.
- If you reach age sixty-five with nary a health issue and you don't end up needing your HSA to fund medical expenses tax-free, it effectively morphs into a traditional IRA and allows you to make withdrawals penalty-free for anything—you'll just need to pay taxes on them, as you would with other pretax withdrawals.
- And in the event you *do* have qualified medical expenses in our dystopian hellscape of a for-profit healthcare marketplace, your money goes in tax-free, grows tax-free, and comes out tax-free! It's like the consolation prize for having the world's most exploitative system. Yay!

Plus, there's one more hack worth knowing with your HSA if you want to take your implementation to Level 1,000. Since your invested HSA funds become so valuable in the back half of your life for the reasons outlined above, it's beneficial to let them continue to compound, rather than withdrawing the contributions early in life to cover medical expenses as they occur. If you're able to cover your medical expenses throughout your life with your regular cash flow, hang on to the receipts. There's no time limit for applying for reimbursement from your HSA, which means your expensive shoulder surgery from 2007 that you paid $3,000 for can function a little bit like a "Get $3,000 Tax-Free" coupon in 2027. All you have to do is save your itemized receipt, submit it for reimbursement from your HSA (even if it's twenty years later!), and cash out.

This is valuable because of exponential compounding. If you contribute the maximum to your HSA only once and it compounds for a few decades, your $4,300 contribution could be worth $15,000 by the time you go to use it. By paying for your surgery with $3,000 of regular, post-tax money, you've effectively given yourself the ability to let your invested funds grow and multiply for years, so by the time you reimburse yourself, you're using money that your money made for you—and then some. (Of course, if you're the world's least organized human, don't stress about this—but if you're down to scan your receipts into an external hard drive or Google Drive, this can be another supplemental source of tax-free income later.)

INVESTMENT ACCOUNTS IF YOU WORK INSIDE THE HOME INSTEAD OF OUTSIDE IT

I talk to people frequently who think they're unable to save for retirement in something like a 401(k) or IRA plan because they aren't employed outside the home. But if you or your spouse are (or intend to become) a stay-at-home parent, you can open a **spousal IRA** to invest for retirement using your *household* income. To be eligible, you must:

- File a joint tax return
- Have a spouse with earned income

- Open the account in your name using your Social Security number

It works the same way other IRAs do (e.g., the contribution limit rules mirror other IRAs), but it allows a stay-at-home parent to save for retirement, too.

Post-tax investing: Where we'll be investing our tax savings

Now that we've explored all the titillating ways you might choose to generate more investable income with pretax investment vehicles, we've finally arrived at the point in which you can both double down on the amount of income you're investing *and* secure some sweet, sweet tax flexibility for yourself later in life. Our first major player is the Roth IRA.

ROTH IRA

My ultimate recommendation to (lovingly) leave the IRS in the dust is to invest your tax savings in a Roth IRA (and if you're already contributing the maximum to a Roth IRA, you can also use a taxable brokerage account).

Rather than *spending* the $5,640 in tax savings that Early Retiree Katie generated from her 401(k) contributions, she's going to double down on her good deeds and invest that amount in her Roth IRA—money that she otherwise would've spent on taxes just became extra income to invest! Work smarter, not harder. And boom—with one $23,500 contribution to her 401(k), she now *also* has another $5,640 to contribute to her Roth IRA (or, if she's self-employed and using the solo 401(k), $12,000 in tax savings).

The Roth IRA has an annual contribution limit in 2025 of

$7,000, so it's not exactly large enough *on its own* to fund your retirement—but when employed as part of this strategy, you're cleaning up in the present year *and* in the future. One other nice-to-know element of a Roth IRA: You can access your **cost basis** (e.g., the contributions that you put in) at any time. While you can't touch the *growth* on those contributions before you're 59.5, your original contributions are always[†] fair game. Withdrawing your Roth IRA contributions isn't really advised, but it creates a nice little loophole that we're going to use later.

THE BACKDOOR ROTH IRA

If, like ERK and her spouse, you make more than $165,000 single or $246,000 married filing jointly after deducting your 401(k) contributions from your gross income, you earn too much money in 2025 to contribute to a Roth IRA in the "regular" way (the ultimate tiny violin problem). But fear not: You can always conduct a backdoor Roth IRA, which is both a tax strategy and an opportunity for countless innuendos. We'll leave the latter to the imagination, but regarding the former . . .

All ERK would have to do is:

1. Make a nondeductible contribution (using her post-tax cash that's just hanging out in her checking account) to a traditional IRA at any point in the year. This involves opening a traditional IRA, contributing money, and then *not* claiming the deduction on her tax return the following April. (When she files her taxes, her tax filing software will probably prompt her to fill out Form 8606 to report a nondeductible IRA contribution, which she'll duly fill out.)

---

† We'll talk shortly about an instance where this is not true.

2. Wait a couple of days for the funds to settle—she won't invest the money.

3. Then, she'll *convert* the entire sum to Roth—she'll just need to have a Roth IRA open at the same institution to do this seamlessly, so if she doesn't already have one, she'd open it during step 1. Most major brokerages will literally have a "Convert to Roth" button, but to be safe, she'll Google her brokerage firm and "backdoor Roth IRA" ahead of time to make sure.

4. That's it! She's ready to invest the funds in the holdings of her choosing.

Candidly, I'm not sure why Congress hasn't closed this loophole yet (and of course, we could probably write another book about the ethical implications of taking advantage of it), but for whatever reason, the back door is still unlocked as of January 2025. And now even ERK can get some Roth dollars on the board, like my plan suggests.

Things to watch out for when sneaking through the back door

There's just one IRS rule to be aware of when you're doing your backdoor Roth IRA, and it's a little convoluted. It's called the **pro rata rule**. To understand it, imagine your various IRAs are all held in one big bucket, and your pretax contributions are milk, while your post-tax contributions are Mountain Dew (I hate this analogy already). If you've dumped pretax and post-tax contributions—milk and Mountain Dew—into your various IRAs at any point, the IRS looks at that disgusting mixture in its entirety and goes, "All right, some portion of that mix is pretax and some is post-tax." But since the funds are "mixed together" in the eyes of the IRS (yes, even if they're in different IRAs, and even if the contributions were made years ago), they can't be sure what portion of your backdoor Roth IRA conversion was post-tax (i.e., money you've already been taxed on and don't need to be taxed on again) and what's still pretax (i.e., money that has never been taxed). To solve this issue, they just look at the *overall* concoction of your pretax and post-tax holdings across *all* your IRAs—all the milk and Mountain Dew together—to assess what percentage of *the whole mixture* is pretax, and assume that percentage of your Roth conversion was also pretax. That's how they determine what percentage of your Roth conversion to tax (which was entirely post-tax in actuality).

Now that we're all nice and nauseous, all you need to know is this: You probably want to avoid doing a backdoor Roth IRA if you have pretax funds lying around in any IRA (traditional, rollover, SEP, or otherwise). If you do and you'd like to clear those pretax funds out, you'll just need to roll them over into another type of pretax account where they can live instead: For example, if you have an employer or solo 401(k) plan, you can move the funds there, as these types of accounts—bewilderingly—are not affected by this "gotcha" rule.

How taxable investing fits into this strategy

Early Retiree Katie has now contributed the maximum to her traditional 401(k) and Roth IRA, but if she really wants to take full advantage of the tax-free drawdown strategy we'll unpack next, she's going to contribute whatever else she can manage to a regular taxable **brokerage account**. You might also choose to prioritize this type of flexible, standard-issue investing account earlier in your own implementation for a few reasons:

- You don't have access to an employer-sponsored retirement plan, and you're not self-employed, so there's no big pretax bucket you can focus on.
- You make too much to contribute to a Roth IRA but can't go through the back door because you have too many pre-tax funds in IRAs already.
- You really value the flexibility of being able to contribute or withdraw whenever and however you want.
- You, like ERK, want to maximize your tax flexibility later and have the income and savings to swing it.

Because what a taxable brokerage account lacks in tax advantages, it more than makes up for in unfettered flexibility. Even the name "taxable brokerage account" is a hair misleading, because it conjures the image of a man in an ill-fitting suit hacking away at your earnings much like your W-2 paychecks. A taxable account is actually a pretty tax-friendly place to grow your wealth. It's also a necessary puzzle piece in a totally tax-free retirement, because it completes our flexibility triumvirate of tax-deferred (like in a 401(k) or otherwise pretax account), tax-free (as in a Roth IRA or HSA), and taxable accounts.

This is where we venture into "art and science" territory, because the amount of income one needs to earn to contribute the maximum to all tax-advantaged accounts *and* still make meaningful contributions to a taxable account is—make no mistake—a lot, like Early Retiree Katie's income of $150,000. You don't have to contribute the maximum to tax-advantaged accounts before you begin funding a taxable account, but be conscious of your overall breakdown. Depending on the lifestyle you hope to live in retirement (early or otherwise) and the overall expenses you want your investments to support, it's entirely possible you might need just as much (if not more!) in a taxable account as in pretax or Roth funds.

The taxable brokerage account is lovely in retirement because of a little something called **capital gains taxes**, a vestige of the tax code from a time when a rich man got pissed about his investment income being taxed like regular income and basically complained until it changed. True story! #USA! (Like I said, a whole different book could be written examining the ethics of investment tax breaks, as it's the reason why extremely rich people pay such low rates.) The capital gains tax brackets are exceedingly forgiving, *especially* if you have no other earned income (i.e., you're retired).

If you sell an investment in a taxable brokerage account after owning it for 365 days (one year) or more, you'll pay the long-term capital gains tax rate on your gains.

- If you (as a single person in 2025) have $48,350 or less in total declared income, you won't pay any taxes on your long-term capital gains. That's right. **Zero percent.** For married filing jointly, the 0 percent bracket is up to $96,700 in total income.
- If you have between $48,351 and $533,400 in income (not a typo), you'll pay **15 percent**. For married filing jointly, it's an income range between $96,701 and $600,050.
- And if you have $533,401-plus in income, you'll pay **20 percent**. If you're married, it's a total income above $600,051.

Compare this to the top marginal tax rates on earned income of 37 percent.

Moral of the story: While you'll pay annual taxes on your dividend income, taxable brokerage accounts are an incredible place to grow your money, and they're a necessary component of creating as close to a tax-free early retirement as possible.

We know ERK will be taking $23,500 of her $150,000 income and investing it in her 401(k), which unlocks approximately $5,640 in tax savings that she'll be contributing via the back door to a Roth IRA, but that still leaves her with around $7,500 per month in take-home pay. She's going to make it a goal to invest around $750 per month in her taxable account, depending on her other priorities.

Where Early Retiree Katie stands after twenty years of investing

Let's imagine Katie keeps up this charade (adjusting upward for inflation) for twenty years, until she's fifty years old. Not only would she be sitting on a 401(k) worth around $1.2 million, but she'd also have *another* account—the one she funded entirely with her 401(k) tax savings, which we'll assume is her backdoor Roth IRA—with an *additional* $290,000, for around $1.5 million total:

YEAR	401(K) CONTRIBUTION	24% MARGINAL TAX BRACKET SAVINGS	AVG. RETURN	401(K) BALANCE	"TAX SAVINGS INVESTED ELSEWHERE" BALANCE IN HER ROTH IRA
1	$23,500.00	$5,640.00	7%	$23,500.00	$5,640.00
2	$24,205.00	$5,809.20	7%	$49,350.00	$11,844.00
3	$24,931.15	$5,983.48	7%	$77,735.65	$18,656.56
4	$25,679.08	$6,162.98	7%	$108,856.23	$26,125.50
5	$26,449.46	$6,347.87	7%	$142,925.62	$34,302.15

6	$27,242.94	$6,538.31	7%	$180,173.36	$43,241.61
7	$28,060.23	$6,734.45	7%	$220,845.72	$53,002.97
8	$28,902.04	$6,936.49	7%	$265,206.96	$63,649.67
9	$29,769.10	$7,144.58	7%	$313,540.54	$75,249.73
10	$30,662.17	$7,358.92	7%	$366,150.55	$87,876.13
11	$31,582.03	$7,579.69	7%	$423,363.12	$101,607.15
12	$32,529.50	$7,807.08	7%	$485,528.04	$116,526.73
13	$33,505.38	$8,041.29	7%	$553,020.38	$132,724.89
14	$34,510.54	$8,282.53	7%	$626,242.35	$150,298.16
15	$35,545.86	$8,531.01	7%	$705,625.17	$169,350.04
16	$36,612.23	$8,786.94	7%	$791,631.17	$189,991.48
17	$37,710.60	$9,050.54	7%	$884,755.95	$212,341.43
18	$38,841.92	$9,322.06	7%	$985,530.79	$236,527.39
19	$40,007.18	$9,601.72	7%	$1,094,525.12	$262,686.03
20	$41,207.39	$9,889.77	7%	$1,212,349.27	$290,963.83
21	$42,443.61	$10,186.47	7%	$1,339,657.33	$321,517.76
22	$43,716.92	$10,492.06	7%	$1,477,150.27	$354,516.06
23	$45,028.43	$10,806.82	7%	$1,625,579.22	$390,139.01
24	$46,379.28	$11,131.03	7%	$1,785,749.05	$428,579.77
25	$47,770.66	$11,464.96	7%	$1,958,522.14	$470,045.31

And, as we know, she's been investing around $750 per month in her taxable account, giving her approximately $500,000 in her brokerage account by age fifty.

This assumes she:

- Continued to earn an income in the inflation-adjusted 24 percent tax bracket, as though she always made the equivalent of $150,000 today. No big raises necessary.
- Continued to contribute the maximum to her traditional 401(k) every year, an amount that's also increased for

inflation, and invested those tax savings in her Roth IRA via the back door.

- Used her take-home pay to sock away $750 of flexible funds in her brokerage account each month (also adjusted for inflation over time).
- Got an average 7 percent rate of return on her investments, which is in line with conservative historical averages for buy-and-hold investing in the stock market.

This is where the exponential power of compounding begins to really show off. If she calls it quits at age fifty, she can sail into the sunset with her $1.5 million in her tax-advantaged accounts and another half million in her taxable account. But if she keeps it up for just *five more years* (until she's fifty-five), she'd end up with over a *million dollars more*: $3.1 million total.

This is, in itself, an outrageously impressive feat, and the vast majority of it ($1.5 million of the $2 million at age fifty) is made possible by a single choice: contributing the maximum to her pretax retirement account. Since she was interested in retiring early and using our patented Big Daddy Tax Strategy, she invested even more of her $90,000 post-tax, post-401(k), post–Roth IRA income in her taxable brokerage account, which, as you'll see, plays a substantial role in funding the "early" portion of her early retirement.

Pulling the rip cord on Early Retiree Katie's totally tax-free early retirement

ERK's been rockin' and rollin' with this strategy for a solid twenty years, and now she's fifty and ready to transition to a different type of life. But wait—don't most of these accounts delay her access until she turns 59.5? I'm glad you asked! It's now time to get specific about how she can take advantage of all the saving and investing she's done.

Assuming she's ready to begin a traditional work-free retirement (albeit early) and start living fully off her investment income, she's going to leverage something called a **Roth conversion ladder** in tandem with **the standard deduction** to get her tax-free, penalty-free retirement party started. In 2025, the standard deduction—i.e., the amount the IRS will wipe clean off a single person's taxable income—is $15,000. For married filing jointly, it's $30,000.[†]

Important note: The Roth conversion ladder is a method we're using to access pretax funds early because ERK's not yet 59.5. Someone who begins using their money after age 59.5 could skip this Roth conversion ladder step and just withdraw the funds directly. Additionally, executing an "entirely tax-free" drawdown assumes there's no other taxable income from any other source coming in (pensions, part-time work, etc.). This is because income from other sources will interfere with the amount of control you can exercise over your tax rate, so it makes it a little more challenging to create a net $0 tax bill. Still, understanding how your various sources of income are taxed—which is what we'll review in this section—will help you make more strategic decisions about how and when you use your investment income.

Finally, the "totally tax-free retirement" strategy we'll explore is technically the most optimal outcome from a tax standpoint—

† Tax law is written in pencil, not pen, and as of this writing, it is assumed that the standard deduction will remain as is through at least 2028 as the Tax Cuts and Jobs Act is extended. It's possible that it'll be cut someday, but then it could go back up by the time you're retiring early. We don't know what the future holds, but it's worth noting that meaningfully lower standard deductions in the future would diminish the ability to convert large swaths of pretax funds to Roth with a 0 percent tax rate.

but the amount of money it can generate isn't endless, so we'll go through the most tax-efficient ways to create additional investment income if the maximum amount you can access while paying $0 in taxes isn't enough. Even if you only decide to implement this strategy directionally, you'll still benefit from a lower lifetime tax bill and net more overall wealth as a result of understanding how your income is taxed.

Now that I've sufficiently caveated my case, get ready: because the tax code is very specific (down to the dollar!) about how much tax-free income you can generate, and our goal is to strategically combine our withdrawals from our pretax account, like our 401(k), with taxable withdrawals from our brokerage account and eventual Roth distributions in order to make the most of the boundaries we're playing within. In 2025, based on our current limits for the 0 percent capital gains tax brackets and the standard deduction, the maximum tax-free incomes you can draw from your investments looks like this:

- A single person's most optimal tax-free outcome is generating **$63,350** in tax-free income per year ($15,000 from your pretax account and $48,350 from your brokerage account), enough to spend **$5,279** per month. A single person *earning* $63,350 will pay more than $10,000 in income taxes—but a single person generating that income from their investments will pay $0 in taxes. (Like I said, this country loves its capital class.)

- A married couple's most optimal tax-free outcome is generating **$126,700** in tax-free income per year ($30,000 from your pretax accounts and $96,700 from your brokerage accounts), enough to spend **$10,558** per month. A married couple *earning* $126,700 would pay more than $20,000 in income taxes—but not you, dear married millionaires. You're rewarded for your responsible saving and investing for retirement and will pay $0 in taxes on your investment income.

Keeping these limits in mind, let's dive into the steps that Early Retiree Katie will take to put this plan in motion.

Step 1: Preparing your funds

In Year 1 of Early Retiree Katie's early retirement, she'll prepare her funds to execute her Roth conversion ladder. This will enable her to begin accessing her pretax account ahead of schedule, as she's not 59.5 yet.

First, ERK will roll over her musty old 401(k) into a traditional IRA (also called a rollover IRA; for the purposes of this breakdown, I'll be calling it a rollover IRA moving forward). She does this because she needs to take over management of the account to properly execute her grand plan after leaving her job.

She'll also open a *new* Roth IRA, separate from the Roth IRA she's been contributing to for the last twenty years. This way, she can keep her Roth conversion funds separate from her funds that were Roth from Day 1. This will help her avoid accidentally pulling out the "wrong" funds. (You can open as many Roth IRAs as you want, though you shouldn't need more than two. The limits only apply to how much you can contribute each year.)

Step 2: Starting your Roth conversion ladder

Once she has her 401(k) in a more malleable format (the rollover IRA), ERK will convert a sum of money that matches the current standard deduction to Roth (allowing it to land in her *new* Roth IRA). If she were beginning this process in 2025, this would be equivalent to $15,000 for people filing single and $30,000 for married filing jointly couples.[†] By converting the funds to Roth, the *entire* conversion amount now becomes her cost basis in her new Roth IRA. And what have we learned about our cost basis in a Roth IRA? It can be accessed at any time! She's now successfully weaseled her way into accessing her pretax funds early! Congratulations, Katie.

As long as ERK has no other earned income, she can convert the entire standard-deduction-sized amount of $15,000 or $30,000 from her rollover IRA to her new Roth IRA—eating up her "get out of tax free" card benefit for earned income and completing the entire conversion tax- and penalty-free. That means her money went into her pretax accounts tax-free, grew tax-free, and came out tax-free.

Of course, age, timing, and other taxable income matters here, and the earlier you start, the more tax-advantageous this strategy becomes. If you won't be retiring until you're already taking Social Security and a few years away from required minimum distributions, you'll have a lot less flexibility than someone who begins making conversions early. But early retirees should theoretically have a reasonably easy time converting much of their rollover IRA to Roth before they hit age seventy, when they'd need to begin Social Security, or age seventy-three, when they'd have to start taking the required minimum distributions. Moreover, if you take sabbatical years during your working life in

---

† There's no limit to how much money you can convert to Roth in any given year, unlike the limit on Roth contributions. We just choose to manage our conversion amounts in this way to keep our tax liability low.

which your earned income is very low, that provides another opportunity to begin rolling over any pretax funds you may have in rollover IRAs into Roth IRAs to take advantage of your *temporarily* lower tax rate.

There's only one catch: Roth conversions must "settle" for five years before you're allowed to use them. *Womp womp.* Technically, ERK would be able to access and withdraw her Year 1 conversion on January 1 of Year 6. For example, since she's starting this process at age 50, she'd have access to her entire first year's conversion amount on January 1 of the year she turns 56. In doing so, she's accessed funds in her 401(k) before age 59.5 without paying a 10 percent penalty, and with $0 in tax liability.

Step 3: Repeating this process in Years 1–5 of early retirement

But wait, you might be wondering, *if she has no other earned income and she can't use her Roth conversions for five years, what's she supposed to do for money in Years 1–5?*

This is where her taxable brokerage account comes into play to bridge the gap. To support her spending in Years 1–5, she'll withdraw enough from her taxable brokerage account to take full advantage of the 0 percent capital gains tax brackets: $48,350 in capital gains for single and $96,700 in capital gains for married filing jointly.

If for some reason she doesn't *need* that much money to live on—if their spending as a married couple is only, say, $85,000—she could theoretically withdraw a lot less than the maximums allowed by our tax code at the 0 percent capital gains tax rate (though I'd recommend that ERK withdraw all of it anyway and reinvest what she doesn't use; that way, she's "stepping up" her cost basis and reducing the amount of gains she'll owe taxes on later).

And if you spend more than that (as my husband and I do, and I imagine most people with dependents do), you can withdraw more from the taxable brokerage account, knowing you'll just pay the 15 percent capital gains tax on any gains above $96,700 (still not a bad deal, in this reporter's opinion). It's also possible you might be withdrawing the cost basis (that is, the money you originally put in), which is money you won't owe any taxes on. You can simulate different scenarios for your own situation using the TaxAct tax calculator[†] by plugging in income from "Taxable IRAs" (your rollover IRA, formerly your 401(k) or equivalent account) and "Capital Gains" (from the taxable account) to double-check your work and get an estimate for your total tax bill.

In Early Retiree Katie's case, we know her brokerage account—the one she funded with her post-tax take-home pay after her regular retirement accounts were stocked—has around $500,000 in it, which means she risks depleting it before Year 6 if she pulls out the maximum $96,700 each year. Using our 4 percent guideline from Chapter 3, we know that—at around $2 million in investments—her safe withdrawal is around $80,000 per year, which is a lot less than the maximum tax-free amount possible for married couples of $126,700.

At this point, there are two upper limits to be aware of—the lower of which will guide the maximum you withdraw and spend if both a 0 percent tax rate and investment longevity are important to you:

---

† To estimate your total tax bill based on your withdrawals from investment accounts and any other income, check out the calculator at taxact.com/tools/tax-calculator.

1. **The maximum amount you can withdraw, per** *your* **4 percent safe withdrawal rate.** E.g., ERK's safe withdrawal amount at age fifty is around $80,000, a withdrawal composed of the $30,000 standard deduction for married filing jointly couples and $50,000 in the 0 percent capital gains tax bracket from her bridge brokerage account. Again, this is quite a bit lower than the amount of capital gains the tax code would allow them to realize for free ($96,700).

2. **The maximum amount you can withdraw tax-free under the tax code.** If ERK were to hold out for another five years and skid into early retirement with $3.1 million, her safe withdrawal amount would be around $124,000, which is coincidentally almost identical to the optimal tax-free outcome for a married couple of $126,700.

To safely pull off the maximum allowed by the tax code without violating the maximum allowed by your own personal safe withdrawal rate based on how much money you've invested, you'd be shooting for around $1.5 million as a single filer using 2025 data (such that you can withdraw around $60,000 per year) and $3 million as a married filing jointly couple (such that you can withdraw around $120,000 per year).

Step 4: The real party starts in Year 6

After Year 6, ERK can use her first $30,000 chunk of converted Roth funds *and* her $96,700 of 0 percent capital gains from her brokerage account (though as we noted, in her case, she might want to withdraw less, given her total portfolio balance).

To summarize, your tax-free retirement income could look like this:

		SINGLE TAX-FREE INCOME		MARRIED FILING JOINTLY TAX-FREE INCOME	
RETIREMENT YEAR		**ROTH CONVERSIONS (FROM ORIGINAL 401(K) PLAN)**	**0% TAXABLE GAINS FROM BROKERAGE ACCOUNT**	**ROTH CONVERSIONS (FROM ORIGINAL 401(K) PLANS)**	**0% TAXABLE GAINS FROM BROKERAGE ACCOUNT**
	1	$0	$48,350	$0	$96,700
	2	$0	$48,350	$0	$96,700
	3	$0	$48,350	$0	$96,700
	4	$0	$48,350	$0	$96,700
	5	$0	$48,350	$0	$96,700
	6	$15,000 from Year 1	$48,350	$30,000 from Year 1	$96,700
	7	$15,000 from Year 2	$48,350	$30,000 from Year 2	$96,700
	8	$15,000 from Year 3	$48,350	$30,000 from Year 3	$96,700
	9	$15,000 from Year 4	$48,350	$30,000 from Year 4	$96,700
	10	$15,000 from Year 5	$48,350	$30,000 from Year 5	$96,700
	11+	$15,000 from Year 6	$48,350	$30,000 from Year 6	$96,700

These numbers would adjust upward for inflation each year, but for the sake of simplicity, this is generally how the tax-free income would be created. Some people who are *really* committed to a tax-free early retirement (usually out of a strategic devotion to the game, rather than a true aversion to taxes) might build up a little extra cash savings on the side in the last year or two of work to supplement their 0 percent long-term capital gains in the first five years. This might mean investing a little bit less and hanging on to more of your savings in an account that's easy to access as you're about to send the two-weeks-notice paper airplane into your boss's boss's corner office.

As for the Roth IRA that ERK funded throughout her life, she'll toss that to the back burner and allow it to continue compounding until she needs it to supplement her pretax conversions (whether because the taxable account is tapped or she's simply ready for more tax-free income). Depending on how many years it compounds untouched, she might be able to supplement her income in retirement with a *lot* more tax-free Roth income. For example, if she lets it rip for fifteen years untouched after retiring, by the time she's sixty-five, it will have ballooned from around $285,000 (its balance when she quit working) to $780,000 in tax-free funds.

Since the original Roth dollars are the most valuable (as they can be used in any way without taxation and aren't subject to required minimum distributions), it's the account that gets used last. This is also why it's okay if you're slowly depleting the taxable brokerage account as you execute this plan.

To summarize how you might enact this for yourself:

1. Put your original Roth IRA on the back burner, unless you absolutely need its cost basis in Years 1–5 to supplement your taxable brokerage account withdrawals.
2. Roll over your traditional 401(k) plan(s) to rollover IRA(s) so you can use them.
3. Open a new Roth IRA(s) with the firm where you've opened your rollover IRA(s).
4. Check the standard deduction for your filing status.

5. Convert a standard-deduction-sized amount of your roll-over IRA(s) to your new Roth IRA(s) every year moving forward (and reinvest it if it's not already invested post-conversion). If you itemize your deductions and you can deduct even more than the standard, you could convert more!

6. In Years 1–5, try to keep your spending under the 0 percent capital gains tax allowance threshold for your filing status, only withdrawing and using funds from your taxable brokerage accounts, though know that your tax burden on capital gains above those thresholds will only be taxed at 15 percent (so it's still a pretty good deal).

7. In Year 6, your Roth conversion from Year 1 becomes available, and you'll still have access to the full 0 percent capital gains tax bracket in your taxable accounts. In this example, ERK would've been fifty-six years old in Year 6; still three years away from the "normal" access point and still almost twenty years away from required minimum distributions.

This tax strategy—standard-deduction-sized withdrawals from your pretax accounts paired with 0 percent capital gains withdrawals and supplemented with any amount of income from a Roth IRA—works regardless of when you retire, but you might be forced (as in, by the Feds) to take more from the pretax accounts after age 73 thanks to the aforementioned required minimum distributions (which is why this strategy is most valuable for someone who intends to retire early). As one final reminder, those who retire after 59.5 get to skip the Roth conversion ladder step and withdraw their standard-deduction-sized funds directly from their rollover IRAs, since the ladder's only purpose is to get your pretax funds into a post-tax form you can use before they'd ordinarily be available to you.

Between you and me, I doubt that most people who know about this strategy ever actually execute it to its full potential. Sure, it's an idealized interpretation of the way our tax code treats our various investment vehicles, but it also functionally illustrates the interplay between these three tax statuses when it's time to start using your money. As with much of what we covered in this chapter, even if you're only letting it guide you directionally, you'll still lose a lot less investment income to taxes than if you were withdrawing your money willy-nilly. For example, I've encountered recommendations that prescribe emptying your entire brokerage account first, followed by pretax accounts, then using Roth accounts last. In doing so, you'll almost certainly pay more of that investment income in taxes than if you combine steps one and two the way we did here.

What about Social Security?

Early retirees don't need to stress much about Social Security in the beginning of their retirements, because they can delay its effects until age seventy if they'd like to—but at some point, your income from Social Security will impact your taxable income. Even though it's estimated Social Security will only pay out between 75 percent and 83 percent of benefits after the trust runs out in 2035, my own back-of-the-napkin math reveals that ignoring it entirely probably means you're overshooting the amount you need to save and invest by around 30 percent. If you're planning to retire at the traditional retirement age of between sixty-five and sixty-seven, you can factor this in by:

1. Going to SSA.gov
2. Getting your estimated monthly benefit
3. Calculating what you'd expect to receive each year
4. Multiplying that annual number by 25
5. Subtracting it from your financial independence goal

That's your new financial independence goal with Social Security income factored in, as that additional income will fill in the gaps.

Some people like to eliminate it from consideration entirely because they're going to retire many years before Social Security eligibility, they're nervous about relying on it, or they figure ignoring it will allow them to amass enough money to easily cover the *new* expenses of early retirement, like paying for health insurance out of pocket.

In conclusion

Early Retiree Katie went from $0 invested to financial freedom in about twenty years, thanks to pairing her strong income with a savvy understanding of the tax code and a propensity to save money. Had she not executed this strategy during that time (and instead just took all her income home, then saved or invested it less intentionally), it would've taken her at least 15 percent† longer. (Early Retirement Katie, now in her fifties, wants us to know that your fifties are the new forties, and she's working on self-publishing a romance novel from her Parisian flat on a three-month Eurotrip. Well done, ERK.)

---

† Without her tax savings invested elsewhere, it takes twenty-three years of work to accumulate $1.5 million, not twenty.

Because men have long been the de facto decision-makers about how resources are allocated in mixed-sex households, it's common for women to find themselves financially lost in their fifties, sixties, and later, particularly after a divorce or a spouse's death. By arming ourselves with the right tools to step into the driver's seat of our long-term financial planning, fewer women will face financial duress later in life. Part of that plan is investing in a tax-advantaged way, which supercharges our path to long-term independence.

Now that we've got our key puzzle pieces on the table and know how we can most meaningfully assemble them, let's talk about how to implement this plan in your life *today*.

7

Rich Girl for Life: Putting It All Together

I met one of my closest friends—we'll call her Eleanor—when I was teaching group fitness in Dallas, Texas. She was the type of instructor that Peloton builds ad campaigns around. Her classes reliably transported all fifty attendees to another dimension, so she was a *very* popular draw for the studio. Of the ten or so classes she taught each week, they were almost always waitlisted. As a full-time instructor in her early twenties, she was making north of $80,000 per year, about $20,000 more than I was earning at the time at my Big Girl corporate job.

One early morning after class in 2019, we were sitting outside the Starbucks down the block before I headed to work. We started talking about money. Her car had recently needed unexpected work, and she was stressed about paying for it. Before I knew it, we had my laptop open on the table, examining her bank statements. To my surprise, while she had been haphazardly saving some of her money, she hadn't started investing yet. Thanks to my newfound obsession with all things personal finance, I realized quickly she was the perfect candidate for a set-it-and-forget-it plan.

She hadn't been sure where to start—but after talking it over, she agreed to let me set up an automatic transfer from her checking account to a Roth IRA and a brokerage account with a robo-adviser I liked.

"So it's just going to take the money out and invest it, and I don't have to remember to do anything?" she asked, incredulous.

"Yeah," I replied, "I know it sounds too good to be true, but that's it."

We didn't speak much of it again, and our relationship mostly reverted to its original form. Fast-forward about eighteen months to late summer 2020: The studio had been closed for months, leaving her without steady income, save for a few PPP-loan-fueled paychecks. She was building out her own online digital space to teach meditation and mat-based classes, but she knew she'd need to tap her savings soon, and she was anxious about her financial situation.

But then, one hot August afternoon, I received a text. "Dude, holy shit," it read. "I just remembered those Betterment accounts you set up for me. I checked and there's $30,000 in them!"

She was floored. Honestly, I was floored. I had seen automated, set-it-and-forget-it investing pay off in my own life, but I didn't realize she had kept it up (and not checked it). Because the money had been whisked away from her checking account before she had the chance to do anything with it, she felt as though she had hardly noticed the several hundred dollars disappearing with each paycheck. (This also illustrates the relative ease of saving and investing when you earn a strong income in a medium cost-of-living city, as you may have gathered.)

In the years since, I've heard a lot of stories like this one. Every single day, I read emails or podcast reviews or comments about how using a Wealth Planner (or something like it) has radically changed someone's financial life, or how understanding their best tax strategy unlocked thousands in previously untapped savings. I've heard from women who started over after divorces from financially abusive men, now with hundreds of thousands of dollars invested. One such woman recently reached out to tell me she got divorced at forty-five with hardly anything in savings, $320,000 in mortgage debt, and no plan—and twelve years later, she's a millionaire. Women who were once living above their means would write to tell me that understanding their numbers helped them make the decision to downgrade their vehicles and move into a less luxe apartment for a little while to build up their safety net, and they were happier for it. It was most meaningful when I heard from women who had overcome serious obstacles, like first-generation Americans who were supporting family members.

Sometimes I can scarcely believe these success stories myself, or the resilience required to make them a reality. But it's true: Having an informed plan (and using it to take informed action) can go a shockingly long way. People with basic financial literacy and a plan for retirement end up with two to three times as much wealth as those without it, and approximately 30 percent of wealth inequality in retirement is attributable to financial literacy.[†] It's not the whole story—hell, it's not even the majority of the story— but it's the best shot we have at lives of economic dignity in the midst of cultural and economic legacies that are poised to disadvantage us (and tend to benefit from our ignorance of how "the

---

† The paper that produced these figures used the Health and Retirement Study, a nationally representative longitudinal dataset of Americans over the age of fifty.

system" works). Individualized personal finance advice doesn't exist in a vacuum, nor does it fix failures of policy—but it might have the power to change *your* life.

The amount of money we have access to is one of the most impactful determinants of our quality of life. We know that by navigating consumer landscapes that are squarely directed at women with wisdom and skepticism, planning for the future in a way that generates the biggest bang for our buck *without* falling into the classic pitfalls, and building careers (and families) that ensure our basic needs will always be met and we'll never be trapped, we can exert more control over our outcomes.

Because before I started interrogating *my* money management systems (or lack thereof) proactively, my monthly plan looked a lot like Eleanor's:

1. Get paid.
2. Spend with reckless abandon as my threadbare Discover card was out there in the Dallas streets fighting for its life, eyeballing my checking account to determine whether I could afford things.
3. Pay off the statement at the end of the month (only after staring at the bill summary PDF for no less than twelve minutes, wondering how I had managed to spend so much).
4. Shuffle a meager amount of money into savings with whatever was left, if anything.

To state the obvious: Your girl was going nowhere fast. She was paying bills, but she was treading water: There was no plan beyond the bare minimum. If you had asked me back then whether I had enough money to start investing for the future, I would've told you—unequivocally—no. I wasn't swimming in free cash flow every month, nor did I really know how much my life cost. I didn't think I had any room in my budget for the future because the present was such a question mark. After all, there was rarely much left over at the end of the month in my checking account, so how could I have invested? *Surely* I needed to earn more first, right?

Of course, once I sat down and mapped my fixed expenses onto my income, I was faced with math that was hard to square with reality—I had nearly a thousand bucks that was going unaccounted for each month after I removed my big-ticket items like rent, a car payment, insurance, groceries, and gas. Where was all of it going? "Hmm," I thought, brow furrowed, "let me double-check that." I punched the numbers into my phone calculator again and saw the same answer on the screen in front of me, and once again, it assured me: I *could* afford to save and invest, but since the money hadn't been proactively rerouted elsewhere, it sat in my checking account until I spent it. It's this brand of financial aimlessness that's most ripe for education and strategy—as a single person (with a roommate!) earning around $55,000 per year in pretax income in 2018 Dallas, Texas, I was not suffering from resource scarcity. I just didn't have a plan.

In this chapter, we'll weave together everything I've covered in the previous six to build a holistic view of these ideas. Then, we'll talk about some of my favorite ways to check in and stay on track. Personal finance doesn't have to become your whole personality and namesake like it did mine—because this strategy, when implemented, requires less than $150 and twenty hours per year to execute in its entirety.

It all begins with spending according to where you derive the most joy and value

That's why I began our adventure together by discussing the consumer industries that tend to most successfully market to women—those that keep us polished and shellacked on the Hot Girl Hamster Wheel, sometimes without our explicit, conscious permission or recognition. Because even though our romp through the metaphoric aisles of Ulta was specific to beauty and self-care, the larger message is this: *Spending with discernment can make your life better.* The Hot Girl Detox exercise we performed in Chapter 1 with respect to your beauty spending can be conducted more agnostically, too: Look at the *entirety* of your spending and consider where the value exchange no longer feels good.

At the end of 2020, I reviewed my spending for the previous year—only to learn that of the $30,000 I had spent, nearly $6,000 went to one line item: my car. Between payments, gas, maintenance, and insurance, 20 percent of my spending was being funneled into my little red jelly bean of an Audi A3. As I reflected on how often I used my car in 2020 (spoiler alert: not often), it was clearly an area where my spending far outweighed the value I was receiving. I knew some of that $6,000 could've gone a lot further on fun takeout meals or new novels to break up the monotony of 2020 life, or inside a brokerage account for after the world opened back up. I decided to sell my car, and we became a one-car household for several years. I relied instead on my bike when I needed to get around the Colorado mountain town we had recently moved to, and discovered the wonders of not worrying about parking, traffic, or check engine lights.

There's no real shortcut to analyzing your spending, and it's often an area we resist because it feels punitive. *Yeah, I know I spent too much on fast-casual dining and new luggage last month,* we might intuit before diving headfirst into the AmEx statements. But I encourage you to question that instinct: You probably *think* you know where you spent "too much" from a general eyeballing of the cardboard boxes stacked by the back door or the wilting organic arugula in your fridge's faulty airtight drawer. But "too much" is a subjective judgment we should interrogate—if your online shopping delivered a mountain of mind-expanding books and necessary household goods to your door, is that really a bad thing? If your grocery bill is higher than average but cooking is one of your most earnest passions, does it really represent an area where you need to cut back? Spending a lot on something is only behavior that needs to change if the value exchange is no longer fair or it's actively undermining your future self's security.

The next step

If you've never gotten curious about or familiar with your spending patterns before (or maybe you're interested in revisiting them in your current life stage because it's been a while and you've #evolved), now's the time. Our goal is to observe and reflect on our behavior and patterns with spending not because spending is bad or we should necessarily do it less, but because we want our money to serve a greater vision for our lives.

To start this deep dive on spending habits, I like using software that automatically links to my credit cards and checking accounts for ongoing tracking because it's easier (like Copilot Money, which costs $95 per year), but keeping a manual log in a journal or spreadsheet is often the most effective way to get curious about and familiar with your spending patterns. A ninety-day period will give you the most exhaustive view, but one month is the minimum effective dose so it captures a full "cycle." You can even jot down observations in the notes app on your phone if you don't feel like going high-tech. In the moment of (or soon after) the purchase, you'll want to capture a few attributes:

Purchase (aka, what did you buy?):

Amount:

Mood you were in when you made the purchase:

For example:

Purchase: *Premium cat food*

Amount: *$66*

Mood you were in when you made the purchase:
Responsible

Then, at the end of each week, go back and answer this question for your more notable purchases:

ROI (return on investment)?: *Giving Sam cat food that's high quality feels like an investment in his health and lower medical bills in the future. Spending on my pets feels really good.*

In retrospect, how much value did a purchase bring you? If that thing were taken away from you now, would you buy it again? Do you regret it? For example, I noticed that when I paid for professional help to clean my home, I always felt a sense of profound gratitude and relief. This was psychologically instructive: I experimented with other areas of outsourcing, like meal delivery (and eventually settled on grocery delivery as the happy medium). I also noticed that when I get into "self-improvement"-y moods, I tend to feel compelled to buy new clothes (did someone say reinvention?), which I usually regretted when "Western-forward Christian Girl Autumn" was no longer my aesthetic. For a little while, I circumvented this tendency by subscribing to a clothing rental company that allowed me to "try on" different styles without permanently acquiring a bunch of new stuff that would sit in my closet untouched or end up in a landfill after the phase passed.

The result of this exercise is not necessarily that you should be spending less—just that you might be better served by spending differently. If you're unsure whether something is "too much," we can look to the math-heavy best practices as a starting point, using your current income as our guide.

Developing an honest, strategic relationship with your income

Chapter 2 is the longest chapter in this book for a reason. The more you earn, the easier it is to rearrange the puzzle pieces. If you were only going to take one thing and run with it, increasing your income is likely where your energy will go furthest.

In 2020, I focused on increasing my income through finding additional work (freelance, part time, you name it) and interviewing whenever possible for higher-paying full-time jobs. At $30,000 of spending per year, there wasn't much more I could cut without subjecting myself to arbitrary deprivation, so I shifted my focus to the income side of the equation.

I began my career as an ad copywriter—a position that didn't pay very well. I toyed with the idea of starting an agency or trying to ascend the ranks to a position like creative director, but that didn't really appeal to me, and the road looked *long*. I wanted to make more money in the next year or two, not fifteen years from now. Instead, I leaned into my interest in broader creative strategy. I ended up working closely with the principal user experience designer on my team, who gave me a valuable piece of insight: *UX writers get paid a lot more than ad copywriters do.* My position in the company shifted as I worked more with her, until the point at which my role was almost entirely UX copy. I pivoted internally, which positioned me to pivot *externally* for a much larger salary elsewhere. This process took about two years: My total compensation when I left my previous "internal pivot" role was around $70,000, and my new total compensation was $140,000.

Earning more money immediately enables higher savings rates, which is the first step toward investing meaningful sums of money. As soon as I had my spending, saving, and investing system in place with my newfound healthy income, it mostly maintained itself. That's not to say it's not possible on below-median incomes, just that all else held equal, the return on your effort to increase your income is often larger than expending that same energy on cutting costs at the margins.

The next step

Usually, people fall into one of two camps at this juncture:

1. They're one negotiation or redirection away from increasing their income (as was the case in my UX-writing anecdote, which was a slight, concerted pivot in experi-

ence and framing that did not require additional formal education).

2. They're in a field that's not well paid and feel they're at a crossroads.

I see number two most with readers who work in fields that are dominated by women, like physical therapy, nursing, and education (and per our conversations about occupational segregation, that's no coincidence). In these instances, there often isn't an easy corporate rebrand; you can't press the "pivot to tech" button and sail away to six-figure land. But if you *are* in a field like these, I think it's important to reflect on a few questions:

- **Do I love what I do?** Am I happy in my profession? If so, am I comfortable operating within the supposed bounds of the lifestyle it can provide to me?
- **Can I see any path to higher pay?** Are people much further along in this field paid substantially more, or is the salary progression relatively flat regardless of skill level?
- **Would entrepreneurship change the financial outcomes?** Do I know *anyone* in my field earning the type of money I'd like to earn, or is the limit on income real?
- **Am I willing to do other work part time** that *is* more lucrative or has more upside to fill in the gaps (for example, a teacher becoming a part-time tutor), or is that a lifestyle compromise I'm uninterested in for personal or professional reasons?

These aren't always easy questions, and crucially, there are no right answers. Some people decide their job is their vocation and they're comfortable working within its financial parameters;

others conclude the lifestyle they envision for themselves is not possible on their current path and they need to make a bigger change. Working a job you hate for a lot of money is no walk in the park, either; I don't recommend abandoning a career you love for one that's lucrative but soul-sucking. Regardless of where you land, there are guidelines that can help shape *how* you allocate your income.

Breaking down the individual pieces of your income

Since taxes are one of our largest expenses, it makes sense to begin by contextualizing how much we're devoting to taxes off the bat. Add up your estimated total income from all sources (base pay, commissions, bonuses, side hustles, etc.) to get a full understanding:

1. As I mentioned in Chapter 6, I like to use the SmartAsset income tax calculator[†] to quickly get an estimate for take-home pay based on my zip code and a few quick deductions (if you're going to make contributions to pretax accounts, include those in the deductions section so your tax estimate is accurate).

2. Divide the result for take-home pay by twelve to get a sense for your average monthly take-home pay. For people who are paid biweekly or folks who get bonuses at certain times of the year, this will help normalize your income

---

† Which can be accessed at smartasset.com/taxes/income-taxes.

and present it holistically (versus thinking about bonuses or commission checks like "extras" throughout the year).

Once you've identified your average monthly take-home pay, this baseline plan functions as scaffolding you can modify based on your situation and goals:

IDEAL BREAKDOWN

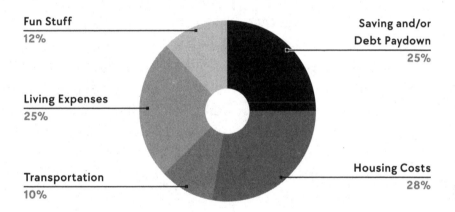

Fun Stuff
12%

Living Expenses
25%

Transportation
10%

Saving and/or Debt Paydown
25%

Housing Costs
28%

We might have a solid sense for what specific type of conscious consumption tickles our fancy or how to earn more over time, but identifying a savings target often works in tandem with figuring out where the rest of your income is going.

I use the word "target" because life is messy. Some years it'll be higher. Other years it'll be lower. Missing the target is not a referendum on your morality or goodness, just like exceeding it isn't, either. In one survey we did of Rich Girl Nation in 2023, we heard from a couple that didn't hit their savings rate goal for the year . . . because one of them was undergoing cancer treatment. Another was way behind because she had split from her partner and was rebuilding her life in a new city. Talk about not losing the forest for the trees, huh? We use things like pie charts and percentages because they help us direct our efforts, but your plan can, should, and will adjust. **Your physical, mental, and emotional health and safety all supersede money on the priority list, so if these things are suffering in service of a spreadsheet, we've officially taken a wrong turn.**

I say this explicitly as my preamble before building a savings plan because I've personally shied away from doing things like hiring professional help for my mental or emotional well-being or going to doctors (and witnessed close friends do the same) out of fear that it would become expensive. This is self-defeating: Having a bunch of money later in life is only fun if your body and mind are healthy enough to enjoy it. You do not serve under the jurisdiction of a pie chart.

That said . . . let's explore this sacred pie chart.

Saving, investing, or debt paydown with 25 percent of your net income

All three of these activities—saving, investing, debt paydown—increase your net worth, in the first two cases by bolstering your assets and in the third by lowering your liabilities. I like 25 percent because—if you adjust all income and spending for inflation over time but otherwise stay on the same course—a 25 percent save rate means you can retire in twenty-six years. Of course, this is one of those things that works better in a book about personal finance than in the lumpiness of real life. A thirty-year-old paying for a wedding and having their first kid is probably going to have a harder time saving 25 percent of their income than a forty-five-year-old who's now in a director-level position at work and whose kid just got a scholarship to a state school, but like I said, this is a baseline.

As we noted in Chapter 3, if you're really trying to get "optimal" and early retirement is your primary financial goal, 40 percent is technically the save rate that I think strikes the most efficient balance between the "now" and the "later." My suggestion? If you think it's within your range, shoot for 25 percent to begin with, then adjust over time depending on where you are in your financial life cycle and how your income picture shakes out. If you're a high earner and can work your way up to 35 percent or 40 percent, incredible.

It's also normal for that "25 percent" to be split between various medium- and long-term goals (for example, you might be paying off student loans, saving for a vacation, putting away money for childcare, and investing for retirement simultaneously), so if you're trying to calculate your savings rate for the purposes of identifying your long-term financial freedom timeline specifically, be sure to remove the savings that are going toward other large, medium-term expenses.

Saving and investing with a highly irregular income

If you have a highly irregular income, you might want to introduce a personal slush fund to act like a second source of income in slow months. It's different from your emergency fund, because a slow month isn't an emergency—it's just the reality of owning your own business or working in sales.

To establish yours, aim to save at least two months' worth of expenses in an overflow account (it can be a savings account attached to your main checking account, or somewhere else) that can help supplement your income during a slow month. During the beefy months, you fill it back up. For example, if your life costs $5,000 per month but your net income every month varies from $2,000 to $10,000, you'd spend a few good months shuffling any amount over $5,000 into your overflow savings—from which you'll pay yourself the difference when the $2,000 months hit. Anytime the number in the overflow account drops below around $10,000 (a two-month slush fund), you'll make refilling it the top priority the next month you've got excess incoming cash.

For people who have irregular wages or business owners who have boom-and-bust cycles, this ensures you always have the cash on hand to pay yourself before you get overzealous about investing in accounts that can't be easily tapped. To flesh out our previous example, imagine you've got $8,000 in your overflow account and you know you need to top it off with another $2,000. The next time you have a good month, your non-spending priorities are:

1. Replenishing the overflow account +$2,000
2. Any high-interest debt payoff
3. Other medium- and long-term investing

Depending on the nature of your work and your comfort level with risk, you might decide to keep more than two months of expenses in your overflow account.

Ideally, the goal is to—over time—establish a baseline of income (even in irregular circumstances) that is *always* more than enough to support your lifestyle. If you're regularly not earning enough to pay your bills for whatever reason, it might signal you're either living beyond your means or have an income challenge that needs more immediate attention.

Housing costs comprising no more than 28 percent of your net income

I include *all* costs related to housing in this category, and my reasoning is very simple: When too much of your net pay goes to the roof over your head, you're going to have a really hard time *also* having fun and saving money. Conventional lending criteria typically allows you to borrow such that 28 percent of your *gross* income goes toward the mortgage alone, but that means—after taxes and insurance—many people are spending 40 percent of their take-home pay on housing. It's important to remember the incentives with which lenders are operating: to loan you the maximum amount of money they're confident you'll be able to pay back.

Of course, I don't live under a rock (and even rocklike accommodations are expensive these days). The cost of housing has outpaced wage growth for the majority of the US—so again, this is baseline guidance that can serve as a starting point if you're apartment hunting and have options all over the price band. Depending on how you spend in other areas, going higher here might be totally reasonable.

The rest of your living expenses under 25 percent of net income

Think food, childcare, pets, etc. I know those of you with multiple children in childcare might be cursing my name right now, so I'll reiterate that there will be stages of life where this category gets totally blown out of the water—and that's okay.

Total transportation costs at 10 percent or less

Similarly, this is in reference to your car payment, car insurance, gas, maintenance, etc. This rule of thumb simply creates boundaries that prevent you from stretching yourself to afford a car that looks fine on paper but ends up torpedoing your ability to absorb other unexpected costs by chewing up too much of your monthly net income. If you live in a very high cost-of-living city with public transportation, you might consider skipping the vehicle altogether and reallocating most of this 10 percent to your housing costs or other living expenses.

And finally, "fun stuff" at 12 percent

Since the relationship between our savings rate and fun spending is flexible, you'll have to adjust the dial accordingly based on what you're prioritizing more of right now. Different seasons of life are going to call for different versions of you. Some years you may prioritize saving more than you prioritize the sort of fun that costs money—other years, it might be the opposite. But beginning at 12 percent gives you a sense for the ballpark you're working with.

Putting it all together

Those are, of course, the large categories under which you're going to have a lot of subcategories, so if you've never taken the time to flesh out your plan at a more granular level, I suggest you do so now, if only so you have a basis for annualizing your expenses. You don't need to track at this level of granularity every month if seeing these line items makes you break out into hives, but it's a healthy step toward getting a *real* picture of how much the life you want to live costs.

On the next two pages is an example of our categories and subcategories from a few years ago.[†]

---

† For a blank, editable version of the budget table and financial independence calculator, go to moneywithkatie.com/chapter-7-budget-template.

Plan Your Monthly Spending

Housing		Amount	Recurring Fixed Bill?
Rent	▼	$3,000.00	☑
Cleaning	▼	$250.00	☐
Electric	▼	$250.00	☐
Water	▼	$125.00	☐
Internet	▼	$75.00	☑
Phone	▼	$60.00	☑
Trash	▼	$25.00	☐
	▼		☐
	▼		☐
	▼		☐
Total		**$3,785.00**	

Food		Amount	Recurring Fixed Bill?
Groceries	▼	$500.00	☐
Restaurants	▼	$500.00	☐
Coffee	▼	$75.00	☐
	▼		☐
	▼		☐
	▼		☐
	▼		☐
	▼		☐
	▼		☐
	▼		☐
Total		**$1,075.00**	

Transportation		Amount	Recurring Fixed Bill?
Car Insurance	▼	$300.00	☑
Rideshare	▼	$100.00	☐
Gas	▼	$50.00	☐
	▼		☐
	▼		☐
	▼		☐
	▼		☐
	▼		☐
	▼		☐
	▼		☐
Total		**$450.00**	

Pets		Amount	Recurring Fixed Bill?
Daycare	▼	$100.00	☐
Food	▼	$150.00	☐
Veterinary	▼	$100.00	☐
	▼		☐
	▼		☐
	▼		☐
	▼		☐
	▼		☐
	▼		☐
	▼		☐
Total		**$350.00**	

Debt Payments		Amount	Recurring Fixed Bill?
			☐
			☐
			☐
			☐
			☐
			☐
			☐
			☐
			☐
			☐
			☐
Total		**$0.00**	

Personal Care		Amount	Recurring Fixed Bill?
Haircut/Hair Color	▼	$100.00	☐
Personal Care Items	▼	$50.00	☐
Gym	▼	$40.00	☐
	▼		☐
	▼		☐
	▼		☐
	▼		☐
	▼		☐
	▼		☐
	▼		☐
Total		**$190.00**	

Family ♡	Amount	Recurring Fixed Bill?	Travel ✈	Amount	Recurring Fixed Bill?
▾		☐	Airfare ▾	$500.00	☐
▾		☐	Hotels/Accommodations ▾	$500.00	☐
▾		☐	Ground Transportation ▾	$200.00	☐
▾		☐	Airport Parking ▾	$100.00	☐
▾		☐	▾		☐
▾		☐	▾		☐
▾		☐	▾		☐
▾		☐	▾		☐
▾		☐	▾		☐
▾		☐	▾		☐
Total	**$0.00**		**Total**	**$1,300.00**	

Medical ✎	Amount	Recurring Fixed Bill?	Donations & Giving ◌◌	Amount	Recurring Fixed Bill?
Doctor's Visits ▾	$120.00	☐	Giving Fund	$500.00	☐
▾		☐			☐
▾		☐			☐
▾		☐			☐
▾		☐			☐
▾		☐			☐
▾		☐			☐
▾		☐			☐
▾		☐			☐
▾		☐			☐
Total	**$120.00**		**Total**	**$500.00**	

Entertainment ▣	Amount	Recurring Fixed Bill?	Miscellaneous ◍	Amount	Recurring Fixed Bill?
Streaming ▾	$100.00	☑	Guilt-Free Spending ▾	$500.00	☐
Subscriptions ▾	$50.00	☑	Miscellaneous ▾	$250.00	☐
Books & Media ▾	$50.00	☐	▾		☐
▾		☐	▾		☐
▾		☐	▾		☐
▾		☐	▾		☐
▾		☐	▾		☐
▾		☐	▾		☐
▾		☐	▾		☐
▾		☐	▾		☐
Total	**$200.00**		**Total**	**$750.00**	

The broader categorization (e.g., how these example categories and subcategories fit into the pie chart) might look like this:

HOUSING—*total less than 28 percent of take-home pay*
- Rent
- Cleaning
- Electric
- Gas
- Water
- Internet
- Phone
- Trash

LIVING EXPENSES—*total less than 25 percent of take-home pay*
- Food (groceries)
- Medical (doctor's visits)
- Pets (daycare, food and medication, litter and supplies, veterinary)
- Miscellaneous (donations, gifts, and other stuff that stubbornly resists categorization)
- Personal care (gym, haircuts, personal care items)

TRANSPORTATION—*total less than 10 percent of take-home pay*
- Car payment
- Car insurance
- Maintenance
- Gas

FUN STUFF—*total less than 12 percent of take-home pay*
- Food (restaurants and coffee)
- Travel (airfare, hotels and lodging, ground transportation, parking)
- Entertainment (streaming, books and media, tickets)

I adjust our spending almost as often as I change my underwear, but the main reason what you regularly spend matters is that it tells you a lot about:

- How much money your desired lifestyle will cost to maintain in the *future* (i.e., your financial independence number)
- Your current margin between expenses and income, and therefore the amount you're able to save and invest now

. . . which, taken together, can be used to triangulate your timeline, as we covered in Chapter 3 in more depth.

Depending on what you find, you may decide it's appropriate to pull back your spending a little bit (or hell, maybe even ramp it up!).†

It may feel like overkill, but getting these steps ironed out before you begin attempting to meaningfully track anything moving forward will increase your chances of success. In my own life, I found I was far more likely to stick to my best intentions when I knew with some level of certainty they'd deliver me to the outcome I wanted most.

---

† There's a robust Financial Independence tab in the Money with Katie Wealth Planner that takes all these numbers and spits out a timeline, but you can access a simpler version of the calculator at moneywithkatie.com/chapter-7-budget-template.

Understanding your current net worth picture

Finally, there are a few important things to clarify about where you are today before deciding where you'd like to allocate those future savings. The first is your **assets and liabilities**.

ASSETS VS. LIABILITIES

Assets that impact your long-term financial picture include:

- Your cash (checking, savings, and other liquid sources)
- Your investment accounts (qualified, tax-advantaged accounts for retirement and taxable funds)
- Any stock options or equity you may have with your employer
- Any equity in a business you own
- Any real estate you own
- Some people count cars or expensive belongings in this category, but I tend to think those things—unless you're about to sell them—often don't hold their value in a way that makes a measurable difference.

Typical liabilities that impact your long-term financial picture include:

- Consumer or credit card debt and other revolving lines of credit
- Student loans
- Auto loans
- Mortgages
- Home equity lines of credit

While there's no perfect allocation that works for everyone, there are good rules of thumb to prevent common pitfalls. For example, you probably don't want to be sitting on more than between three and twelve months' worth of expenses in cash—three if you're a renter without dependents, six if you're a homeowner with kids, and up to twelve if you're self-employed (between your emergency fund and the irregular income slush fund). I've noticed over the last six years that women tend to be excellent at cash flow management; they're "good savers." I've met countless women who only spend $3,000 per month and have $50,000 in a savings account who wonder whether they're ready to start investing. All that to say: Be on the lookout for an unnecessarily cash-heavy allocation at this step.

HIGH-LEVEL ASSET ALLOCATION

Where is the bulk of your money? In your house? Your retirement accounts? Your checking account? Most people are overexposed to one asset class and underexposed to others. For example, roughly 95 percent of my net worth is in the stock market, and 5 percent is in cash. I have basically no exposure to real estate, except indirectly through REIT ETFs (real estate investment trust ETFs). If you notice that your primary residence makes up 90 percent of your net worth, you might decide you actually *don't* need to upgrade your home next year, and that other financial goals (like retirement) might need to take precedence.

TAX DIVERSIFICATION

Of your investments, how do the various tax statuses break down? Do you have mostly pretax funds? Roth? Because I didn't start earning a higher income until the last few years, most of my savings are in taxable brokerage accounts. This type of analysis can help reveal where you may need to shift your future contributions to help beef up an underweight position. There's no one "correct" breakdown of pretax versus Roth versus taxable dollars, but if you have $0 in any one tax status (pretax, Roth, or taxable), that can be a signal you may lack flexibility later.

DEBT DEETS

If you have debt, understanding the various interest rates you're paying is key to your strategy. Rates higher than 7 percent should be treated with more urgency, because the interest you're accruing on the remaining balance is probably growing faster than your money in the market after inflation is considered. As a reminder, debt payoff fits into your "25 percent of saving, investing, and debt paydown" because all three activities increase your net worth.

The next step

Once you've determined what your overall save rate is and where your net worth currently stands, you get to make decisions about which goals are most important. As we covered in Chapters 5 and 6, it's beneficial to start investing in accounts that are more flexible early in life (read: not just retirement accounts, but taxable accounts, too).

Even if you're not sure you ever want to do something incredibly expensive like, *I don't know*, buy a home or have children, contributing *something* to your brokerage account provides optionality—a necessity if you intend to retire early. For example, if 25 percent of your monthly income was $2,000, you might do something like this:

1. 401(k)—$800 (10 percent of your total income, and a little less than half of your total savings each month for retirement)
2. Roth IRA—$300 (also for retirement)
3. High-yield savings account earning 5 percent—$450 (child-care fund)
4. Brokerage account invested in 80 percent equity ETFs and 20 percent bond ETFs—$450 (for early retirement or an eventual down payment on a home)

As a rule of thumb, I like to make sure at least half the savings are for the long-term future (in this case, $1,100 of the $2,000 was for retirement). As noted in Chapter 3, robo-advisers like Betterment or Wealthfront can help you easily adjust your asset allocation *within* each account based on the timeline; e.g., your allocation in your Roth IRA should be more aggressive than your allocation in a brokerage account you're going to need three years from now. If you're using a robo-adviser, the platform will ask you questions during account setup about how you intend to use the money— and will invest the funds accordingly.

Involving another whole-ass human in these accounting decisions

Managing something as personal and psychological as money on your own can be complicated. Adding another person to the mix can turn it into a *Wipeout*-style relationship obstacle course. If you're not yet married (but intend to be), pursuing the prenuptial agreement is likely the easiest way to protect yourself in one fell swoop. But for those of us skating by in prenup-less marriages on shared accounts and a prayer, there are two levels of due dil' to be aware of:

1. **The accounting you just did for your own assets? You'll probably want to do the same with your partner.** As we covered in Chapter 4, marital property affects both of your lives, and if you're diligently saving but your spouse has a penchant for the finer things with no savings to counterweight it, you might be unpleasantly surprised when you *skrrrrt* into early retirement and they're expecting you to foot the bill for their retirement, too.
2. **The "shared ambitions" conversations we covered in Chapter 4.** If you've never asked for transparent access to someone's balance sheet before, step 1 might need to be preceded by the conversations we outlined in Chapter 4. Namely, those about shared goals and ambitions and how you and your spouse are building a financial life together.

I asked Stacy Francis, founder of Savvy Ladies, for her perspective on how to successfully manage your finances within marriage in an ongoing way, and she told me about the trends she's observed over the last few decades working with women who are dealing with financial challenges while going through divorce. "The typical fact pattern is that the person who does not work has no clue about the finances. If they *do* have any clue about them, they're managing the bill paying. But that's it. And they're not coming together for decisions. They're not coming together to see where they are in relation to their goals. [Transparent finances] is an important pillar for a trusting, healthy relationship that's about being together as a team."

She also emphasized how much relationship therapy and counseling can help if this is a topic you don't feel equipped to navigate on your own. Stacy, who's been married to her husband for twenty-five years and works with money for a living, talks openly about how much financial counseling improved her marriage. As much as I wish I could promise that this is a onetime sit-down negotiation of terms that you can check off a list and be done with forever, maintaining money health in your relationship is probably going to be an ongoing dance.

The next step

Depending on your relationship status, your next steps likely involve conversation and couples accounting . . . but it might also involve opening joint accounts or setting up different individual accounts. This is the type of stuff that's easy to deprioritize on a to-do list, but taking an inventory of what you have and where you have it can be an anxiety-*relieving* process—especially if you feel an ambient sense of disarray about the state of your combined finances. You might decide to begin consolidating things, but be careful to avoid unintentional commingling if you'd like certain assets to remain separate.

Other (financial) family planning and negotiating labor within your home

It's at this point you probably feel like I'm giving you an insurmountable amount of homework, so allow me to apologize and check myself real quick: Our end goal in excavating our financial lives is to rebuild them in a way that serves us, not to place even more of a burden on you, the person who is likely already (statistically) doing more than your fair share.

Part of what enables you to have the time, energy, and freedom to prioritize things like a forensic accounting of your assets or scheduling financial counseling is *not* bearing a disproportionate load of unpaid labor in your family situation. At first, this might feel like I'm saying, "Hey, it's *your* fault you never have any time for yourself! Figure it out, babe! Have you tried bubble baths?" But much like the reward for always being on top of it at work is more work, sometimes being the person in your household who brings the Big Executive Assistant Energy means you become the de facto household manager (or maybe your spouse is the one bearing the unfair load). If you're single, you've got no choice but to bring the BEAE for yourself. I am the poster child of BEAE, so I made the unfortunate mistake of immediately setting a precedent that household management was my domain when I got married, which meant we had to consciously unwind that assumption of responsibility later.

This is why it felt important to directly address the realm of children and unpaid domestic care work in this book, because it's the largest (though too often invisible) force in many women's financial lives. It's also the one that most resists neat, individualized solutions because it's so deeply ingrained in our culture and national policy framework that women are primary caretakers; that raising a family and running a household are "women's work." If we don't think that impacts our relationships, financial resources, and energy levels at the aggregate, we're kidding ourselves.

I wish I could tell you there's a special account you can open or a secret cheat code I possess that will erase this challenge from your life. The truth is, one of the only solutions I'm aware of that helps address this systemic shortcoming is saving in advance, whether for childcare in the direct sense or for the type of help that can buy back time or energy. (I know, those of you who are already moms are like, "Gee, thanks, Katie! Brilliant advice, I'll hop in my time machine," and to that I say, "I know, I'm sorry; let's form a PAC.") If this is an area of your life or finances that feels untenable, remember, that's because it is—American women (and American parents more broadly) are expected to shoulder an impossible load, and do so with a smile on their faces.

The next step

First and foremost, remember to go easy on yourself. Second, if you're in a position where you *can* begin preparing for children you don't yet have, remember to create the savings carve-out in your budget. We talked about analyzing the amount you'd need to set aside in Chapter 5, but in the theater of rugged individualist "every parent for themselves" American childcare, any small amount you can set aside as a buffer for later will help.

And if you're not saving for kids (maybe because you don't want them, or maybe because you've already had them), use this opportunity to check in with any other medium-term goals you might have.

By this phase, you'll have a sense for your "margin," as well as what your priorities are, so finally, let's automate the investing of that margin.

Building and automating a robust investing routine that helps you reach your goals efficiently

Knowing what to invest in (and knowing that you should do so as often as possible) is a good starting point—but how do you implement an investing strategy within your broader financial plan? Before we talk about what we *should* do, let's talk about what we probably *shouldn't* do, which is the mistake I made for a long time: using your checking account as a proxy for what you can spend, and therefore what you can invest. Anytime I wanted to buy something, I'd just log into my Chase app and see how much I had. If things looked okay, I'd feel good about buying it. This approach is common but flawed, because it doesn't consider all the things that money is probably already earmarked for (whether that be an upcoming bill or a contribution to an investment account).

If you find yourself contemplating a purchase and logging into your checking account to decide if you can afford it or not, we've gone off course. But it's a bad habit that sneaks up on all of us sometimes, and creating automatic outgoing transfers to your investment accounts that quickly follow paydays is the easiest way to prevent it. Such transfers whisk the money away and put it to use earning more money for you, so it's not sloshing around in your checking account creating a false sense of boujtastic spendability.[†] This, combined with a spend-tracking app like Copilot, can reduce mindless overspending.

---

† Yes, this is an industry term.

Putting your investment strategy on autopilot

If you have regular income (read: you make a predictable amount of money every month), putting your investment strategy on autopilot will be very simple. Here's an example of the first strategy I implemented:

1. I was paid on the fifth and the twentieth of each month.
2. My 401(k) contributions were deducted before I got my paycheck.
3. I had an automatic transfer contribution go from checking to savings on the fifth and the twentieth (on payday) for any smaller, short-term purchases I was saving for, like flights or concert tickets.
4. I had an automatic transfer contribution go from checking to my Roth IRA set for the sixth and the twenty-first, the day after payday.
5. Finally, I had *another* automatic transfer go from checking to my taxable brokerage account with an asset allocation designed for more flexible, medium-term goals set for the seventh and the twenty-second.

It's up to you how much you want to auto-transfer—if you're feeling apprehensive, start small. For example, my first batch of automatic contributions were less than $200 each. After a few months passed and I realized I didn't really "feel" the loss (but saw my balance chugging steadily upward), I got competitive with myself. Could I try $300? What about $400?

These habits allowed me to almost effortlessly accumulate an investment portfolio worth more than $100,000 in just under three years on an income peak of about $70,000 (it didn't hurt that I began investing during a bull market). Because my Roth IRA and brokerage account were set up with Betterment, my contributions were automatically deployed to my correct asset allocation without any additional work from me, which made the entire process take about half an hour of setup time and little else.

Automations with a highly irregular income

If you make an irregular income, fear not. While I automated all of our contributions for a long time, now my income is too irregular for that—so instead, I do something a little simpler: At the end of every month after I record our take-home pay and spending, I assess how much money is "left over" and distribute it accordingly. For example, our 401(k), HSA, and Thrift Savings Plan (the federal government version of a 401(k) plan) contributions come out of our paychecks automatically, but then the remainder of our excess income is invested in our taxable brokerage account. I manually transfer what's left over each month into the account. Because we have high-level spending and investment goals, it's obvious to me when we're falling short of them during this monthly manual transfer process.

The next step

Depending on what your net worth analysis turns up, you might decide you need to open new accounts (like a taxable brokerage or Roth IRA) or switch your paycheck contributions from one tax status to another. You might also want to use the online financial independence calculator I built to plug in your existing invested assets and other data to see how your current work-optional timeline is shaking out, and if you'd like to throw more money at that goal (or less).

This might also be the time to adjust your investment allocation if you realized through this deep dive that your current approach is way too conservative (or, less likely, too aggressive). Once you know what your plan is, the most important thing is turning it on: Set up those automatic contributions.

Checking in with your goals regularly

You may have highly specific, short-term savings goals you're focused on, like buying a new car or furnishing an apartment—and my guess is you'll be attuned to how you're tracking toward them, given the innate urgency you probably feel every time your butt sinks into the deflated spot in your old curb couch. But human beings do a pretty bad job of intuiting their progress toward long-term goals, because our brains weren't designed to plan for things years down the road or think exponentially. We've got some ancient hardware powering our prefrontal cortexes within the modern context of the "life expectancy is seventy-six years old" software.

I recommend you follow one of two cadences, depending on your personality. I'm a type A planner who used to sleep with her agenda under her pillow, so I do light check-ins with my progress at the end of every month. This is not necessary, but it feels good to me, so I do it. While you could stretch your check-in timelines to annual assessments, I find sometimes this is too infrequent and leaves too much of an opportunity to get off track and lose a bunch of time. Annual check-ins work best for people who have their financial situation locked 'n' loaded and whose goals are already well underway. The best cadence for deeper dives will most likely be quarterly.

Regardless of how often you decide to check in, there are a few things I track monthly so I have the data when I need it:

- Our take-home pay (I add back in our paycheck contributions to employer-sponsored accounts so the save rate calculation I run is accurate)
- Our total spending (I record transactions by category so I can go back later and observe trends)
- Any contributions to short- or medium-term savings goals (inclusive of big vacations, but also things like saving for future childcare or housing)
- Any contributions to long-term investing goals (eventual freedom)

You can use the following framework for your check-in. I'm including some example numbers below. Overall, you want to examine three major things:

1. A balance sheet check-in that determines how your net worth is changing
2. Noteworthy spending trends

3. Upcoming noteworthy events and expenses you'll want to plan for

It looks a little something like this:

Q1 BALANCE SHEET CHECK-IN
- **Q1 Income:** $15,000
- **Q1 Spending:** $9,000
- **Save Rate:** 40%
- **Q1 Investment Contributions:** $6,000
  - *Katie's 401(k) with Match: $3,500*
  - *Katie's HSA: $750*
  - *Katie's Roth IRA: $1,500*
  - *Katie's Brokerage Account: $500*
- **Net Worth:** $75,000
- **Q1 Net Worth Change:** +12%
- **Cash Position:** $15,000
- **Investments:** $60,000
  - **Liquid/Accessible:** $25,000

Ideally, you're checking in to get a sense for how you earned, how you spent, and where your money was invested—as well as how things like your net worth changed.

Crucially, it's not that your spending review must be able to identify down to the penny how much you spent on shampoo in November 2018—it's meant to help recognize broad trends before things unintentionally deviate too far from the plan. We often think we have a handle on these things, but I'm still routinely surprised by what I find when I do my big annual deep dive after a year of monthly check-ins (which is why I continue to do it; also, it's just fun).

Finally, look ahead toward the next quarter's noteworthy events—where are you traveling? What big purchases will you be making that are out of the ordinary? What goals are you actively saving toward? Looking to the horizon can help you dial in what needs to be planned for now; that way you're not suddenly six bachelorette parties deep with an AmEx bill to prove it.

Q2 NOTEWORTHY EVENTS

- We'll be paying our estimated tax bill of $5,500
- This will lower our cash position by about 33%
- Katie will receive a cash bonus of $7,000 in June
- Moving in Q3; estimated expenses of $4,000 to move (begin saving in May)

TRAVEL & OTHER BIG EXPENSES

- Going to McCall's wedding in May; need to budget about $1,000 for flights and hotel
- Invited to Rachel's baby shower in April; will need to purchase a gift from her registry ($250)
- Resources to consider
  - Gift card to Nordstrom: $100
  - 35,000 Chase Ultimate Rewards points
  - 15,000 Marriott Bonvoy points

End-of-year reviews

While the monthly tracking for quarterly reviews is sufficient, I love doing annual reviews of our finances, because it always amazes me what I learn looking at the holistic picture. The end of the year is also a good time to collect copies of your end-of-year financial documents, per Lisa Zeiderman's advice about creating a paper trail of your separate and marital property over time. Use this opportunity to reflect on your treasure trove of financial data:

- What was your total take-home pay for the year, and what were the sources of income? If you work multiple jobs or have side hustles, is there anything worth noting about the ROI on time spent? (E.g., if your side hustle is earning half as much as your full-time role but in 20 percent of the time, that might be a sign you *could* pivot to self-employment.)
- What was your effective tax rate for the year? Did you take full advantage of your pretax accounts?
- What percentage of your planned spending happened? (Another way to ask this: Of all the money you thought you'd spend, did you spend more or less?) Did you spend it in the way you figured you would? (E.g., I said at the beginning of the year that travel was most important to me, but I spent most of my money on online shopping and takeout.)
- What was your overall savings rate for the year? How did it compare to what you set out to do, and if you were to maintain that rate moving forward, how would it impact your timeline to financial independence? How did it feel? (Doable or tight?)
- Are there any areas of opportunity that jump out at you in reviewing a year's worth of expenses? (For me, the car was a big one in 2020, restaurant spending was the biggest one in 2022, and miscellaneous entertainment was the biggest thing in 2023.)
- Which accounts did you contribute the most to? Which accounts grew the most? Does your asset allocation still

look appropriate for your goals? Have you accidentally accumulated a bunch of cash you need to invest?

- How did your liabilities change this year? Are you making progress toward debt paydown, and are you still prioritizing the "correct" debt? (E.g., maybe the 3 percent fixed rate mortgage is *not* the debt to stress about; you'd have to pry a 3 percent mortgage out of my cold, dead hands.)
- When are you projected to hit your financial independence goal given your current standing?
- Are there any major goals or changes coming next year that you'd like to start preparing for now?
- Where did the money you spent go the furthest in the previous year? Where was your return on spending highest? (I remember one year we spent $2,000 on a temperature-controlled mattress, which felt absurd at the time but ended up being our favorite purchase—to this day, it remains one of the best investments in our sleep quality.)

In conclusion

If you've been getting your finances dialed in for a long time already, you may have picked up a few new pointers in the previous seven chapters that you're ready to implement right away—but if this was the first book about personal finance you've ever read, you might be feeling like I just handed you a copy of the Magna Carta in its original Latin and said, "See? It's so *easy!*"

Take it from me: It took several years of reading, digesting, trialing, and erroring to get to the point where I felt competent and comfortable enough with my finances to give it my all. While much of this is second nature to me now, I recently started working with a personal trainer and nutritionist. In the first few weeks, they were loading my plan with all sorts of words and instructions that were completely foreign to me. Macros? Reps and sets? The meal planning required so much math that it took me an entire afternoon (and more executive functioning than I'd like to admit) to make a coherent grocery list. I felt like I was learning a second language, and it was totally overwhelming—I left the store the first day sporting a headache and a bad mood.

But much like you wouldn't try to learn how to speak Japanese in one or two sittings, you also wouldn't try to implement major financial, dietary, or lifestyle changes in under a week. Learning the language of money takes time—and it's only once you learn it that you can begin speaking it fluently in your daily life. Would you ever say, "Wow, I'm forty years old and I don't know how to speak Japanese yet . . . how *embarrassing!*"? No, of course not. If you've never earnestly attempted to learn, why would it be embarrassing that you don't know how? Money is the same way. Nobody emerges from the womb with a diversified portfolio, and "proficiency at thriving under capitalism" is not a natural skill.

I'd encourage you to implement things a little bit at a time. Start with the highest-priority change first and focus on making that second nature before you move on to the second-highest-priority shift. Rome wasn't built in a day, and your net worth won't be, either. To the extent that you can, try to enjoy the journey— the ability to build wealth of your own is a privilege that wasn't available to our great-grandmothers. You have a unique opportunity simply by nature of being alive in the year 2025. Might as well have a little fun with it, right?

Invite Your Friends

*Six years after Kylie invited me
to that fateful* Money Diaries *event*

A few months ago, I attended a friend's launch party for her new fintech app in New York City. I had become friends with Lindsay because of my outspoken posture online about women's financial health, and she had reached out expressing a similar vision. She wanted to know what I felt was missing in the financial technology world, and as we chatted more, she presented me with the opportunity to become an adviser to her venture-backed startup for an equity stake. I was in.

For the launch, we hosted a panel about investing for a room full of women. There were conversation-starter cards strewn around with prompts about asset allocation and savings rates, and I observed as women met one another and formed fast friendships. It struck me as I stood there that *this*—women talking to one another, dragging their finance-phobic friends to investing events, and gathering to share tips and tricks—is how we transmit cultural change like an antidote. After all, six years prior, *I* was the ignorant friend coaxed out on a weeknight to an event about personal finance, and now I was the one sitting onstage with a microphone.

In the six years that followed my attendance at the *Money Diaries* book tour, I went on a radical financial journey: from naive faith in "personal finance advice" as the only component necessary to live a myopically rich life, to disillusioned helplessness and rage that our system necessitates mastery of such advice in the first place, to the realistic middle ground where I now find myself, believing that radical, progressive change is necessary, *and* we are not without agency. Such an evolution was only possible because of other women in the financial space who weren't afraid to marry their discussions of fiscal prudence with the uncomfortable recognition that such prudence is not enough. I got to learn, evolve, and grow because of other people who were publicly committed to reckoning with not *just* the tactical steps, but the implications of a world that requires "wealth-building" to succeed.

I learned from people who put their money where their mouth is, like Chelsea Fagan. As CEO of the company she cofounded, she pays herself the fifth-highest salary at her firm and instituted a four-day workweek with no change in pay.

I learned from financial professionals who explicitly tackle the ethics of wealth accumulation, like Paco de Leon. Paco believes that "the most radical thing is to be hopeful" for a better future; to not cede victory to the likes of extractive private equity firms and predatory lending companies and the incessant cultural drumbeat of unchecked, rampant consumerism.

I learned from women who devote their lives and private, for-profit businesses to the running of *non*profit organizations that help women from all walks of life in impossible financial situations for free, like Stacy Francis. After witnessing her grandmother die at the hands of her grandfather's physical abuse because she was financially trapped, Stacy founded Savvy Ladies in 2003 and has since changed the stories of more than twenty-five thousand women.

I've learned from people like every single one of you in Rich Girl Nation, who engage thoughtfully with the work I'm doing, email me to share more reading or recommendations or reflections you think I'll find interesting, and consistently challenge me to push until we reach the truth of the matter.

We talk often about how individual solutions fall short in the face of systemic inequities or structural opposition, but that makes it sound as though we, as individuals, are incapable of joining together to spark cultural and political change from the ground up. For example, it wasn't a specific policy that shifted my perspective on our healthcare system; it was thanks to another individual private citizen, T. R. Reid, who wrote *The Healing of America* and helped me understand that our American healthcare marketplace is uniquely punishing. I didn't learn that the poverty of many is a trap that enriches the few in some publicly shared curriculum—I learned it because Matt Desmond has worked tirelessly to educate the public about how our predatory financial system profits from others' despair. It was *one* woman's work (and the persistence to write a book called *Money Diaries*) that gave me the confidence to pursue financial education and entrepreneurship.†

Our ability to influence one another's choices, values, perspectives, and lives is our superpower. "Awareness" alone may be insufficient, but it's also the most important ingredient required for change. To change, we must first be moved, and movement

---

† In a particularly full-circle moment in August 2024, I hosted an online event with Lindsey Stanberry (the founding editor of *Money Diaries*) and Lindsay Dorf, the founder whose fintech startup I advise.

requires the collectively shared, profound revelation that the status quo is not acceptable, followed closely by the capacity to imagine something better.

Recognizing our shared goals and struggles is a key step toward progress of any kind, and if there's anything I've learned as a public-facing writer and podcaster over the last several years, it's that we're more alike than we are different—whether our ultimate goal is home ownership or total financial freedom or simply being able to travel outside the small town where we grew up, we're all doing the best we can with the cards we've been dealt. Now that you understand some of the most pressing drivers of financial disparity in women's lives, the work begins: We find our footing. We find ourselves. Then we find each other. Our ambitions for our lives and those who come after us will only be as strong as the interconnected support system we can build around them.

We must loudly, proudly, and publicly align ourselves with one another. We have to keep talking about money, questioning why some receive so much and others receive so little, pursuing positions of influence, and using our newfound resources to support one another and groups that have historically been barred from accruing resources of their own. **We have to keep inviting our friends.**

Acknowledgments

This book exists because of dozens and dozens of brilliant, tenacious women, and I want to thank a few of them.

My editor at Penguin Random House/Portfolio, Megan McCormack, who believed that it would be possible to write a personal finance book for women that went beyond the tactics—and displayed endless patience and faith as we wrote and rewrote it, until we got it right.

My agent from Arc Literary Management, Kate Davids, whose insistence that we meet "just to talk about the literary process" ended up producing a book proposal that became something great, and who was doggedly in my corner in the moments when it seemed like it might not pay off.

It was possible for me to spend two years writing *Rich Girl Nation* while writing and producing for a full-time personal finance media brand because of the fine folks at Morning Brew, like my producer, Henah Velez, whose attention to detail across all Money with Katie channels meant I never had to worry about rogue em dashes. This book was made indirectly better by the editorial mentorship of Mallory Rice, who has taken my writing to the next level, and Caroline Burke, whose brilliance has made me a better critical thinker.

Thank you to my English teachers at Notre Dame Academy—

especially Linda Bricking, Emily Sampson, and Lynn Dickman—who encouraged and challenged me, even when I complained about the number of summer reading books (I mean, honestly, four is excessive, don't you think?).

And thank you to my family: Mom, for all those quiet days spent sitting on the floor of the Lents branch library or wandering the stacks at Barnes & Noble. Dad, for spending your time after work at the kitchen table with me every time my homework involved numbers and for being my number-one fan. Grandma Jean, for being a feminist icon before it was cool. Ellie, for being my sister who takes the words right out of my mouth.

And to Thomas, Sam, and in memory of Beans: I love you, and none of this would mean anything without you.

Notes

INTRODUCTION: THE INVITATION

9 **"Women be shoppin'!":** *The Nutty Professor*, directed by T. Shadyac (Imagine Entertainment, 1996).

9 **"bad at math":** J. Bohannon, "Both Genders Think Women Are Bad at Basic Math," *Science*, March 10, 2024.

9 **"gold digger" trope:** "Signs of a Gold Digger," WebMD, December 3, 2022.

9 **marketed to women also cost more:** *From Cradle to Cane: The Cost of Being a Female Consumer; A Study of Gender Pricing in New York City* (New York City Department of Consumer Affairs, 2015).

9 **earn the high incomes:** J. Yavorsky, L. Keister, Y. Qian, and M. Nau, "Women in the One Percent: Gender Dynamics in Top Income Positions," *American Sociological Review* 84, no. 1 (2019): 54–81.

9 **bear a disproportionate amount:** R. Fry, C. Aragão, K. Hurst, and K. Parker, "In a Growing Share of U.S. Marriages, Husbands and Wives Earn About the Same," Pew Research Center, April 13, 2023.

10 **fifty-five cents in median wealth:** A. Hernández Kent, "Gender Wealth Gaps in the U.S. and the Benefits of Closing Them," *Open Vault* (blog), Federal Reserve Bank of St. Louis, September 29, 2021.

10 **56 percent of husbands:** S. Hanna, K. Kim, S. Lindamood, and S. Lee, "Husbands, Wives, and Perception of Relative Knowledge About Household Finances," *Financial Planning Review*, January 2021.

10 **women's wealth lags men's:** Hanna et al., "Husbands, Wives, and Perception."

10 **married white women have:** Hanna et al., "Husbands, Wives, and Perception."

11 **more than twice as much:** Fry et al., "In a Growing Share."

12 **after women become parents:** J. Staff and J. Mortimer, "Explaining the Motherhood Wage Penalty During the Early Occupational Career," *Demography* 49, no. 1 (2012): 1–21.

12 **Women typically outlive men:** S. Dattani and L. Rodés-Guirao, "Why Do Women Live Longer Than Men?," Our World in Data, November 27, 2023.

12 **in poverty following divorce:** "Marital Status and Poverty," Social Security Administration, May 2016.

12 **less than one third:** "2024 Pulse of the American Retiree Survey," Prudential, June 24, 2024.

13 **less than $20 per hour:** "Low-Wage Workforce Tracker," Economic Policy Institute, January 2024.

13 **plunges hundreds of thousands:** S. Gottlieb, "Medical Bills Account for 40% of Bankruptcies," *British Medical Journal* 320, no. 7245 (2000): 1295.

13 **rates of all high-income nations:** "Insights into the U.S. Maternal Mortality Crisis: An International Comparison," The Commonwealth Fund, June 4, 2024.

13 **have their own bank accounts:** I. Rose, "A Bank of Her Own," *JSTOR Daily*, January 11, 2023.

CHAPTER 1: THE HOT GIRL HAMSTER WHEEL

15 **Dr. Renee Engeln,** *Beauty Sick*: R. Engeln, *Beauty Sick: How the Cultural Obsession with Appearance Hurts Girls and Women* (Harper, 2017).

18 **"My desire becomes a market":** T. Cottom, "In the Name of Beauty," in *Thick: And Other Essays* (New Press, 2019), 65.

19 **the opportunity cost is $1,001,728.88:** "Compound Interest Calculator," investor.gov, accessed August 2024.

19 **around $200,000 in savings:** "Retirement Accounts: Median Balances by Demographic and Population Groups," Federal Reserve Board Survey of Consumer Finances, 2022.

19 **average of $1,907 per month:** "What Is the Average Monthly Benefit for a Retired Worker?," Social Security Administration, January 2, 2024.

19 **$3,756 per year on beauty:** "Looking Good Isn't Cheap: Groupon Finds People Will Spend Almost a Quarter of a Million on Their Appearance over Their Lifetime," Groupon Investor Relations, June 21, 2017.

20 **$100 billion industry in the US:** "Beauty & Personal Care—Worldwide," Statista, September 2024.

21 **"appear as white as possible":** A conversation with Jessica DeFino via Money with Katie, "Beauty Is $$$: How to Hop Off the 'Hot Girl Hamster Wheel,'" *The Money with Katie Show*, August 8, 2023.

21 **Mikki Kendall describes:** M. Kendall, *Hood Feminism: Notes from the Women That a Movement Forgot* (Penguin Books, 2020), 104.

23 **a community's efforts toward equality:** A. Harris, "A History of Self-Care," *Slate*, April 5, 2017.

23 **probably worth around $11 billion:** C. Lieberman, "How Self-Care Became So Much Work," *Harvard Business Review*, August 10, 2018.

27 **0.5 percent *higher* than "average":** R. Hernández-Julián and C. Peters, "Student Appearance and Academic Performance," *Journal of Human Capital* 11, no. 2 (2017): 247–62.

27 **weight requirements for flight attendants:** T. Lewin, "USAir Agrees to Lift Rules on the Weight of Attendants," *The New York Times*, April 8, 1994.

27 **earn 12 percent less:** "The Obesity Pay Gap Is Worse Than Previously Thought," *The Economist*, November 23, 2023.

30 **possesses naturally blond hair:** "Blonde Hair Percentage by Country/ Blond Hair by Country 2024," World Population Review, 2024.

30 **women serving as CEOs:** M. Zetlin, "Why Are Female CEOs Disproportionately Blonde? Here's the Answer, According to Science," *Inc.*, August 30, 2016.

CHAPTER 2: THE TRUTH ABOUT EARNING MORE

37 **I heard the bewildering statistic:** E. Peck, "At the CEO Level, Women Finally Outnumber Men Named John," *Axios*, April 27, 2023.

39 **correlation between income and savings:** K. Dynan, J. Skinner, and S. Zeldes, "Do the Rich Save More?," Harvard University, November 2000.

40 **60.7 percent as much:** "The Wage Gap over Time: In Real Dollars, Women See a Continuing Gap," National Committee on Pay Equity, September 2020.

40 **83.6 percent of what all:** "Women's Earnings Were 83.6% of Men's in 2023," US Bureau of Labor Statistics, March 12, 2024.

40 **For example, Hispanic women:** R. Kochhar, "The Enduring Grip of the Gender Pay Gap," Pew Research Center, March 1, 2023.

42 **still paid disparately:** "2024 Gender Pay Gap Report," Payscale, 2024.

43 **six math whizzes:** K. Kleiman, "These 6 Pioneering Women Helped Create Modern Computers," *TED Ideas* (blog), April 17, 2018.

43 **rote, and, well, "women's work":** R. Cohen, "What Programming's Past Reveals About Today's Gender-Pay Gap," *The Atlantic*, September 7, 2016.

44 **low-wage shift work:** J. Tucker and K. Patrick, "Low-Wage Jobs Are Women's Jobs: The Overrepresentation of Women in Low-Wage Work," National Women's Law Center, August 2017.

44 **the gap is eighty-nine cents:** C. Goldin, "A Grand Gender Convergence: Its Last Chapter," *American Economic Review* 104, no. 4 (2014): 1091–119.

44 **it leads to lower pay:** A. Levanon, P. England, and P. Allison, "Occupational Feminization and Pay: Assessing Causal Dynamics Using 1950–2000 U.S. Census Data," *Social Forces* 88, no. 2 (December 2009): 865–91.

44 **Women in unions make:** "Median Weekly Earnings of Full-Time Wage and Salary Workers by Union Affiliation and Selected Characteristics," US Bureau of Labor Statistics, 2023.

45 **earned just shy of $400,000:** M. Bertrand, C. Goldin, and L. Katz, "Dynamics of the Gender Gap for Young Professionals in the Financial and Corporate Sectors," *American Economic Journal: Applied Economics* 2 (July 2010): 228–55.

46 **gender wage gap is largest:** "Gender Earnings Ratios and Wage Gaps by Age since 1960," US Department of Labor, March 2024.

46 **women under thirty now outearn:** R. Fry, "Young Women Are Out-Earning Young Men in Several U.S. Cities," Pew Research Center, March 28, 2022.

46 **stated wages were negotiable:** A. Leibbrandt and J. List, "Do Women Avoid Salary Negotiations? Evidence from a Large-Scale Natural Field Experiment," *Management Science* 61, no. 9 (September 2015): 2016–24.

47 **"holding background factors":** B. Artz, A. Goodall, and A. Oswald, "Research: Women Ask for Raises as Often as Men, but Are Less Likely to Get Them," *Harvard Business Review*, June 25, 2018.

47 **doesn't work for women:** M. Konnikova, "Lean Out: The Dangers for Women Who Negotiate," *The New Yorker*, June 10, 2014.

47 **Four different studies:** H. Bowles, L. Babcock, and L. Lai, "Social Incentives for Gender Differences in the Propensity to Initiate Negotiations: Sometimes It Does Hurt to Ask," *Organizational Behavior and Human Decision Processes* 103, no. 1 (May 2007): 84–103.

48 **Feminist philosopher Kate Manne:** K. Manne, *Down Girl: The Logic of Misogyny* (Penguin Books, 2018), 112–15.

48 **I asked Kathryn Valentine:** A conversation with Kathryn Valentine via Money with Katie, "It's Officially Negotiation Season—Here's What Works," *The Money with Katie Show*, January 9, 2024.

55 **salary transparency data:** "Pay Transparency Laws by State," GovDocs, June 2024.

58 **"If women can demonstrate":** K. Valentine, interview by the author, December 2023.

65 **supervisors, or financial professionals:** J. Bakija, A. Cole, and B. Heim, "Jobs and Income Growth of Top Earners and the Causes of Changing Income Inequality: Evidence from U.S. Tax Return Data," Working Paper No. 2010-22 (Department of Economics, Williams College, 2012).

69 **reported $75 million:** S. Fischer, "Exclusive: Insider Inc. Buys Majority Stake in Morning Brew in All-Cash Deal," *Axios*, October 29, 2020.

CHAPTER 3: KNOWLEDGE IS POWER

80 **their husbands take responsibility:** "UBS Own Your Worth Report Finds That Only 20% of Couples Participate Equally in Financial Decisions," UBS, May 6, 2021.

80 **just "less natural" for them:** "UBS Own Your Worth Report 2023: Women Primary Breadwinners Face Challenges Embracing Their Financial Power," UBS, June 13, 2023.

81 **managing their finances alone:** B. Stewart, "Suddenly Single: How to Plan with Female Clients," *Enterprising Investor* (blog), CFA Institute, October 18, 2019.

85 **rounded down to 4 percent:** W. Bengen, "Determining Withdrawal Rates Using Historical Data," *Journal of Financial Planning* 7, no. 4 (October 1994): 171.

85 **a *100 percent* historical success rate:** A conversation with Bill Bengen via Money with Katie, "Does Early Retirement Still Work with 2023 Inflation? Featuring Bill Bengen," *The Money with Katie Show*, April 11, 2023.

92 **it's less than 4 percent:** US Bureau of Economic Analysis, "Personal Saving Rate [PSAVERT]," FRED, Federal Reserve Bank of St. Louis, 2024.

102 **about 10 percent per year:** J. Royal, "What Is the Average Stock Market Return?," NerdWallet, May 3, 2024.

102 **Apple represents 7.10 percent:** G. Alpert, "Top 10 S&P 500 Stocks by Index Weight," Investopedia, August 29, 2023.

105 **[total world stock market] fund:** A conversation with JL Collins via Money with Katie, "The Easiest Way to Build Wealth with JL Collins, the Godfather of Financial Independence," *The Money with Katie Show*, February 13, 2024.

105 **the top 25th percentile globally:** E. Dimson, P. Marsh, and M. Staunton, "Long-Run Global Capital Market Returns and Risk Premia," February 2002.

106 **cap was around $70 billion:** Market capitalization of Amazon (AMZN) in September 2010.

108 **annualized 13.6 percent per year:** B. Porche, "7 Small-Cap Value ETFs to Buy in 2023," *U.S. News & World Report*, August 21, 2023.

109 **top performer only 20 percent:** J. Kloepfer, "The Callan Periodic Table of Investment Returns: Year-End 2023," Callan, 2024.

111 **0.25 percent of your balance:** As of August 2024, Betterment charges 0.25 percent per year for accounts with more than $20,000 in assets or with recurring monthly deposits of more than $250; accounts with lower balances or monthly deposits cost $4 per month (betterment.com/help/fees). Wealthfront charges 0.25 percent per year (wealthfront.com/pricing).

113 **iShares by BlackRock:** "BlackRock Transforms Access to Retirement Solutions for Millions of Americans," BlackRock, October 19, 2023.

115 **June 1932 (the biggest ever):** N. Maggiulli, "Even God Couldn't Beat Dollar-Cost Averaging," *Of Dollars and Data* (blog), February 5, 2019.

117 **spending tends to decline:** "How Much Will You Spend in Retirement?," *Fidelity Viewpoints*, November 14, 2023.

118 **93 percent of all wealth:** J. Sor, "The Wealthiest 10% of Americans Own 93% of Stocks Even with Market Participation at a Record High," Yahoo! Finance, January 10, 2024.

CHAPTER 4: I THEE WED (AND SPEND THY BREAD)

123 **As attorney James Sexton said:** S. Illing, "A Divorce Lawyer's Guide to Staying Together," *Vox*, November 25, 2019.

123 **poverty after a divorce:** T. Leopold, "Gender Differences in the Consequences of Divorce: A Study of Multiple Outcomes," *Demography* 55, no. 3 (June 2018): 769–97.

123 **caretaker for her family members:** "Women Caregivers Age 40 and Older in New York: Their Challenges, Struggles, and Needs," AARP, 2023.

124 **man's permission in the US:** The Equal Credit Opportunity Act, 15 U.S.C. 1691, Civil Rights Division, US Department of Justice.

125 **some other dude's kids:** "The Origins of Marriage," *The Week*, January 8, 2015.

125 **idea known as "coverture":** "The Origins of Marriage."

126 **spousal rape became illegal:** R. Bergen and E. Barnhill, "Marital Rape: New Research and Directions," National Online Resource Center on Violence Against Women, February 2006.

132 **Kim Davis recommends:** A conversation with Kim Davis via Money with Katie, "To Prenup or Not to Prenup? With the Fiscal Feminist, Kim Davis," *The Money with Katie Show*, June 1, 2022.

133 **"When you get married":** A conversation with Stacy Francis via Money with Katie, "How Marriage Legally Changes Your Financial Rights," *The Money with Katie Show*, February 28, 2024. Quotes from this interview were edited for brevity and clarity but faithfully reflect the content of Francis's advice.

136 **role of a "traditional" housewife:** T. Hekker, "The Satisfactions of House-

wifery and Motherhood In 'an Age of Do-Your-Own-Thing,'" *The New York Times*, December 20, 1977.

137 **small, peripheral household expenses:** T. Hekker, "Paradise Lost (Domestic Division)," *The New York Times*, January 1, 2006.

138 *Disregard First Book:* T. Hekker, *Disregard First Book* (iUniverse, 2009).

140 **"Mumford & Sons":** @damienkronfeld, "the four wedding themes are mumford & sons, money, beach vacation, and gender," Twitter (now X), October 14, 2020, https://x.com/damienkronfeld/status/1316473503210704896.

140 **average cost of a wedding:** J. Chertoff and G. Darling, "How Much Does the Average Wedding Cost in 2024?," Zola, April 22, 2024.

141 **average bride spends around $2,000:** S. Hanlon, "This Is the Average Cost of a Wedding Dress Today," The Knot, March 13, 2024.

142 **clocked in at $4 million:** H. Scott, "7 of the Most Expensive Celebrity Weddings, from Kim K to Paris Hilton," Tie the Knot Scotland, July 1, 2024.

145 **"Courts are not always":** L. Zeiderman, interview by the author, February 2024.

148 **"Using separate accounts":** A conversation with Bill Nelson via Money with Katie, "Rich Girl Roundtable: Money, Marriage, & Risks of Combined (and Separate) Finances (with a CFP!)," *The Money with Katie Show*, October 9, 2023.

148 **"You don't want one person":** Francis, "How Marriage Legally Changes."

152 **"talk to your lawyer":** Francis, "How Marriage Legally Changes."

CHAPTER 5: EVERY MOM IS A WORKING MOM

159 **Sociologist Jessica Calarco:** J. Calarco, *Holding It Together: How Women Became America's Safety Net* (Portfolio, 2024).

160 **cooked and cleaned for him:** K. Marçal, *Who Cooked Adam Smith's Dinner? A Story of Women and Economics* (Simon & Schuster, 2012).

160 **Wages for Housework movement:** J. Kisner, "The Lockdown Showed How the Economy Exploits Women. She Already Knew," *The New York Times*, February 17, 2021.

161 **"rediscover what is love":** S. Federici, *Wages Against Housework* (Falling Wall Press and the Power of Women Collective, 1975).

161 **leisure time is nearly double:** "Chapter 6: Time in Work and Leisure, Patterns by Gender and Family Structure," *Modern Parenthood*, Pew Research Center using data from the US Bureau of Labor Statistics, March 14, 2013.

161 **four hours more leisure time:** "Chapter 6: Time in Work and Leisure."

161 **unpaid household and caretaking labor:** US Bureau of Labor Statistics, American Time Use Survey (18), US Department of Labor, 2023.

162 **retirement income overall:** Women's Bureau, "Living on Less: Persistent Gender Disparities in Income Levels, Sources for Older Adults," US Department of Labor, May 2023.

163 **household income on childcare:** "This Is How Much Child Care Costs in 2024," Care.com, January 17, 2024.

163 **gender pay gap is less than half:** "Gender Equality and Work," Organisation for Economic Development, 2023.

163 **Seventy percent of families:** R. Fry, C. Aragão, K. Hurst, and K. Parker, "In

a Growing Share of U.S. Marriages, Husbands and Wives Earn About the Same," Pew Research Center, April 13, 2023.

163 **49 percent in 1972:** Fry et al., "In a Growing Share."

163 **Of these dual-income households:** Fry et al., "In a Growing Share."

164 **keeps the "greedy" job:** G. Gavett, "The Problem with 'Greedy Work,'" *Harvard Business Review*, September 28, 2021.

165 **94 percent of childcare workers:** J. Vogtman, "Can We Rewrite the Shameful History of Undervaluing Child Care Workers?," National Women's Law Center, March 29, 2019.

165 **97 percent of prekindergarten:** M. Coffey, "Still Underpaid and Unequal," Center for American Progress, July 19, 2022.

166 **"look at the bigger math":** A conversation with Farnoosh Torabi via Money with Katie, "How Kids Impact Financial Independence," *The Money with Katie Show*, October 4, 2023.

167 **one in five divorced women:** B. Butrica and K. Smith, "The Retirement Prospects of Divorced Women," *Social Security Bulletin* 72, no. 1 (January 2012): 11–22.

167 **a rate 56 percent higher:** "Marital Status and Poverty," Social Security Administration, May 2016.

167 **compared to 37 percent of men:** C. Miller and L. Alderman, "Why U.S. Women Are Leaving Jobs Behind," *The New York Times*, December 12, 2014.

167 **a staggering 95 percent:** J. Yavorksy, L. Keister, Y. Qian, and M. Nau, "Women in the One Percent: Gender Dynamics in Top Income Positions," *American Sociological Review* 84, no. 1 (February 2019): 54–81.

171 **$300,000 to raise a child:** R. Torchinsky, "It Now Costs $300,000 to Raise a Child," *The Wall Street Journal*, August 19, 2022.

171 **Living Wage Calculator's 2024 data:** J. DeJohn, "Cost of Raising a Child in the Largest U.S. Metros—2024 Study," SmartAsset, June 11, 2024.

171 **childcare was $13,187 per year:** DeJohn, "Cost of Raising a Child."

172 **inflation-adjusted dollars since 1980:** C. de Brey and K. Donaldson, *Digest of Education Statistics: 2022* (National Center for Education Statistics, 2022), comparing inflation-adjusted cost of higher education at a four-year public university including total tuition, fees, room, and board for the 1979–1980 school year to the same measure for the 2020–2021 school year.

172 **four-year public university undergraduate:** de Brey and Donaldson, *Digest of Education Statistics: 2022.*

173 **rate of 8 percent per year:** H. Rivera, "College Tuition Inflation: How the Cost of College Has Risen over Time," Bankrate, July 26, 2023.

178 **cursed viral Reddit post:** Posted in 2023 on r/TwoHotTakes: "AITA for expecting my partner to pay half of my hospital bill? (The original post was deleted but I have a screenshot)," accessible at reddit.com/r/TwoHotTakes/comments /11iih05/aita_for_expecting_my_partner_to_pay_half_of_my.

CHAPTER 6: DON'T OUTLIVE YOUR ASSETS

196 **"Two Funds for Life" strategy:** P. Merriman, "2 Funds for Life: Strategic Planning for Investing at Every Stage of Life," Merriman Financial Education Foundation, 2020.

221 **75 percent and 83 percent:** A. Markowitz, "Social Security Report Projects Trust Fund Shortfall in 2035," AARP, May 6, 2024.

CHAPTER 7: RICH GIRL FOR LIFE: PUTTING IT ALL TOGETHER

227 **People with basic financial literacy:** A. Lusardi and O. Mitchell, "Financial Literacy and Planning: Implications for Retirement Wellbeing," Working Paper No. 17078 (National Bureau of Economic Research, May 2011).

252 **"The typical fact pattern":** A conversation with Stacy Francis via Money with Katie, "How Marriage Legally Changes Your Financial Rights," *The Money with Katie Show,* February 28, 2024. Quotes from this interview were edited for brevity and clarity but faithfully reflect the content of Francis's advice.

CONCLUSION: INVITE YOUR FRIENDS

268 **"the most radical thing":** A conversation with Paco de Leon via Money with Katie, "The Cognitive Dissonance of 'Getting Rich' and Imagining a Better 'American Dream,'" *The Money with Katie Show,* July 3, 2024.

Index